RATCHET & CLANK ALL 4 ONE

OFFICIAL STRATEGY GUIDE

ACROSS THE UNIVERSE:
THE HISTORY OF RATCHET & CLANK

RATCHET & CLANK

Date Released: November 6, 2002   **System:** PlayStation®2 computer entertainment system

"Using our highly sophisticated technology, which you can't possibly understand, we will extract a large portion of your planet and add it to our new one. Unfortunately, this change in mass will cause your planet to spin out of control and drift toward the sun where it will explode into a flaming ball of gas, but, of course, sacrifices must be made. Thank you for your co-operation."

In a robot manufacturing plant on the planet Quartu, Chairman Drek of the Blarg race was in the process of creating sentry-bots. But, one of the sentry-bots didn't come out a sentry-bot at all. Instead of a large, deadly machine, the plant's computer created XJ-0461, a much smaller, less deadly robot later known as Clank.

The pint-size robot discovered Drek's plans to create the ultimate Blarg home world by stealing the best parts of other planets (and destroying those planets as a result). Knowing he had to escape and find help, Clank ran for it. But, he didn't get far. Drek's minions shot down Clank's ship over the planet Veldin.

Down on the Veldin's surface, an orphaned Lombax named Ratchet was working hard to repair a spaceship when Clank crash-landed. Ratchet discovered the mini-robot in the wreckage and was shown a Holo-Vision of Drek's devious plan. It didn't take much for Clank to convince the adventure hungry Lombax to leave Veldin and help stop the Blarg chairman. Using Ratchet's fixed up ship, the two took off.

Clank knew that for a plan this evil, they needed more assistance. They needed help from an experienced hero known the universe over. They needed Captain Copernicus Leslie Qwark. When Ratchet and Clank finally met the famed Captain Qwark on the planet Rilgar, they discovered there was much more to the legend than the man. In fact, he was working for Drek! In the end (or near the end) Qwark left Ratchet and Clank's fate in the hands of Blargian Snagglebeast and jetted away to continue Drek's bidding.

Furious, Ratchet could only think of getting his revenge on Qwark and was ready to abandon their quest in order to get payback. But, Clank acted as the voice of reason and the two continued with their plans to stop Drek. As luck would have it, Ratchet got his revenge later in their adventure when Qwark was sent to ambush the duo.

Ratchet and Clank finally cornered Drek and stopped the planet plunder once and for all. In the wake of their success, the two became instant celebrities and heroes.

RATCHET & CLANK: GOING COMMANDO

Date Released: November 11, 2003   **System:** PlayStation®2 computer entertainment system

"Dr. James D. Fullbladder reporting on Megacorp experiment number 13. This update is strictly classified, if you are watching this, you're fired."

After Ratchet and Clank's impressive victory over Chairman Drek, they were the talk of the universe. However, the spotlight soon faded and the two returned to everyday life. That all changed after their filming of *Behind the Hero* when Abercombie Fizzwidget, CEO of the you-name-it-we-make-it company, Megacorp, teleported the former galactic saviors to the Bogon Galaxy.

It turned out that Fizzwidget was in a pickle. An experiment, known as the Protopet, had been stolen and he wanted for nothing more than for the heroes to get it back. Ratchet, ready for another adventure, was on the job. Clank, however, wanted to sit this one out. Unfortunately, Clank had no say in the matter once the thief Ratchet was after kidnapped his robotic companion. After being rescued, Clank decided to join Ratchet in stopping the thief and get back the Protopet.

Being the heroes they are, Ratchet and Clank successfully defeated the thief, retrieved the Protopet, and delivered the experiment to Fizzwidget. Strangely enough, Fizzwidget had a funny way of showing his appreciation, as he "accidentally" ejected the duo from his ship. Shortly after, the thief confronted the heroes, demanding the experiment returned to her. This thief turned out to be Angela Cross, a Lombax just like Ratchet.

Angela was a former employee of Megacorp and worked on the Protopet, but was fired from the team when Megacorp decided to release the Protopet before a flaw could be fixed. In its current state the Protopet could lead to galactic doom! Having discovered the truth, Ratchet and Clank try to persuade Fizzwidget to put an end to the Protopet. Their efforts were in vain.

Fizzwidget turned on his former comrades, had his thugs lockup Ratchet and Clank, and capture Angela. But the duo's stint in jail wasn't long lived. They soon escaped and freed Angela. Reunited, the group traveled to Megacorp HQ with the Helix-O-Morph, Angela's invention that would repair the fatal flaw in the Protopet. But once at the company's headquarters, they witnessed another shocking twist. Fizzwidget was actually the faux-superhero, Captain Qwark.

Snatching the Helix-O-Morph, Qwark zapped the Protopet, but instead of being rendered harmless, the experiment grew into a gigantic monster! Luckily, the heroes were able defeat the Protopet before it could go on a rampage. Afterward, Clank discovered that the batteries in the Helix-O-Morph were in backwards, which was what caused the mishap. With this knowledge, Angela was able to finally fix the Protopet and everyone (minus Qwark) had their happy ending.

RATCHET & CLANK: UP YOUR ARSENAL

Date Released: November 2, 2004   **System:** PlayStation®2

"To think, they called me insane, Lawrence. We'll see who's insane... when my pets have exterminated all life on this miserable planet!"

Enjoying some well-deserved time off after their last adventure by flipping through Holo-Vision channels, Ratchet and Clank stumbled upon a disturbing news report: Ratchet's home world, Veldin, was under attack from an army of Tyhrranoids and their robotic leader, Dr. Nefarious. Spurred into action, Ratchet and Clank took off immediately for Veldin, hoping to join the battle.

Upon their arrival, Ratchet was appointed the new sergeant for the Galactic Rangers and given an audience with the President. The President tasked the duo with finding the only man who ever fought Dr. Nefarious and lived: the Florana Tree Beast. The only problem was that the Florana Tree Beast was actually Captain Qwark. Apparently, the fake hero lost his memory while trying to save the Florana Jungle's fauna and thought he was a monkey.

On Florana, the heroic duo battled through the Path of Death to find the confused Captain Qwark. Ratchet and Clank packed up Qwark and his one-eyed monkey pal Skrunch, and met with Captain Sasha Phyronix and the Starship Phoenix to continue their quest.

Meanwhile, Dr. Nefarious had interrupted galactic transmissions in order to declare war on all organic life forms, or "Squishies" as he prefers to call them. The Starship Phoenix set a course for the planet Marcadia to meet up with the rest of the Galactic Rangers. Here, Ratchet and Clank's crew grew to include Big Al, Helga, Skidd McMarx, and a fully recovered Captain Qwark to their rosters. Together, they formed the Q-Force!

The Q-Force set out to infiltrate Nefarious' base on the planet Aquatos. There, they discovered the not-so-good doctor's secret weapon, a device called the Biobliterator that could turn organic life into robots. Ratchet and Clank, along with the rest of the Q-Force, faced many challenges on their quest against Nefarious' evil plans. Through trials and tribulations the team finally destroyed the Biobliterator, and with that the Q-Force thinks they won the day. Oh, how wrong they were! As it turned out Nefarious had built two Bioliterators.

Ratchet, Clank, and crew blasted through Nefarious' secret bases, massive Tyhrannoid monsters, and scores of dim-witted robots, until they finally confronted Nefarious himself. Armed with the second Biobliterator, Nefarious gave the heroes a valiant battle before falling and begging for mercy. Ratchet and Clank began to show just that when Dr. Nefarious made a final attack. Thanks to a last minute save by Qwark, Nefarious' weapon self-destructed and warped him to an unknown location.

Victorious, the Q-Force and friends sit down to watch the newest *Secret Agent Clank* Holo-Film and finally get that much needed rest.

RATCHET:
DEADLOCK

Date Released: October 25, 2005   **System:** PlayStation®2

"Now I'm going to do what I should have done a long time ago... I'm going to give DreadZone fans the finale they always wanted... It's a little one-act play I like to call... Death of a Lombax."

Gleeman Vox had a dream: to create the highest rated show ever to hit Holo-Vision. That dream became a reality with the creation of DreadZone. This gladiatorial show pitted hero against hero in a series of fights to the death, and before Ratchet knew it, he was the newest contender!

Ratchet was placed on Team Darkstar along with Clank, Big Al, and two combat bots: Merc and Green. No one thought Ratchet would make it far in DreadZone, but the hero was an expert in all types of combat and weaponry. Ratchet defeated opponent after opponent until he reached the legendary Exterminator of DreadZone and former hero, Ace Hardlight.

While Ratchet was busting up bots and taking names, Big Al and Clank were searching for a way out of the Deadlock collars that kept Team Darkstar (and all other contestants) in Vox's clutches. Hardlight discovered Big Al's plan and shot the technical engineer with his blaster. Later, Al returned to DreadZone with robotic features.

After Ratchet defeated Hardlight, Vox was particularly upset. How was he supposed to sell Hardlight merchandise if he was defeated? Vox offered Ratchet a deal to use the Lombax's image to sell merchandise and make a profit out of the situation, but Ratchet declined. Now furious, Vox sent Ratchet on a death mission. When the Lombax once again returned victorious, Vox was beside himself with anger. Desperate for ratings and money, Vox gave Ratchet one last mission. The price of failure was complete destruction of DreadZone Station.

Ratchet eventually defeated Vox, destroyed the station's containment fields, and freed all the imprisoned heroes. Team Darkstar, along with the rest of the DreadZone Station inhabitants, escaped and the station exploded with only Vox left on it.

RATCHET & CLANK:
SIZE MATTERS

Date Released: February 14, 2007/March 11, 2008   **System:** PlayStation®Portable/PlayStation®2

"Nothing is stronger than the power of the mind!"

After the events on DreadZone Station, Ratchet and Clank took a vacation on the tropical planet Pokitaru. By now you'd think the duo would know that any vacation they take will end in trouble, and this one was no exception. While relaxing, Ratchet was approached by a young girl named Luna who was working on a school report about heroes. Ratchet agrees to help her with a few things, but Luna is kidnapped by a robot during her assignment. Ratchet and Clank immediately set off to save the little girl.

After an intense robot battle, Ratchet and Clank discover a race of tiny inventors known as the Technomites. These underappreciated technical maestros may have been behind Luna's kidnapping, so the heroic duo followed a trail of artifacts to their home base. Ratchet then discovered that Luna was no more than a robotic puppet built to lure him into a trap.

Ratchet and Clank defeated the robot girl and uncovered the truth behind the Technomite plot: the Technomite leader, Emperor Otto, wanted to create an army of Ratchet clones to kidnap intelligent beings across the galaxy so he could absorb their smarts. Battling through a multitude of clones, Ratchet finally turned the tide on Emperor Otto, transferring all his raw intellectual power into Captain Qwark's chimp pal, Skrunch.

SECRET AGENT CLANK

Date Released: June 27, 2008/May 26, 2009   **System:** PlayStation®Portable/PlayStation®2

"Bravo, Hector, Serpentine; the turkey is in the dishwasher."

Between adventures with Ratchet, Clank donned a snazzy tuxedo and became his debonair alter ego, Secret Agent Clank. The mission: infiltrate the Boltaire Museum to stop the theft of the priceless Eye of Infinity gem. Clank arrived at the museum too late, but he did manage to identify the thief who was none other than his best friend, Ratchet! Ratchet was then quickly apprehended by local authorities and thrown in jail and forced to fight the minions he's put behind bars over the years. Clank swore his friend was innocent, and set out to find the real culprit of these crimes.

Traipsing across exotic locals, Clank found information on a new criminal master-mind known to locals only as The Kingpin. The crime lord was rumored to have a gun capable of destroying the galaxy. As Clank's investigation brought him closer this mysterious figure, The Kingpin revealed himself to be Klunk, Clank's evil twin. Klunk planned to use the Eye of Infinity to act as a refractor for a massive laser system, destroying every planet in the galaxy with a single shot!

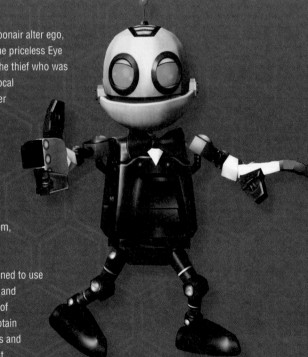

As for Ratchet, Klunk had controlled his actions with a mind-control helmet and planned to use the unwitting Lombax as a scapegoat. Ratchet would be the one to activate the laser and Klunk, posing as Clank, would stop Ratchet and win the love, adoration, and control of the people of the galaxy. Clank, with a little help from the serendipitous arrival of Captain Qwark, managed to put a stop to Klunk's schemes. Ratchet was cleared of his crimes and Klunk was transformed into a new vacuum cleaner for Ratchet and Clank's apartment.

RATCHET & CLANK FUTURE:
TOOLS OF DESTRUCTION

Date Released: October 23, 2007   **System:** PlayStation®3

"Emperor Percival Tachyon… Crown Prince of the Cragmites… and… pending the destruction of a few insubordinate species… ruler of the universe!"

While spending some free time working on an old rocket sled, Ratchet and Clank received a distress call from Captain Qwark. A large army of robots, lead by Emperor Tachyon, had unleashed a full-scale assault on the capital city, Metropolis. Tachyon revealed that he was searching for Ratchet, the last Lombax in the galaxy. Outnumbered and outgunned, Ratchet and Clank flee to learn more about the mysterious Tachyon.

Shortly after starting their quest, Clank was visited by tiny beings (that only he can see) called the Zoni. The Zoni come and go, upgrading Clank and telling him that he is special. They also tell Clank that he must soon help Ratchet make a difficult decision.

During their adventure the duo learned a bit of shocking history, as well. The Lombaxes had wiped out a destructive race known as the Cragmites, banishing them to another dimension and becoming heroes across the galaxy. One Cragmite egg was left behind, however, and raised by the Lombaxes. This Cragmite grew up to be Tachyon. After learning what the Lombaxes had done to his species, Tachyon launched an attack on his adopted home world. Fearing defeat, the Lombaxes used a device known as the Dimensionator to escape to an alternate dimension. There were only two Lombaxes left behind: The Guardian of the Dimensionator and his son, Ratchet.

Determined to put an end to Tachyon's plot for revenge, Ratchet and Clank fought from planet to planet until they confronted the vengeance-driven emperor. But, during their meeting Tachyon made an offer to Ratchet. It was an offer Ratchet had wanted to hear his whole life. Tachyon used the Dimensionator to open a portal to the Lombaxes new home and offered to send Ratchet to his people.

Ratchet was torn. Would he reunite with the family and community he thought was forever lost? Or would he stay in the current universe with the only friends he's ever known? With the help of Clank, who received warning from the Zoni, Ratchet realized that no world is safe while Tachyon holds the Dimensionator. During the ensuing battle the Dimensionator became damaged, creating a black hole that sucked Tachyon into oblivion.

Ratchet, Clank, and their friends gathered to celebrate the victory, but the Zoni had other plans. Now visible to everyone, the robots say they will take Clank "home" and show him who he truly is. Clank agrees (possibly not of his own free will), leaving a stunned Ratchet behind as he goes with the Zoni towards his destiny.

RATCHET & CLANK FUTURE: QUEST FOR BOOTY

Date Released: August 21, 2008   **System:** PlayStation®3

A year after Clank was kidnapped by the mysterious race known as the Zoni, Ratchet and his friend Talwyn were still on the hunt for their pintsized pal. Their journey took them to the pirate planet Merdegraw in search of Captain Darkwater, a rumored expert on Zoni culture. The pair encountered an old friend, Rusty Pete, whose boisterous demeanor attracted the attention of some nearby pirates. Under attack from Sprocket and his pirate horde, Ratchet and Talwyn managed to trick the pirates into launching them out of a cannon toward Hoolefar Island, where Rusty Pete claimed they would find what they've been looking for.

On the shore of Hoolefar Island, Ratchet had a vision of Clank suspended in mid-air by blue energy. Before Ratchet could attempt to communicate with Clank, Talwyn shocked him back to reality. The duo then met the Mayor of Hoolefar Island who agreed to give Ratchet a powerful telescope called the Obsidian Eye after he performed a few tasks for the people. Ratchet completed the tasks, and received the Obsidian Eye, built by Captain Darkwater to communicate with the Zoni. However, the Obsidian Eye was missing its power source, the Fulcrum Star, and was useless without it. It was then that Rusty Pete arrived on the scene, offering to take the pair to Darkwater's ship, where the Fulcrum Star was hidden.

It was rumored that Captain Darkwater's ship was cursed and if anyone disturbed it he and his crew would return from the dead. The trio discovered the ship and Darkwater's severed head. Upon picking up Darkwater's head Ratchet found a map. Rusty Pete, while checking for booby traps, placed the severed head of his friend, Captain Slag, on Darkwater's body and unknowingly resurrected the ancient captain.

Ratchet, Talwyn, and Rusty Pete discovered just how true the curse was and fended off the attacks from the resurrected pirates. Making their exit, the group followed the map they found to Darkwater Cove, an island where Captain Darkwater hid all of his treasure.

At the pirate's cave, Ratchet spied the Fulcrum Star almost immediately and rushed toward it. However, in the Lombax's haste he triggered a trap door and fell deep into an underground cave. It was at this time that the persistent Captain Darkwater/Slag caught up to the heroes and renewed his attack.

Ratchet escaped and defeated Darkwater, ending the curse. With all threats removed, Ratchet is finally able to collect the Fulcrum Star. Using the object to activate the Obsidian Eye, Ratchet peered in. There, he saw his best friend, Clank, floating in same beam of light as before, speaking gibberish about "The Doctor" coming to fix him. Ratchet then saw a shadowy figure coming down the stairs toward Clank, and when the shadow stepped into the light "The Doctor" was none other than the villainous Dr. Nefarious!

Ratchet discerned that Nefarious was holding Clank in the Breegus Nebula and immediately sets out to rescue his friend before it's too late.

RATCHET & CLANK FUTURE: A CRACK IN TIME

Date Released: October 27, 2009   **System:** PlayStation®3

"With the clock under my control, I'll be able to wrong all the rights in the universe. Every villain who has ever stumbled will get a do-over. Every protagonist's triumph will be reversed! Until, finally, a new present is created... in which the heroes always lose!"

The Zoni wanted nothing more than to protect their master, the next keeper of the Great Clock, Clank. They thought that the robotic stranger they met would help them, and the Zoni relied on Dr. Nefarious to "fix" Clank. However, the pintsized bot was the key to opening the Great Clock's innermost room, the Orvus Chamber, and Nefarious wanted in.

The Zoni did not like what Nefarious was up to and soon their partnership was dissolved. Clank finally awoke from his deep sleep and wanted nothing more than to get away from his longtime nemesis.

A clock caretaker name Sigmund freed Clank and took him to the mnemonic chamber where the small robot discovered that his own father, Orvus, built the clock to fix a rift in time caused by improper time travel. He also discovered that something terrible happened to his father on Zanifar.

While Clank was discovering his past, Ratchet and Captain Qwark crash-landed on a planet while searching for their robot friend. On the planet Qwark revealed the existence of another Lombax named General Alister Azimuth, a friend of Ratchet's father. From Azimuth, Ratchet learned that Emperor Tachyon's army killed his father, Kaden, and his mother before they could escape. Since Tachyon had tricked Azimuth into helping build the army that led to the isolation of the Lombax, he took responsibility for their deaths. That was why Azimuth was left behind when his race fled. As they searched for a way to contact Clank, the general promised Ratchet he would use the Great Clock to bring back his parents.

They used an Obsidian Eye to contact Clank, who begged Ratchet to go to Zanifar and use a time portal to help his father. Ratchet traveled back in time, where he watched Orvus vanish after refusing Dr. Nefarious entry into the Orvus Chamber and discovered that only Clank could enter it safely.

Back at the Great Clock, Dr. Nefarious immobilized Clank and Sigmund, and led Ratchet and Azimuth into a trap. However, Ratchet still managed to save Clank, who explained that using the clock to save the Lombaxes would cause a time crisis. Ratchet sadly accepted the news, but Azimuth did not and left.

Ratchet, Clank and Qwark continued their quest and thwarted Nefarious' plan to alter time so that the villains always won. Ratchet and Clank narrowly escaped death when Azimuth returned to take them to the Great Clock.

Fearing catastrophe, Ratchet refused to help Azimuth change the past to undo his wrongs. Lost in his plan, Azimuth turned on his fellow Lombax and did the unthinkable. He killed Ratchet. Unable to stop himself, Clank broke the rule against time travel and used the Orvus Chamber to save Ratchet. Azimuth pushed past them into the chamber and almost tore apart the Great Clock trying to rescue the Lombaxes. Realizing he was unhinging the universe, Azimuth sacrificed himself to stop the destruction.

After the dust cleared, Clank decided to leave the clock and repairs in Sigmund's care and resolved to help Ratchet find his people.

UNLIKELY FOURSOME

RATCHET

SPECIES: LOMBAX   HEIGHT: 5'1''
SPECIAL WEAPON: DOPPLEBANGER

Ratchet has come a long way since first leaving the planet Veldin. It seems like eons ago when the Lombax first met his pint-size robot companion, Clank, and left to travel across the universe, trademark wrench in hand.

As Ratchet flew across the universe stopping one villainous plot after another, he met countless races, but never found another Lombax. He had heard that they had all been destroyed, and that he was the last of his kind. Then, during his last adventure, Ratchet met one of his own. The truth about his race and family was revealed, giving Ratchet a sense of completion.

Ratchet has always been known to leap before he looks and has a hard time resisting an adventure. But, through his travels he's matured, transforming from a know-it-all who cared only about himself to reliable friend who puts others before himself. Although forever impulsive and quick to add in a sarcastic remark, Ratchet has become a true hero, saving several galaxies from utter destruction more than a few times.

After visiting nearly every planet worth going to (and loads not worth the fuel it took to get there), and making many close friends and nearly as many enemies, Ratchet has decided to retire from hero work.

At least that was the plan before he got roped into another one of Dr. Nefarious' botched schemes. Now he's marooned on a distant planet with his best friend, Clank, the ever-ridiculous President Qwark, and the evil Dr. Nefarious.

CLANK

SPECIES: ROBOT   HEIGHT: 2'2''   SPECIAL WEAPON: ZONI RAY

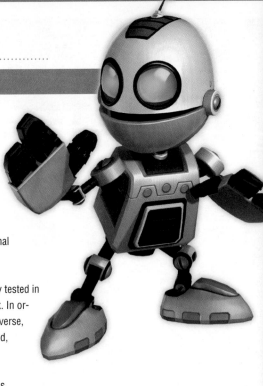

Clank has been with Ratchet since just after he was created. Clank was born in a robot factory on the planet Quartu, and shortly after gaining consciousness, he discovered his creator's devious plans to create a new planet using other planetary compounds. Barely escaping Quartu with this information, Clank crashed on Veldin. Here, he met Ratchet and the two began their first adventure.

From that day on, Clank has traveled all across the universe, acting as Ratchet's companion, voice of reason, and fellow hero. Clank is known for his loyalty, sense of humor, and scholarly knowledge. And for a small robot, Clank has a big heart. He played a large part in Ratchet's personal growth and maturity. He constantly places others before himself.

Clank has stuck by Ratchet through thick and thin, and his friendship with the Lombax was greatly tested in the duo's last adventure where Clank discovered he was initially created as heir to The Great Clock. In order to take on the duties of managing the time-keeping relic in the (approximate) center of the universe, Clank would need to leave his best friend. Unable to part, Clank decided to remain with Ratchet and, although a bit reluctant, agreed to join him in his retirement.

Now, Clank finds himself forced back into action after an ambush by legendary villain Dr. Nefarious. However, the devious booby trap has gone awry and now Clank, Ratchet, President Qwark, and Dr. Nefarious all end up on an unknown planet.

QWARK

SPECIES: UNKNOWN   HEIGHT: 10'5''   SPECIAL WEAPON: QUANTUM DEFLECTOR

Many know Copernicus Leslie Qwark as a selfless hero who stands for justice in the face of all evil, but that couldn't be farther from the truth. In reality, Qwark is nothing more than a coward looking to gain fame and fortune by riding on the backs of real heroes, which is why he is so often in the company of Ratchet and Clank.

Qwark has a unique past, to put it politely. When he was young, Quark's family put him up for adoption. Shortly after he was taken in by a family of monkeys and raised on the planet Florana. Qwark went through his schooling slowly and while still in 9th grade at the age of 26, he met the young Dr. Nefarious. Qwark greatly enjoyed his time with Nefarious in their shared biology class, and would often humiliate the younger student; somehow unaware of the torment Nefarious was experiencing. These actions had a profound influence on the adolescent Nefarious and eventually helped lead him to a life of revenge and villainy.

Nowadays Qwark is just as oblivious and greedy as ever. He recently used Ratchet and Clank's latest victory over Nefarious to propel himself into the spotlight and the hearts of the Polaris Galaxy's citizens. He earned their trust and votes, and now acts as the Galactic President of the Polaris Galaxy.

At the onset of this current adventure, and unbeknownst to Qwark (as most things are), Nefarious has been plotting revenge since his last defeat and is now ready to cause some havoc for the new Galactic President. Unfortunately for everyone involved, Nefarious' plan backfires and Qwark is stranded on an unknown planet with Ratchet, Clank, and Nefarious. Will Qwark finally step into a true hero role in this new adventure? Or will he continue to burden everyone around him?

DR. NEFARIOUS

SPECIES: ROBOT   HEIGHT: 6'
SPECIAL WEAPON: CLOAKER

Dr. Nefarious is egotistical, cunning, maniacal, and just plain evil. After enduring constant humiliation at the hands of Qwark during his youth, and at the hands of colleagues during Nefarious' attempt at a legitimate scientific career, the doctor decided to become a super-villain and mad scientist. Nefarious swore revenge on all who wronged him, and declared himself Qwark's arch nemesis. However, shortly after starting his revenge, the big green menace accidently sent Nefarious plummeting into a pit of churning gears. Most creatures would have been killed in the machinery, but Nefarious stayed alive and transformed into a robotic being. Nefarious' new form made him stronger and he extended his hatred from the beings who had picked on him to all organic life forms or, as Nefarious calls them, squishies.

However, none of Nefarious' attempts to destroy all squishies and rid the universe of Qwark have been successful, thanks to the two adventurers and galactic heroes, Ratchet and Clank. By now, these two have skyrocketed to the top of Nefarious' must-destroy list along with Qwark.

After Nefarious' most recent failure, he traveled to planet Luminopolis with another devious plan. Successfully tricking Qwark, Ratchet, and Clank into visiting Luminopolis, Nefarious unleashed a Z'Grute on the city. But when the Z'Grute went out of control, Nefarious had to join his hated enemies in stopping it.

The Z'Grute's rampage caught the attention of a powerful interstellar machine known as the Creature Collector. That's when Nefarious' plan completely backfired. After being dumped by the Creature Collector on an unknown planet with Ratchet, Clank, and Qwark, Nefarious comes to the horrifying realization that his only way out of this unexpected mess may be teaming up with his most hated enemies.

PLANET IGLIAK
LUMINOPOLIS

OBJECTIVES

ROOFTOP AMPHITHEATRE

- Chase Down the Z'Grute
- Apprehend the Z'Grute Using the Air Taxi

SKYWAY

- Fend Off the Minions
- Complete Weapon Certification Program

POWER STATION EXIT

- Access the Fusion Turrets atop Zogg Tower
- Defeat the Z'Grute

NEW ENEMIES DEFEATED

ROOFTOP AMPHITHEATRE

Lumenoid

SKYWAY

Cleaner Minion

Scout Minion

Intrepid heroes Ratchet and Clank arrive in the glittering city of Luminopolis on Planet Igliak in their sleek intergalactic ship. They're reluctantly escorting President Qwark to a ceremony where he's being given the Intergalactic Tool of Justice award. Oddly, Qwark is being rewarded for stopping a light-eating Z'Grute, a feat he can't actually recall.

Ratchet wonders aloud if accepting an award for an accomplishment he didn't do is deceitful. Concerned only about his approval ratings, Qwark continues practicing his speech. Clank questions whether the award exists at all, noting he's never heard of it before.

They arrive at a podium with a rather unusual backdrop—the massive light-eating Z'Grute looms over it, apparently frozen in cryosleep. At the last minute, Ratchet suggests contacting their robotic pals, Cronk and Zephyr.

It's too late for that, as Dr. Nefarious makes a semi-grand entrance atop a hovercraft piloted by his loyal robotic butler, Lawrence. Shouting through megaphone, Dr. Nefarious cackles maniacally as he springs his trap.

NEW WEAPONS PURCHASED

SKYWAY

☐ Combuster

POWER STATION EXIT

☐ Plasmabomb Launcher

At his command, Lawrence reanimates the Z'Grute with a handheld device. Relishing in his apparent victory, the distracted Dr. Nefarious is caught off guard when the Z'Grute decides to use his vehicle as an appetizer.

Nefarious' plan backfires as he tumbles downward through the air along with Lawrence. As he cries out for his servant's assistance, Nefarious glances up to see Lawrence scurrying away while offering his resignation.

1
MISSION

Ratchet, Clank, Qwark, and Nefarious now find themselves staring down the gullet of the Z'Grute. It bellows a mighty roar into their faces before tearing apart the stadium lights to feed further. After and throws the drained metal aside before bounding off into the city.

The heroes must stop the Z'grute before he destroys the city.

ROOFTOP AMPHITHEATRE

The Z'Grute doesn't quite know where to start. Its hunger for light could take it anywhere in this neon-laced city. Use the left stick to head down the walkway on the right past the bleachers to pursue the terrifying titan.

A toppled lamppost is blocking the path but it's no problem for the nimble Lombax. Simply leap over it by pressing ⊗.

On the other side, the Z'Grute can be seen clinging to the edge of the platform but quickly clambers away. Sprint to catch up by pressing **L3** once while moving to give your character a temporary burst of speed. A bright trail of light is left in his wake as he hurries onward.

Run ahead and leap up to the upper tiers of the platform ahead (indicated by the upward pointing arrows) with some dynamic double jumping. Simply jump once then press ⊗ again at its peak to perform another jump propelling your character even higher.

BE CRATE-FUL

Press ⊙ to perform your character's melee attack. Use it to smash up the stacks of crates along the route here to add valuable bolts to your collection. Bolts are used to purchase weapons and weapon upgrades. Your character's current bolt count appears in the upper-right corner. To see his current total Bolt count, press **L2**.

LIGHTS OUT

Melee attacks also bust the white domed lights lining the path—all the less for the Z'Grute to munch on. While in the swing of things, bash the roving bystander robots nearby. There are trillions of robots and even more lights in the city, so who would notice if a few extra wind up smashed? Just chalk it up to the Z'Grute.

At the end of the path, employ the Swingshot to continue. The Swingshot is a versatile tool capable of latching onto special floating anchor points that pulse with green light.

Press and hold ⬤ when in range of one to deploy the Swingshot. While latched on, use the left stick to swing back and forth to build momentum. Detaching the Swingshot is as easy as releasing ⬤.

CROSS-TOWN TRAFFIC

Swinging safely to the next platform triggers a bridge of light that stops air traffic and spans the distance between Ratchet's location and the Z'Grute up ahead. The Z'Grute's razor-sharp senses react quickly to Ratchet's approach and it flees after flinging a billboard through the air.

SAVING GRACE

Upon landing, your character triggers a bright green hologram of a check mark. This is one of many Checkpoints spread throughout the game.

Passing one ensures that even if the worst should happen, you can count on restarting at the nearest Checkpoint rather than the very beginning of a level.

Checkpoints are only good while within the level. Exiting then reloading progress places your character at the most recent of each level's handful of save points.

BREAK THE BANK

Continue to double-jump onto the higher levels until the next Checkpoint is reached. Your team encounters a series of curious-looking crates beside it. These yellow-framed containers topped with flashing red lights certainly beg to be broken. However, to crack this nut, you need to use some fancier moves.

Jump and press ⬤ mid-air and Ratchet brings his wrench down over his head for a powerful Slam Attack. This brutal blow busts the fancy box open and releases the 45 bolts within.

After collecting the sizable sum, continue onwards where evidence of the Z'Grute is plain as day. In its quest for delicious light, it's torn through the floors to get at the conduits routing the city's lights. Jump over the melted gaps in the flooring in the search for further clues as to where the bounding beast is off to next.

CONTENTS UNDER PRESSURE

Stay Ratchet's furry hand from smashing the yellow-cored boxes here. These explosive crates go boom in a big way even from the slightest nudge. Don't drain your character's health meter by being careless here.

To safely break them without risking life and limb, make use of your character's throw attack. For example, hold **R2** and press ⬤ to hurl Ratchet's wrench through the air at the target and have it safely return.

After crossing the last gap, the Z'Grute reappears and tears a titanic light bulb from the surrounding cityscape with its big, meaty paws. After separating the bulb from its base, the voracious villain tilts its head back and opens wide. Without hesitation, it pours the luminous contents down its gullet before fleeing once more.

The Z'Grute's haphazard buffet has spilled out onto the path ahead. The bright, electricity-generating Lumenoids have been riled up by their traumatic experience.

Looking to pick a fight, they lash out at Ratchet without provocation. Smack them silly with Ratchet's wrench to put them in their place.

JUICE JITTERS

These supercharged critters are filled with electricity. A single touch is all it takes to cost your character a segment of his health bar, so take them out before they get too close.

Keep chugging ahead and dispatch the additional aggressive Lumenoids littering the path. Continue crossing gaps along the platforms until a curving staircase comes into view.

PHONE A FRIEND

When you're playing alone, Clank is hesitant to jump the last gap and timidly waits on the other side. To call him to action, press **L2** and he quickly hookshots to Ratchet's position.

Ignore the staircase and instead double jump up to the ivy-covered platform it winds around. Smash the collection of crates here for plenty of bolts before moving on.

FLIP THEIR LIDS

Keep moving on up to the Checkpoint above where a smiling robot with a pulsing green hat stands idle. He's half of a pair controlling the light bridge here. Across from him, his buddy is taking a nap at his post with only a pulsing red hat visible.

They're both shirking their duties and breaking the circuit. Get them both back to work first by using your character's slam attack to bop the green-topped Slambot on the head and into position.

This wakes up his partner in a hurry, so do the same to him (or let Ratchet's partner pick up the slack). Work quickly because they reset position after a short period of time.

TEAMWORK PAYS OFF

Team actions like this one earn Ratchet and his partner Co-op Points. Flipping these robot switches award the activating players with 5 Co-op points.

With the light bridge in place, Ratchet can safely cross to the other side. A short distance away, the Z'Grute is merrily munching on another Lumenoid conduit bulb.

As soon as it spies Ratchet, it tosses the hefty bulb in his direction and takes off once more. It shatters upon the walkway ahead and releases another cluster of livid Lumenoids looking to pick a fight. Fight past them and hookshot over to the next platform.

MEDICAL SCIENCE

Just ahead of where Ratchet lands is a Nanotech crate. These brightly lit crates contain vital Nanotech used to heal when your character's health is low.

Break it open to release the bright Nanotech spheres. Get close enough and they are automatically drawn to Ratchet, healing him in the process. Nanotech is vital to keeping Ratchet and his friends healthy, restoring their health meters when they are low.

Continue down the path littered with crates, explosive crates, a slam crate, and another Nanotech crate. An Air Taxi call box bobs mid-air just past the Checkpoint there. Ring the call box bell to summon a taxi. To do so, hold **R2** and press ⊙ for a throw attack. Ratchet flings his wrench at the call box and once all his partners do the same, the air taxi appears.

RUNNING UP THE METER

Board the automated taxi that pulls up to commandeer it. While drawing closer to the Z'Grute, it angrily swats a police car out of the sky and prompts them to pull hard to the right.

The steering has gone out, requiring Ratchet and his friends to control the taxi by shifting their weight side to side to bend the gravity coils. Move collectively to avoid the giant spinning fans jutting from the sides of buildings.

After safely navigating past them, the air taxi swings into a crowded tunnel where the taxi must dodge the oncoming police traffic.

Upon reaching the tunnel's exit, a powerful explosion topples a building and forces the taxi to veer hard left and towards the Z'Grute. As they draw close, a huge contingent of police vehicles surround the Critter.

This show of force does little to intimidate the Z'Grute, and it clears the airspace with a massive electrical discharge from its paw. This destroys the air taxi, sending him and his allies falling through the air. Luckily, Ratchet and company lands on a power conduit they can grind along with ease.

NOT A SCRATCH ON HER

Successfully navigate the various obstacles without damaging the Air Taxi to acquire the "Keep the Meter Running" Trophy.

ELECTRIC SLIDE

Watch out for patches of lethal electricity. Use the left stick to lean out of the way of dangers or simply jump over them.

SKYWAY

Your character is deposited at another Checkpoint where he faces three interconnected switch robots surrounded by a number of crates. Smash the Nanotech crate on the left to heal up if necessary before proceeding.

Work with Ratchet's partners to flip the lids on all three Slambots and open the passageway ahead. As they part, a number of strange robots of unknown origin come swarming out.

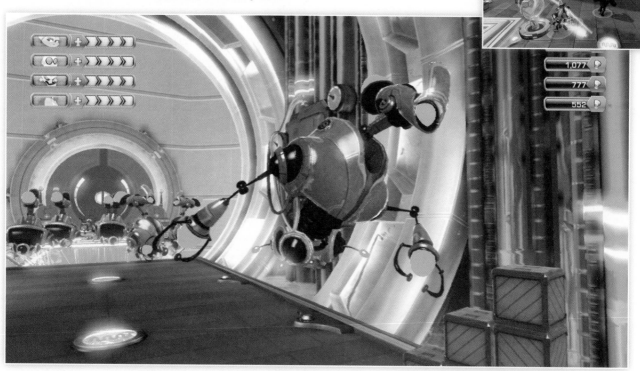

These Cleaner Minions project deadly laser beams that cut across the ground toward their targets. However, their armor is no match for a few swings (or throws) of Ratchet's trusty wrench.

Clear a path through them and march across the light bridge to the circular platform in the middle of a large chamber ahead.

WEAPONS TRAINING

Kip Darling notes that Ratchet and company have found a weapons kiosk left over from Qwark's "Friendship Through Firepower" initiative. Step onto the pad and then press ● to activate it.

Within the store the Combuster is available for the low cost of nothing. Use the left analog stick to cycle through the available weapons until it is selected, then press ● to buy it.

Press ● to exit and return to the game. Now that Ratchet is equipped with a Combuster, the automated Weapon Certification Program begins.

President Qwark's pre-recorded instructions talk Ratchet through the basics of using the Combuster. Fire the Combuster at the stationary targets that appear by pressing or holding **R1**.

Following the first wave, a second appears—this time moving front to back. Thanks to the generous auto-lock feature, tracking these targets is a piece of cake.

After eliminating two waves of targets, it's time to mix things up. The next set of cutouts moves vertically, giving Ratchet a chance to test out the locking mechanism. Hold **L1** to lock onto nearby enemies before firing to unleash punishment with pinpoint accuracy.

There's one last test to pass in order to exit the training program and it's all about teamwork. Two crackling spheres of energy control the exit lock. It takes friends to build up enough of an overload to blast each one.

FRIENDLY FIREPOWER

Locking onto the same target and firing the same weapon simultaneously triggers an exponential increase in participating teammates' rate of fire. Not only that, but damage is also multiplied. Gang up on the bad guys with Ratchet's allies to maximize the mayhem. Every time teammates work together to overload a target, the participating players get 5 Co-op points.

The portal opens onto a walkway filled with more Cleaner Minions. They're even easier to eliminate now that Ratchet is armed with a Combuster.

After clearing the way, advance ahead where a handy new addition can be seen. The bright green hologram of a bullet icon marks an Ammo Pad location. These resupply Ratchet and his allies' arsenal with critical ordnance.

POWER STATION

Rearm at the Checkpoint, taking advantage of the Nanotech crate there if needed, and then proceed down the path to the right. Look through the glass windows on the left to view the mystery robots in pursuit of the Z'Grute. The news anchor notes its destination appears to be the Power Station.

Peeved at its pursuer, the Z'Grute smacks the robot through the window and right in front of Ratchet. This hefty robotic adversary quickly recovers to reveal itself fully as a Scout Minion.

Scout Minions are heavily armored, bipedal robots armed with twin laser cannon arms. Nimbly jump over the incoming fire and use the jutting metal pipes on the left as cover. Ratchet's allies should target a single opponent to dispatch it with maximum efficiency. Don't forget the Ammo Pad nearby in case anyone runs dry.

As Ratchet tromps past the metal wreckage, the doorway ahead opens to reveal more Cleaner Minions. Eliminate them from a distance, and then press onward past numerous crates into the power station.

In the center of the next room is a new type of crate: the Bolt Grabber. The player that breaks the Bolt Grabber glows brightly, automatically breaking any crates within a few paces. The Bolt Grabber also doubles the bolts the players earn while it is active.

The dual-generator door here is sealed shut, so blast its power supplies to force it open. The Ammo Pad opposite the Checkpoint comes in handy if

one of Ratchet's buddies gets a little too trigger-happy.

Through the open door, a pair of Scout Minions immediately opens fire. Reload at the Ammo Pad after blasting them and break the Nanotech crate at the far end of the walkway.

As the group approaches the elevator platform at the far end, Lumenoids leap out of the electrically charged waters. The Combuster sends them packing, allowing a character to step onto the platform. Press ▲ to activate it when all players are in position.

The elevator comes to a stop right in front of several more Cleaner Minions. Shoot them down then reload at the Ammo Pad. Head left take on the solo Scout Minion blocking the circular passageway.

A lonesome Cleaner Minion patrols in the next room but several more arrive, joined by two Scout Minions as soon as Ratchet enters. Use the planter boxes as cover and the Ammo Pads at either end of the room, as needed, to fend off the assault in this tight space.

Once all enemies have been cleared, the exit door's generator shields retract. Fire in conjunction with Ratchet's allies to open the door and pick up the Nanotech crate on the way out.

POWER STATION EXIT

Back outside once again at a Checkpoint, Ratchet eyes another Bolt Grabber ahead. The walkway comes to an end with a Swingcopter hovering overhead.

STACKS ON THE SIDE

Show leadership and charge forward through the exit to safety. Smash the Bolt Grabber there and then backtrack. Explore the walkway to the right of the Checkpoint. A single slam crate and several piles of regular crates are stored here and offer bountiful bolts.

Press and hold ▲ until all Ratchet's teammates have attached their Swingshots. With everyone onboard, the anchor point transforms into a helicopter that whisks them all away.

FACING THE Z'GRUTE

It deposits them directly in front of the Z'Grute just as it crushes a pair of Scout Minions. It's time to confront this monster head on!

BOSS Z'GRUTE

The Z'Grute has been feasting for a while and is now supercharged with electric energy. Unfortunately for Ratchet and company, the platform is made of highly conductive tiles.

When the Z'Grute grasps the platform in both paws, keep an eye on the tiles. Those that glow brightly are about to discharge dangerous electricity.

Alternately, the Z'Grute sends waves of electricity along the length or width of the fenced off area.

SHOCKING SLAPS

Watch the Z'Grutes paws as it swings them down at the walkway. If it brings them together, it's about to pound the center and send an electric wave from front to back. If it raises just one paw, then the electric wave is about to start on that side of the screen.

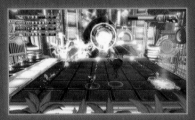

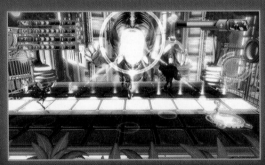

Dodge the dangerous discharges while firing at the Z'Grute with Ratchet's teammates. Only let up the assault to visit the Ammo Pad on the right as needed.

Once half the Z'Grute's health is drained—indicated by its health bar in the upper-right corner—it ceases attacking. Turning to its side, the Z'Grute selects a generator to feed from. Destroy the energy source before the Z'Grute can fully heal itself.

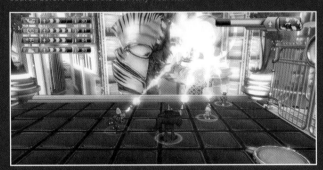

KEEP COMBUSTING!

If the Z'Grute manages to fully heal before the generator is shut down, its armor rises once more and the fight essentially starts over.

The explosion from the overloaded reactor knocks the Z'Grute back into a building. As it falls several stories out of view, the impact of its body causes the tiled walkway to crumble suddenly.

CUT TO THE CHASE

Sprint to the right past the Checkpoint to keep ahead of the collapsing path. The round platform at the end is thankfully secured, giving your character a chance to heal using the Nanotech crate before hopping onto the launcher platform.

Launcher platforms operate in the same manner as elevators and weapon vendors. Step onto the pad and press ⬤. Once all Ratchet's teammates are in position, they are launched through the air and onto a thick conduit.

Within moments, the Z'Grute, presumed defeated, leaps back into the fray. It clambers along the conduit in hot pursuit. Having caught a second wind, it unleashes electrical attacks along the length of the conduit.

Individual bursts along either the left or right side are easily dodged with a lean; however, massive rings of electricity spanning the circumference must be jumped over. The Z'grute can also shoot a burst down the center of the conduit.

After evading the attacks, Ratchet and his allies have a chance to catch their breath when a pair of vertical metal bars cuts off the Z'Grute.

They soon dismount onto an elevated walkway. Reload at the Ammo Pad then clear out the Cleaner Minions ahead to reach another weapon vendor next to a Nanotech crate.

Entering the vendor's area starts an instructional video for the newest available weapon—the Plasmabomb Launcher. It fires grenades filled with unstable plasma to reach enemies who are hiding behind cover. Purchase the Plasmabomb Launcher for 500 bolts, and then exit the vendor to get back to the fight.

Run to the right and jump over the gap onto the next platform where a number of Cleaner Minions quickly descend. Further ahead, a pair of Scout Minions fire from the tiled area. Destroy all the Minions and then step onto the tiled floor to confront the Z'Grute at the far end.

UNEXPECTED ASSIST

Hang back and out of the Scout Minions' line of fire. The Z'Grute's attacks from the other side of the corridor save the team some headache by taking out the Scout Minions from behind.

Try out the new Plasmabomb Launcher against the Z'Grute while dodging its standard array of attacks. The combined might of the Plasmabombs puts the Z'Grute in its place, but the fight is far from over. Forge ahead to the elevator pad, picking up Nanotech as needed, and then ride it up.

STRAIGHT TO THE TOP

As the team ascends, the Z'Grute hops onto the domed cover in an attempt to break through. Unable to penetrate the barrier, it leaps away and begins to climb up an adjacent tower.

During the ride up, the news anchors comment that the tower the Z'Grute is climbing just had a top-of-the-line Lumenoid generator installed, offering plenty of juice for the Z'Grute to feed on.

The elevator swiftly whisks Ratchet and his allies upwards to the top of Zogg Tower. It comes to a smooth stop at the top floor to face an ornery pack of Cleaner and Scout Minions.

Sweep the domed room clear of enemies, then turn to face the four Slambots seated in the floor. Slam attack them in sequence to open the doorway leading to the exterior. The balcony there touts a row of heavy-duty turrets. Don't pass up the Nanotech crate on way out.

BOSS Z'GRUTE

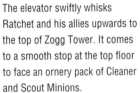

Press ▲ to mount one of the stationary turrets. Aim the turret with the left stick and press **L1** to fire slow, powerful rockets or **R1** to shoot rapid-fire projectiles.

IT'S A TOSS-UP

The Z'Grute is content to attack from the safety of the shielded generator, hurling charged balls of electricity. Your character should use rockets to take out the projectiles the Z'Grute sends their way.

Once the generator's shields have fallen, it's time to concentrate the full combined firepower of all the turrets at the generator.

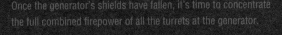

There are four shield generators lined up in view of the turrets. Launch a stream of rockets, coordinating with teammates, to focus on a single target at a time.

Without the shields to protect it, the generator reaches critical mass and forcefully discharges a massive amount of energy. The explosion launches the Z'Grute skyward and directly at Ratchet and his allies.

It sinks its claws deep into the platform and clings fiercely. Be careful as the Z'Grute has enough juice left to send charged attacks through the tiles. Note that its paws are invulnerable while glowing with electricity. Slam attack each of its meaty paws to loosen its grip and send the ravenous rascal packing.

GETTING A GRIP

The Z'Grute is a tough cookie and it can grab back onto the platform a short time after its paw is struck loose.

THE ENEMY OF MY ENEMY?

During the fracas, Nefarious tries to duck out stealthily. But even the slow-witted Qwark isn't fooled that easily. As he begins to confront the megalomaniacal robot, the overhead descent of a giant spaceship distracts the quartet.

They watch in stunned silence as Nefarious observes the space vessel isn't one of his. And with that a giant metal claw extends from the craft to seize the unlikely gang of four in its grasp.

ALDAROS PLAINS

OBJECTIVES

DETENTION CELL
- Complete Gadget Certification
- Regroup with Susie at the South Exit
- Defeat the Minions
- Escape Training Center

OUTSIDE RECEIVING STATION
- Defeat the Gravity Bot to Restore Gravity

ARCHIPELAGO
- Trek to Susie's Village
- Traverse Aldaros Plains

VILLAGE ENTRANCE
- Meet up with Susie
- Explore the Tharpod Village
- Follow the Gravoid!

VILLAGE OUTSKIRTS
- Search for Susie
- Rescue Susie

HERO BOLTS

✓	**DETENTION CELL**
	Under a glass container at the end of lesson three
	Right of the exit door at the end of lesson four
	OUTSIDE RECEIVING STATION
	In the middle of the first stretch of collapsing brown rock
	Head right after landing in a semi-circle of exploding crates atop lava rock
	On the far end of the rock island before the zipline leading to Susie's Village
	VILLAGE ENTRANCE
	On a metal platform between the two bridges to the right of Susie's village entrance
	To the left of the first Pyromite Spawner
	VILLAGE OUTSKIRTS
	Right of the Checkpoint following the fight under the energy shield
	On the left after the Hookshot spring follow Secret Lab #2

Intergalactic adventuring means having to catch shut-eye in some uncomfortable places. So it's understandable when Ratchet groggily regains consciousness that he doesn't immediately realize he's dangling upside down.

Luckily for the foursome, a young galactic scout named Susie shouts to them from the platform below. Chipper and willing to help, she uses a vacuum-powered gadget to release the gang from their bonds and drop them rather roughly to the ground.

NEW ENEMIES DEFEATED

DETENTION CELL

Rift-Jumper Minion

Blade Minion

OUTSIDE RECEIVING STATION

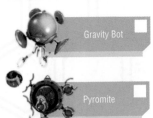
Gravity Bot

Pyromite

ARCHIPELAGO

Gravoid

Gravoid Brute

NEW WEAPONS PURCHASED

OUTSIDE RECEIVING STATION

☐ Arc Lasher

ARCHIPELAGO (VILLAGE ENTRANCE)

☐ Doppelbanger

☐ Zoni Blaster

☐ Quantum Deflector

☐ Cloaker

DETENTION CELL

The young scout knows a great deal about the layout of this massive, mechanical facility. After freeing Ratchet and his allies, she instructs them to regroup with her via the sector seven air vent leading to the south side.

From this floating platform, there appears to be only one exit—a conveniently located launch pad. Follow the on-screen prompts to launch Ratchet and his allies through the air to safety.

2
MISSION

The circular portal before them opens onto a walkway parallel to a rail transport system. Clank observes they appear to be in a creature habitat that collects all manner of species. But with escape as their top priority, there's no time for sightseeing.

A short distance ahead is an elevator pad. Get onboard to be whisked a level below where the group is scanned. Detecting biological life forms, the disembodied female voice of the facility computer prepares to send them to a creature pen for probing and experimentation. Ratchet fools the computer, which redirects them to the training lab for gadget certification.

TRAINING LAB

The foursome is teleported suddenly to the training lab where flickering monitors overhead display the number 1. Proceed to the right past the Checkpoint where the first of many menial maintenance robots wander idly. Smash them for their bolts before encountering a sudden drop-off. There's no danger in falling, because the spring-loaded tiles are quick to send any of the foursome back where they started.

Crossing this area is a simple matter of using the Swingshot to swing from each of the overhead anchor points. The computer voice approves of the group's progress and opens the doorway once they reach the far right.

The doorway opens to reveal Susie. As the group passes through the room, the computer detects an interloper near the sector two training lab. Realizing the computer is referring to her, Susie quickly uses her Vac-U to access a tunnel leading to the nearby equipment room. Before parting ways, she tells Ratchet and his allies that she left a present for them at the recharging station there.

Go through the passageway to the next Checkpoint. From there use the Hookshot to swing easily towards the destination via the overhead anchor points. After landing, proceed through the tunnel. After everyone's on the other side, hookshot across to the walkway ahead. Continue to the right where the foursome find the equipment room entrance.

RESTRICTED AREAS

Though the cavernous complex seems to stretch on forever, you aren't given free reign to roam. Bright blue energy fields appear throughout the area and act as dead ends.

BOLT GRABBER

Beat your teammates to the punch and smash the Bolt Grabber here. Sprint ahead and claim all the bolts before anyone realizes what happened. Then whistle nonchalantly as you quietly count your bolts.

WELCOME TO THE SUCK

Upon entering, Qwark finds a letter from Susie telling them to use the Vac-U units she left for them. After a technical mishap that sends Nefarious across the room, tensions start to run high.

Luckily, Clank is the voice of reason and suggests they work together until they find out where are and how to get home. Nefarious reluctantly agrees—for now.

The computer detects their new acquisitions and readies the next training lesson to familiarize them with the Vac-U. Head right into the next room and step onto the teleport pad.

Ratchet and his teammates rematerialize in front of the second training chamber. Triggering a Checkpoint as they enter, the four find themselves in an incinerator room where a wheeled robot attempts to tidy up a number of loose metal balls.

The clumsy cleaner leaves the job unfinished when it accidentally backs up into the incinerator chute. It's up to the quartet to suck up the debris and deposit it in the chute before they can continue.

Hold ◉ to activate the Vac-U and suck up a ball. Turn towards the chute and press ◉ again to fire it. The arc of light emanating from the Vac-U indicates the projected trajectory.

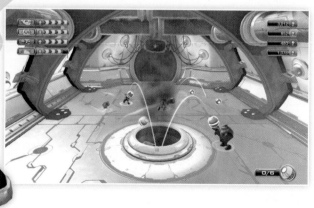

The exit opens once all six balls have been properly disposed. Before they can proceed, the computer informs them the Vac-U can also be used to suck up crates and bolts. Before they can move on, the foursome must suck up the plethora of crates in the next room.

They are greeted in the third testing area by a Checkpoint and a robotic demonstration on the other side of the glass windowpanes. Many machines in the facility can be activated when using the Vac-U to pull the triggering power plunger.

Move to the right past the screen displaying the large number 3 to cross the tiles that rise into position. They lead to a doorway that can only be opened when everyone activates the power plungers with their Vac-U. After offering its congratulations, the computer takes on a sinister undertone saying they are soon ready to oppress the planet's native Tharpods.

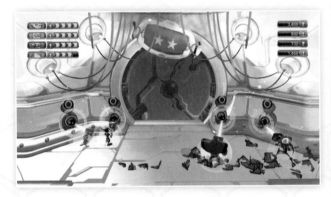

The next room is populated by four adorable critters released from their pens. Collecting critters unlocks the access to secret labs scattered throughout the game. Suck up the critters with Vac-U, but don't worry—patented zepto-srhink technology ensures they are safely stored unharmed.

Another cleanup is in order before Ratchet and his teammates can move on. Tidy up the three metal balls in the next room to raise the glass containers.

Underneath the far right container is a Hero Bolt for each member of the team. Suck it up with the Vac-U to collect it. Beneath the central dome is a teleport pad leading to the next lesson.

DRESS FOR SUCCESS

Hero Bolts are a special kind of currency used to unlock additional skins to change up the quartet's appearance. The more Hero Bolts collected, the more skins become available. Characters' skins can be changed at the Character Selection screen.

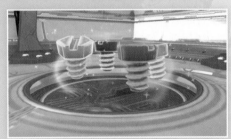

CO-OP CRATES

Sitting in the center of the room is a curious box with green power plungers protruding. Gather up a partner to apply their Vac-U skills to open it and extract the bolts inside. Plus, the two participating players get 15 Co-op Points!

The four reluctant colleagues reappear at a Checkpoint beneath screens indicating this is their fourth lesson. March onwards to the right where the computer voice explains the Vac-U can be used to launch teammates across otherwise impassable gaps.

Simply hold ⊙ until the Vac-U is pointed upward with an arrow pointing at it. Teammates can then leap into the waiting Vac-U until the player holding it presses ⊙ again to fire them off. Aim carefully to hit the concentric circles of the target pad. Both the launching and launched players receive 5 Co-op points for their teamwork. Once the teammate has safely crossed, hold ⊙ to hookshot to their position.

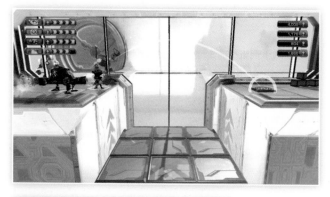

Continue on to the right until a power plunger comes into view. Use the Vac-U on it to pull the needed platform ahead out of the wall. Once it's fully extended, shoot Ratchet's teammate with the Vac-U to the target and hookshot to them.

The next door requires a manual solution to unlock. A Slambot sits in an elevated position attached to the wall. It takes a slam attack to flip its lid and open the door. Accomplish this by shooting a teammate at it as if it were a target pad, and then having the teammate press ⊙ when the button prompt appears. This useful co-op action, the Mortar Toss, is rightfully rewarded with 5 Co-op Points.

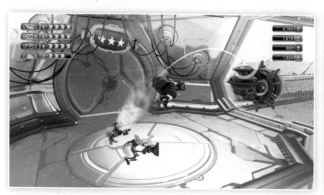

Collect the critters on the other side of the opening door then make use of the teleport pad there. With all their parts in the right place, Ratchet and his companions appear next to another Checkpoint. Proceed forward for lesson five: reviving teammates.

The multi-purpose Vac-U isn't just for keeping clean or getting around. It can actually save lives. When a teammate runs out of health, suck them up with the Vac-U before the ten-second countdown that appears over their body finishes. Hold ⊙ to use the Vac-U's rechargeable nanotech dispersal unit and fill the meter to get them back into fighting shape.

Head to the right where a dangerous, high-voltage sphere descends from the ceiling like a lethal disco ball. Retreat is not an option with a force field that rises behind Ratchet and his teammates. Passing this test requires some brief self-sacrifice. Each teammate must fall victim to the metal ball and let their teammates restore their health.

Once everyone has come back from the grave, the computer happily announces they have finished their gadget certification. The next room opens up where the foursome can claim some nifty rewards.

THE GREAT ESCAPE

Suck up the critters there and don't miss the Hero Bolt to the right of the door straight ahead. Head through the door leading past a Checkpoint, and then hop onto the circular platform. It whisks the quartet away to the right while the computer informs them their destination is a celebratory probing.

Reappearing in the nick of time, Susie manages to divert the platform safely. This doesn't go unnoticed as the computer summons robotic minions to counter the detected intruder alert. Susie opens the door to allow the gang's escape—an escape interrupted by Rift-Jumper Minions. These robots possess teleportation technology and specialize in ambushes. Individually, they're not so tough but they make up for the deficiency by attacking in large quantities.

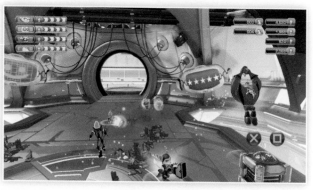

SUCKS TO BE YOU

There's no need to waste ammo on the paper-thin armor of these robots. Instead, turn them into weapons against their own kind. Suck them up with a Vac-U to turn them into makeshift projectiles that can be fired at other enemies.

After clearing the room of the robotic nuisances, team up to trigger the two Mortar Tosses keeping the exit sealed. Collect the critters in the next room and don't miss the Nanotech crate if anyone is feeling under the weather.

Travel through the doorway that opens on the right where a new robotic foe attempts to stop them—the Blade Minion. Like the Slambots, they feature green noggins. Unlike their cousins, however, they move atop sharp blades that spin ceaselessly.

To dismantle these devious destroyers, players must stun it once with a slam attack and then perform another slam attack as the critical blow. To save time, team up with one of Ratchet's allies to launch them into a slam attack the same way Mortar Tosses are dealt with. Not only is this faster, but it also rewards both participating teammates with 5 Co-op points.

APOLOGIZE LATER

Tell teammates that you'd be happy to launch them at the Blade Minions then gleefully send them into any of the orange openings in the floor to their doom. While they're out of play, take out the Blade Minions and claim the bolts for yourself.

Crash the Nanotech crate here if needed then head into the next room where two more Blade Minions arrive on the scene. Send them packing, note the Nanotech crate, and then pass the Checkpoint into the next area.

There are two more Blade Minions along with a gang of Rift-Jumper Minions looking to do some damage. Break them down for spare parts, break the Nanotech crate by the Checkpoint open if they managed to cause any harm, then wait for the next door to open.

A trio of Scout Minions stands at the ready with their gun arms locked and loaded. Rather than waste ammo on them, move behind the conveniently placed

cover and activate the power plunger. This raises another shielded barrier ahead where one of the teammates must activate a second power plunger.

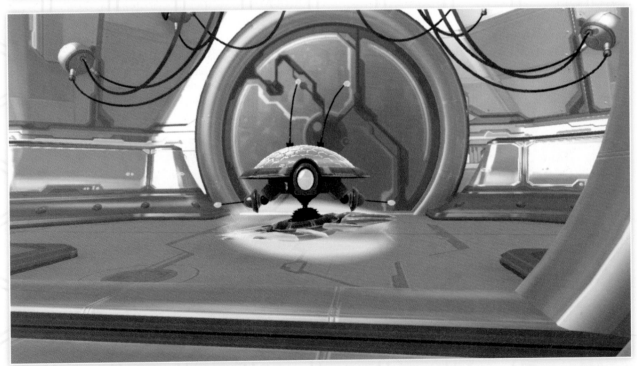

The combination of both activates an extremely convenient compactor mechanism the Scout Minions happen to be standing atop. They're ground up into tiny bits, spraying bolts freely through the air.

This final confrontation marks the last opposition before the group can escape the facility. When the doors behind the minions' open, a Scannerbot flies in to assess the fierce foursome.

SCANNER BOT

At each major leg of the team's journey, this passive robot flies in and sweeps the area with its scanner. After assessing the situation it provides a detailed recap of each players' performance and even awards bonus bolts for the best of the best in each category.

Suck up the critters wandering in the short tunnel that leads to the great outdoors and finally breathe some fresh air outside.

OUTSIDE RECEIVING STATION

Ratchet is awestruck at the massive floating rock formations. Without warning, a machine of extraterrestrial origin plummets to the ground and plants itself before the quartet.

Friendly faces greet them when the holographic projections of Cronk and Zephyr materialize. They explain the device is an Apogee Industries Communication Pod—one of many they've deployed all across the planet's surface. This versatile piece of machinery allows them to communicate with the foursome and even provide supplies.

Qwark is chomping at the bit to be rescued but, as it turns out, Cronk and Zephyr are in a bit of a pickle themselves. One of them fell asleep at the wheel and now they're stranded in an asteroid field.

While waiting for their own rescue, the cybernetic partners managed to establish a comlink to GrummelNet and hacked an old spy satellite. They can monitor the unlikely allies as well as wire bolts to purchase new weapons that are delivered to the surface.

THE GREAT OUTDOORS

Step onto the pod's pads and activate it by pressing △. This takes Ratchet to a familiar weapons vendor screen. Here he and the rest of the team can acquire a new weapon and upgrades for purchased weapons.

LOCK AND LOAD

Everyone with enough bolts gets to add a shiny, new weapon to their arsenal: the Arc Lasher. The Arc Lasher is a supercharged energy whip that stuns enemies.

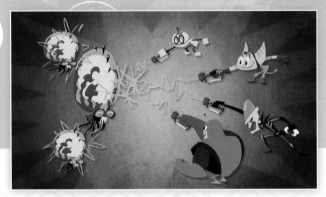

Once everyone has expanded their arsenal, exit the weapons vendor and continue on to explore this strange world. Hop across the floating clusters of rock, collecting the critters along the way.

CRATES OVER CRITTERS

Ignore the critters and sprint past your teammates to get the Bolt Grabber on the next rocky island. While everyone's preoccupied with collecting critters that are counted collectively anyway, you can bolster your bolt count.

Continue along the floating bits of rock to the right where even more critters are found roaming freely. Near the next Checkpoint, Susie appears in a balloon craft being pursued by gravity robots. Susie doesn't seem too concerned as she warns the foursome and takes off. The quartet must now deal with Cleaner Minions that have come to stop their escape.

Past the Checkpoint, launch a teammate across the wide gap to the target pad on the next floating piece of rock. Once everyone is safely across, hookshot over to join them. Just ahead is the next Checkpoint as well as a handy Ammo Pad. After reloading, move ahead and look for another target pad upon a floating island. Launch a teammate to it and hookshot right behind them.

News of the Cleaner Minions' failure to stop the group must have spread; a large group of Rift-Jumper Minions teleports in front of Ratchet and his teammates. Their numbers don't count for much and are soon reduced to zero. In the distance, two eager Scout Minions are standing guard on a metal platform.

CONVENIENT COVERAGE

Several panels ahead provide a protective barrier against the Scout Minions but they aren't perfect. The ones with glass panels in them are indestructible, but the ones on the sides have cracks that compromise their structural integrity. They can only sustain so much damage before shattering.

Equip the Plasmabomb Launcher and approach the Scout Minions carefully from behind the cover and take them out safely. Fortunately, the Scout Minions are foolishly standing behind compromised cover that doesn't last long against the group's combined firepower. There isn't enough cover for everyone, but there is a Nanotech crate on the left.

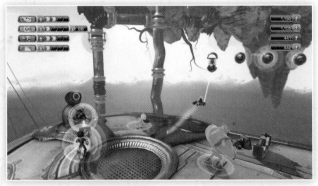

Head to the far end of the metal platform and activate the power plunger to trigger the arrival of a row of Springshots. These anchor points used tightly-wound springs to launch players and require every team member to be attached before they activate. Once everyone on the team has attached their Swingshot, they are sprung swiftly skyward to the next Checkpoint.

SECRET LAB #1

The metal platform to the side is impossible to miss thanks to its bright blue glowing sign depicting a critter with a large number over it. This is the first of six Secret Labs in the game.

SECRET LAB ACCESS

The team must have collected a sufficient number of critters to access the Secret Labs. A counter appears in the lower right when the team approaches a Secret Lab. The number indicates how many critters the team has collected so far.

After their adventures through the training center, the quartet should have plenty to spare. Gather the team on the teleport pad there and activate it to be transported to the Secret Lab. Everyone reappears at a new Checkpoint and are greeted by a pre-recorded message from the lab's creator. In order to complete the puzzle, the creature must be guided safely through it to the end. If the creature falls to their doom or gets hurt, the puzzle resets.

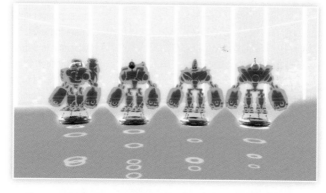

Start the puzzle by activating the power plunger to release the critter. Once it's freed, yellow tiles rise up to form a bridge leading to the right.

Upon the critter's safe arrival, the team is rewarded with the first part of the RYNO blueprint. Having solved the puzzle, the team can hop onto the teleport pad and return to the Aldaros Plains.

ROCKY ROAD

Race across the bridge ahead of the moving critter and simultaneously activate the two power plungers there with a teammate. Each one lowers a section of tubing ahead of the critter so it can safely cross to the end of the puzzle.

Collect the Nanotech crate and reload from the Ammo Pad before double jumping to reach the next rocky platform. Be careful when proceeding, as the ground ahead is not very firm.

ON DEADLY GROUND

The dark brown rock here is highly unstable. As soon as anyone sets foot on it, it starts to crumble. In moments, it collapses entirely leaving only a gaping hole.

THE FOOL WHO FOLLOWS

Don't wait for those lollygagging do-gooders. Leave them in your dust with a speedy sprint. With luck, they won't notice until it's too late to catch up. In their desperate mad dash to reach safety, they fall through the holes left in your wake and lose bolts in the process. Sure, you don't get anything out of it but a supervillain finds happiness in knowing he's made life a little harder for everyone else.

The quartet lands on more unstable ground but don't panic and simply run ahead. Instead, move backwards to the safe, stable ground there to collect a few more critters.

Quickly cross the unstable ground when everyone is ready. You soon encounter a new kind of unsteady rock. Lava rock crumbles to pieces when exposed to an explosion. Avoid touching the stacks of exploding crates unless a lethal fall sounds like good time.

BOOM-ERANG

If you are playing Dr. Nefarious, whip out your green blades to detonate the exploding crates with a throw attack. If the explosion doesn't get your teammates, the fall is sure to.

Cross this area carefully with the team, taking advantage of the more reliable terra firma in the middle. Just ahead are Hero Bolts for everyone but be quick about sucking them up before the ground around it disappears.

After safely crossing to the less unstable ground, another power plunger sits before the team. Activate it to drop in a Spinshot. Use your Swinshot to latch onto this rotating ring. Once everyone is connected, rotate the analog stick in a circle to build up momentum. When every team member has done so, they are whipped through the air.

Advance to the next Checkpoint in the middle of the lava rock field. A Co-op Crate sits right by it to reward two members with bolts and Co-op points. This puts the team inside the attack range of a new robotic adversary in the distance: the Pyromite.

This violent villain consists of two parts. There's a stationary, spinning base that deploys small, round robots that seek out targets before self-destructing. They keep spawning the explosive robots until the base is destroyed so get close to the source to shut it down.

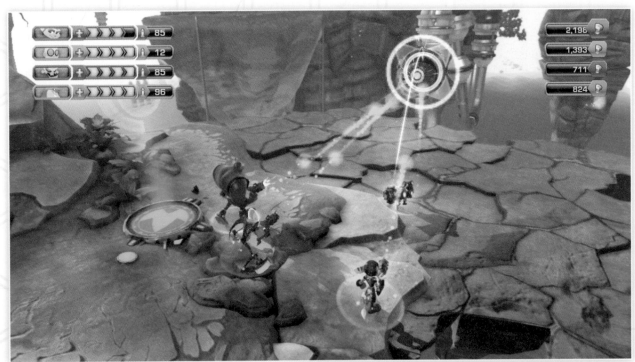

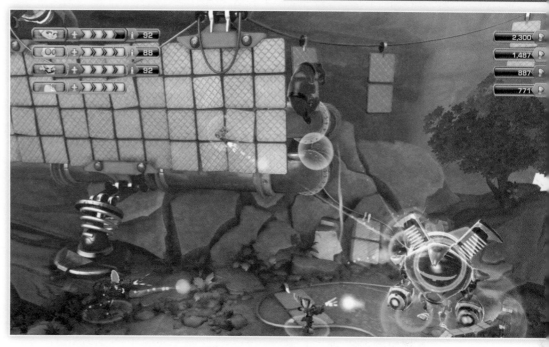

Return to the Ammo Pad to reload before shooting a teammate to the target pad ahead. Follow behind with the Swingshot and then continue up the metal tiles ahead. Thanks to magnetized boots everyone can defy gravity by walking straight up this tiled walkway.

It takes the team to a Scout Minion with its back turned. Surprise it with an assault from behind to take it out before it can even fire a shot in its own defense.

Hop down from the metal tiles and head to the right where a series of anchor points let the team swing to the next area. Recover health with the Nanotech crate there and collect the critters while avoiding the exploding crates that threaten to break apart the lava rock.

INSTANT WEIGHT LOSS

As the team heads to the next Checkpoint, a Gravity Bot swoops overhead and distorts the gravity in the area with its radiation. To return gravity back to normal, chase it down.

Double-jumping between the floating rock islands ahead is much easier thanks to the decreased gravity. They lead higher and higher until the foursome arrives at a metal platform. The source of the gravity disruptions, a Gravity Bot, awaits their arrival. It's armed with more than the ability to distort gravity—it can use its power to levitate rocks and fling them at Ratchet and his allies.

It's fairly heavily armored so don't use the Ammo Pad on the right too prematurely. Eventually, the Gravity Bot's metal plating gives into the foursome's firepower. With gravity returned to normal, the metal platform drifts down to the next Checkpoint.

GETTING BACK YOUR BALANCE

All these changes in gravity really do a number on a superhero. Take the first opportunity to step off this bouncing platform to the adjacent metal platform for the Bolt Grabber there and crush all the crates in the area.

Hop off onto the adjacent metal platforms and heal up with the Nanotech crate from the battle with the Gravity Bot. Collect the critter there and then dismount for the rocky ground towards the Checkpoint past massive quantity of crates. A Scanner Bot appears here to rate the team's progress so far.

ARCHIPELAGO

Cronk and Zephyr have managed to launch another Apogee pod right by the Checkpoint. After purchasing any desired upgrades, pair up with a teammate to open the Co-op Crate, then latch on to the Spinshot spinning overhead.

The team is thrown directly into their next fight with more Scout Minions. The panels here pair well with the Plasmabomb Launcher when used as cover. After defeating them, collect the critters here before attaching to the next Spinshot.

The quartet lands safely at the next Checkpoint surrounded by many more critters. Collect them before mounting up on the launch pad to get flung through the air onto a series of giant, floating metal springs.

They propel the team to the right until they land on a metal platform with a helpful electric resident: the Voltergeist. These electrically charged buddies can be sucked up with a Vac-U and deposited in specially designed receptacles. When nestled inside their destination, they provide power to activate bridges, doors, and other nearby machinery. Placing this Voltergeist in his receptacle extends the bridge from this platform to the next where a Checkpoint awaits and the team can reload using the Ammo Pad. In addition, the player that puts the Voltergeist in its proper place receives 15 Co-op Points.

It flings the foursome to another metal platform patrolled by two Blade Minions. After they are pounded into the pieces, take the Swingcopter

overhead to the team's next destination. While airborne, Susie zips by to warn them about the Gravoids that lurk ahead.

REAL HOMEWRECKERS

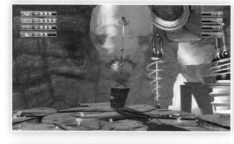

Upon reaching the Checkpoint, the foursome gets their first look at the Gravoids Susie warned them about. These puffed-up pests like to pull up lava rocks and generally make life harder for everyone. Hookshot over to the next floating island's anchor point. Upon landing, a Gravoid

appears and attempts to tear up the ground. Use the Arc Lasher to freeze it in the middle of this terrestrial vandalism and then switch to another weapon to let the air out of its fat body.

Defeating it causes the adjacent rock island bearing the next Checkpoint to lower into view. Launch a teammate onto its target pad and hookshot after them. After triggering the Checkpoint, hookshot to the anchor point ahead.

Once again, the quartet is confronted by more Gravoids looking to sweep the ground right out from under them. After disposing of them, an anchor point moves into position. Using the Swingshot to reach it leads to an encounter with more Gravoids. Blast them mercilessly to secure the ground they stand upon.

Get away from all this lava rock for now by shooting a teammate upwards to the target pad on the next level. Stay on their tail with the Hookshot and reload via the Ammo Pad there. Shoot a teammate and hookshot once more to the next target pad. Hookshot to the anchor point on the right where three more Gravoids attempt to abscond with the lava rock the foursome is standing on. Deflate their monstrous bodies and then move on to the power plunger to the right. Activating it drops a row of Springshot.

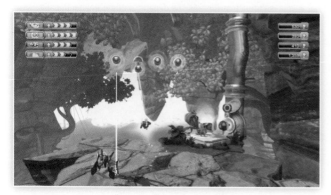

When the entire team has tethered their Swingshots, they are sprung up onto another patch of lava rock that, unsurprisingly, is under attack by Gravoids. Make short work of them and then jump the gap to reach the next Checkpoint. Collect the critters and reload at the Ammo Pad before hooking onto the Spinshot above.

Ratchet and his teammates land in the middle of a precarious situation: they're standing on lava rock and surrounded by exploding crates. Hop over them to solid ground and avoid activating them.

KEEPING DEMOCRACY SAFE

For the good of the galaxy, the President can't be lingering around these dangerous explosives. Head to the left where a Bolt Grabber rests on the ground and gives you the authority to seize all the bolts in the area for reasons of intergalactic security.

HERO BOLT HIDEAWAY

Explore to the right where a Pyromite begins to spew out its explosive robot payloads. Once the threat has been eliminated, double jump up to the metal platform to the right of its old location. Activate the two power plungers there to raise the glass container and reveal Hero Bolts for the team. This fifth Hero Bolt grants everyone a new skin to use!

Backtrack and head to the metal platform to the left where the next Checkpoint awaits. Reload at the Ammo Pad before sucking up the

Voltergeist. However, another teammate must activate the power plunger to raise the Voltergeist's receptacle into position. Once it's put in its proper place, four Springshot descend.

With every teammate's Swingshot attached, the quartet is sprung over to a large metal platform dominated by a large group of Scout Minions quickly joined by a number of Cleaner Minions. Use the Combuster on the Cleaner Minions while keeping a safe distance from the Scout Minions. Once the Cleaner Minions are nothing more than scrap, take cover behind panels and switch to the Plasmabomb Launcher to deal with the Scout Minions.

A late arrival to the party, a lone Scout Minion lands on a metal platform off in the distance. Activate the power plunger at the end of the platform to draw the enemy's perch closer so Ratchet's teammates can blow it away.

Once it's destroyed, a Voltergeist on the platform has the courage to peek its head out. Suck it up and shoot it into the receptacle to the right to extend a bridge. Cross it to the next metal platform and make use of the two Nanotech crates and Ammo Pad there.

Swing from a series of anchor points to the next Checkpoint. Suck up the critter there and then mount the launch pad at the far end. As they approach, the team is confronted by the sudden appearance Rift-Jumper Minions joined by Cleaner Minions that fly in from above. Break them apart for bolts and then take the launch pad to the next Checkpoint.

ZIPPING ALONG

Back away from the Checkpoint to the edge of the area to find a collection of Hero Bolts for the team. Suck it up along with the critters here. An anchor point on the right requires every team member to deploy their Hookshot before it whips them down a zipline to the next Checkpoint where a Co-op Crate can be found.

Two Pyromites a short distance away immediately notice the foursome's landing and begin to ramp up production of explosive flying robots. After they are reduced to rubble, a more sophisticated Gravoid opponent appears: the Gravoid Brute. Unlike its lava rock-pulling cousin, the Gravoid Brute is a flying menace armed with rocket launchers. Each rockets' destination is painted on the ground with a red crosshair.

Shoot down the airborne scourge with the help of the Ammo Pad nearby, then head to the next Checkpoint. Susie flies by to inform the quartet that her village isn't much farther. As she departs, a critter unintentionally demonstrates a new way of travelling: the Cluster Cannon.

To reach it, one teammate must activate the power plunger to the right of the Checkpoint. This reveals a power plunger that controls the powerful grappling hook next to it. Activate that power plunger with a Vac-U to launch the grappling hook and reel in the Cluster Cannon's rocky platform into jumping range.

Hop onto it and then gather the team on the Cluster Cannon. Once everyone is in position, each player needs to rotate the analog stick to ready their tube. Once each tube is primed, all four are fired through the air a tremendous distance to the next Checkpoint where another Scanner Bot appears to rate their progress.

VILLAGE **ENTRANCE**

It's just a short hike to Susie's village, so advance onward to the metal tiled walkway directly ahead. An Apogee pod there packs a nice surprise: new items for the whole team! Not only that, but each member gets their own tailor-made, one-of-a-kind gadget for the price of 5000 bolts.

FOUR FOR FOUR

Each character's weapon plays to their strengths. Ratchet's Doppelbanger is a launcher that deploys a decoy to draw enemy fire. Clank's Zoni Blaster is a high-tech device that slows down its target temporarily. Qwark spends so much time cowering that he can really use the Quantum Deflector that provides him with temporary invulnerability. Dr. Nefarious can pick up the Cloaker that allows him to sneak by enemies unnoticed.

Explore the village center and suck up the various critters wandering about—no one's likely to notice their absence. Then proceed to the right and cross the bridge to the next Checkpoint. Further right from the Checkpoint is a metal platform upon which Hero Bolts for the team can be found.

KIDNAPPING IS A CAPITAL CRIME

As the team heads across the bridge, Susie is about to land when a Gravoid appears out of nowhere and kidnaps her. Not only that, but Rift-Jumper Minions warp in on the other side of the bridge. Tear through them with ease in pursuit of the Gravoid kidnapper and then mount the launch pad by the Checkpoint as a team.

LANDING SITE LOOT

Before taking off via the launch pad, follow the metal cable on the ground to the right. It ends at the edge of floating island and, although it isn't visible, there's an anchor point just out of sight to the right. Hookshot over to it and arrive at Susie's would-be landing site. There are plenty of crates and a Co-op Crate to be found there. To return, suck up a teammate and shoot them at the target pad and hookshot behind them.

The launch pad propels everyone over to another floating island. Head across the unstable brown rocks to the Checkpoint and Ammo Pad ahead.

SECURE BOLTS BEFORE THE BABY

Eagerly rush ahead past the unstable rock to reach the Bolt Grabber on the other side. Your approval ratings are sure to go up when people hear how self-lessly you chased after a little girl's kidnapper.

A string of small floating rock islands bob up and down lazily ahead. Nimbly jump between them to ascend to a large stretch of lava rock. As soon as the team gets there, more Rift-Jumper Minions appear. Watch out for the exploding crates which are all over and just one of them can spell doom. Once the coast is clear, head over to the grappling hook and activate its power plunger to reel in the next necessary chunk of floating rock.

Clamber onto the new extension and head to the right. Launch a teammate from there to the waiting target pad on the other side. As soon as their feet hit the ground, a combination of Gravoids and Rift-Jumper Minions appear. Focus on keeping the ground intact and eliminate the Gravoids first before cleaning up the lingering Minions.

PACKING ON THE POUNDS

Rush across the unstable brown rock to the Springshots ahead and when everyone has attached their Swingshot, the team gets sprung up to a less precarious position. While sucking up the critters here, Cronk and Zephyr notice Glob Lobbers on a neighboring island. These useful tools fire globs of viscous paste that were used to anchor ships in low gravity. To reach them, activate the power plunger of the grappling hook nearby to reel them in. Double jump up to add it to Ratchet's arsenal and then aim it at the Glob Lobber target to the right. This pulls down the rocky island into a position so the team can use it to reach the next Springshots. When every team member is tethered, the foursome gets sprung up to the next Checkpoint.

Break open the Co-op Crate there, reload at the Ammo Pad, and switch back to a weapon before heading on to confront the Gravoid Brute in the distance. Its rockets tear the lava rock to pieces so the best bet is to get right up close and personal on solid ground to open fire on it.

To reach the next Checkpoint, suck up a teammate and shoot them to the target pad by it. After using the Swingshot to follow them, switch back to the Glob Lobber to lower the next two islands on the right and jump from them to the metal platform.

FEELING DOWN

If the metal platform seems out of reach and too far to reach with a jump, just wait. As the Globs slowly disintegrate over time, the island floats right back up.

The platforms needed to progress onward are currently lowered. Activate the power plunger to temporarily raise the glass container encasing the Voltergeist on the neighboring metal platform. As soon as it's fully raised, the power plunger shuts off and the glass container slowly drops back down.

Act quickly to shoot a teammate over to the target pad and suck up the Voltergeist. There's no way to get back while carrying it, so shoot it back to one of the waiting teammates' Vac-U who can then finally deposit it in the proper receptacle. With the circuit complete, the platforms rise into place and the team and hop across them up to the next Checkpoint.

PICKING UP THE TRAIL

After collecting the critter and reloading at the Ammo Pad, the team notices Susie's balloon (sans pilot) dangling from the tree branches. As they forge onward to search for her, a mysterious machine appears. This tri-armed robot drops a domed energy shield around Ratchet and his allies to trap them with the Rift-Jumper Minions that materialize within. After dismantling the minions, two Scout Minions pass through the barrier itching for a fight.

Take cover behind the impervious panels to fire at them from safety. Once they are destroyed, a Gravoid Brute flies in. Dodge its rockets and focus everyone's fire to blast it to pieces. Once it's defeated, the shield drops and a Scanner Bot arrives on the scene.

VILLAGE OUTSKIRTS

Head to the next Checkpoint to the right and use the Nanotech crate. Use the Vac-U to suck up the critters and Hero Bolts in the area. A series of small rock islands float back and forth listlessly nearby. Hop across their tops to get into Glob Lobber range of the target island. Switch to the Glob Lobber and open fire upon it to pull it down to a more reasonable height. Jump up from there to a patchwork of unstable brown rock and lava rock.

SECRET LAB #2

Head to the right to discover the location of the second Secret Lab. This one requires 36 collected critters for entry. The team should have plenty to spare so gather on the teleport pad to jump to the Secret Lab's Checkpoint.

Start by firing the Glob Lobber at the Glob target to lower the first section of tube. Once it's in place, the first power plunger appears for Ratchet's teammate to activate and release the critter. Have a teammate activate the next power plunger to raise the next tube section.

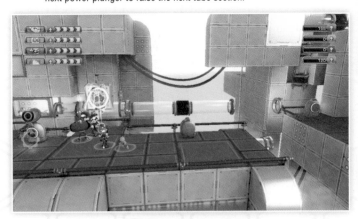

Activate the third power plunger to lower a section of wall to the right. This allows the lead character to reach it with a double-jump up. Release the

plunger to raise everything up to the next level. Hookshot behind them to catch up and then launch a teammate to the target pad across the gap.

Hookshot close behind and team up to fire upon the last two Glob targets. Lower the final tubing sections to safely get the critter to its destination. The team's reward is the next piece of the RYNO blueprint. Head to the teleport pad to exit the Secret Lab.

MOVING ON UP

Back in the plains, head left across the unstable rocks and fight through the Rift-Jumper Minions once more. On the other side, suck up the critter and then activate the power plunger to deploy the grappling hook. Jump up the ledges and note the Nanotech crate en route to the Ammo Pad. When they reach the top, a group of Rift-Jumper Minions appears to greet them. Once they're destroyed, a row of Springshots drops into position.

Ride them up to the next area where the team lands amid more unstable rocks. Immediately open fire at the Gravoids that threaten to destroy this large tract of lava rock. Once the ground is (relatively) secure, head to the left to suck up the Hero Bolts there.

Once the first teammate makes it safely across, a few Rift-Jumper Minions teleport in to start trouble. After dispatching them, activate the grappling hook's power plunger.

Along with the neighboring island, it also draws a Pyromite nearer. After destroying the manufacturing menace, send a teammate to the target pad on the rock island to the right.

The foursome encounters another series of rising, unstable rock platforms. Fortunately, the other side is roughly at the same level so it should be easier than before. However, the other side is just as unstable as the platforms Ratchet took to get there, so keep hustling after crossing until in range of the anchor point by the next Checkpoint.

Round the corner along the field of lava rock and quickly eliminate the Pyromite there before its robots can blast apart the ground. Once it's defeated, an anchor point to safety appears. Hookshot to it and arrive at the next Checkpoint but keep the team's weapons at the ready. Gravoids descend and try to tear up the lava rock here. Without it, the team has no hope of continuing.

At the far end of the lava rock, shoot a teammate at the target pad ahead by the next Checkpoint. Reload at the Ammo Pad before advancing to the right. A never-ending series of unstable rock platforms gently floats upwards there.

The next area is a significantly higher up, so only start jumping when it looks like the second platform is on track to raise Ratchet up a fair distance. It takes precise timing for the entire team to make it across, so it's easier to assign the most skilled player to take point while everyone else rides that player's coattails by using the Swingshot.

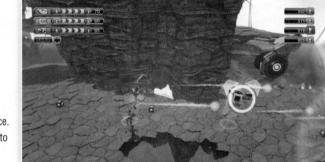

RUSH TO THE RESCUE

With the path ahead secure, advance onward using the Glob Lobber to lower the necessary rock platforms to advance. As the team arrives at the next Checkpoint, the Gravoid holding Susie flies by as she struggles in vain. Chase after it along the drifting chunks of rock to the next Checkpoint. Reload at the Ammo Pad before swinging along the anchor points to two Spinshot in a row. A mysterious warbot is seen and heard in the background at this time.

When the heroes land, they can see the transported creature has been dropped right in their path ahead. It's impossible to avoid this menacing monster with multiple tentacles, so jump across the vertically rising and falling pieces of rock directly ahead.

The group hits the last Checkpoint and Ammo Pad before it's time to face the mysterious monster. Head across the stretch of unstable rock and leap onto the ground immediately in front of the multi-limbed creature to start the encounter.

BOSS
OCTOMOTH

The Octomoth wastes little time before attacking with its sharp-tipped tentacles, which are thrusts upward through the ground. Fire at them before it can tear up the ground from under the feet of your characters.

After you deal with its tentacles, the Octomoth opens its mouth in a rage, indicating it can be attacked directly. Deal as much damage as possible because it soon shuts its mouth and resumes its underground attack. Beat back the tentacles once more and force it to once again expose its mouth to attack.

GREEN MEANS GO (SHOOT)

The color of the ground provides a clue about the tentacle's next appearance. As the tentacles burrow upward, the ground changes from brown to green.

LOSING GROUND

Prioritize the tentacles that have been exposed the longest. Leaving them unchecked is a surefire way to lose the land it's pierced. Don't let the Octomoth eat away at the foursome's meager room to operate.

Once the Octomoth is finally defeated, it collapses and falls far out of sight. Hookshot to the anchor point on the right to reach the next Checkpoint. The good news is that Susie has already taken care of her kidnapper. Rescued by her critter companion, she leads the team away to safety. Suck up the critter here before taking the Swingcopter back to the Checkpoint in Susie's village.

Head past the cheering Tharpods to the Glob target and pull it down with the Glob Lobber to lower the bridge. As they round the corner, a Scanner Bot emerges from a cavern to scan them.

PLANET MAGNUS
THE DEADGROVE

OBJECTIVES

ORTHANI GORGE

- Descend into the Deadgrove

ROOT CAVERN

- Locate the Path into the Mining Camp

ACCESS SHAFT

- Jetpack Down the Access Shaft

MINING CAMP

- Search for the Railway Station

ABYSS

- Defeat the Wigwump
- Find the Subterranean Railway Station

Reunited with Susie, the foursome looks to the sky as a massive vessel passes overhead. The Tharpod Elder later explains to the team that while they know it is called Ephemeris, they do not know who controls it. Susie pleads with the gang to help them but Ratchet is reluctant to take on their cause, claiming to be retired. However, when he discovers Susie was orphaned during one of the raids, he resolves to do whatever it takes to make sure she and her village are both safe.

HERO BOLTS

✓	ORTHANI GORGE
	On a ledge to the right after taking the launch pad following the fight with two Proto Turrets
	ROOT CAVERN
	On a platform after descending upon mushroom tops via the right mushroom top
	Following the collapsing ramp on a platform above the destroyed metal gate
	ACCESS SHAFT
	Behind the glass wall during the first jetpack section
	MINING CAMP
	Next to Secret Lab 3

NEW ENEMIES DEFEATED

ORTHANI GORGE

 Dreadgrubs

 Grove Beetle

 Proton Turret

ACCESS SHAFT

 Proton Excavator

 Mortar Minion

ABYSS

 Wigwump

NEW WEAPONS PURCHASED

ORTHANI GORGE

☐ Warmonger

MINING CAMP

☐ Blitzer

ORTHANI GORGE

The only entrance into the foreboding Deadgrove is the dark and shadowy Orthani Gorge. Even the technological machinations of Ephemeris can reach only so far into its murky depths.

However, don't take this to mean that this area is a safe haven. On the contrary, the diminished presence of robotic foes leaves all the more room for aggressive native creatures to reign unchecked.

3
MISSION

Visit the Apogee pod on the left side of the gorge's entrance. Invest hard-won bolts in weapons and upgrades to fend off the creepy crawlies that are looking for their next meal. The powerful Warmonger is now available and should be purchased without hesitation assuming Ratchet has sufficient bolts.

The impact of the landing draws the attention of the remaining Dreadgrubs that roll down the slope and attempt to bowl over the quartet with their spikes. Luckily, these bugs are used to less aggressive prey and are easily squashed.

MAGIC MUSHROOMS

Don't trip on the hardened, purple mushrooms roughly Rachet's size that appear throughout the Deadgrove. Despite their organic looks, they can be smashed to disperse valuable bolts.

Use the Ammo Pad shining brightly ahead as a beacon. It sits at the rocky edge of the start of the gorge and the only way forward is by leaping onto an unstable rock pile that tilts and sways from the weight upon it.

Continue on to the Checkpoint and then criss-cross the gorge via two sloping surfaces running the width of it. More Dreadgrubs roll up but are easily dealt with. The slopes deposit the team in front of another pack of Dreadgrubs milling around on top of a flat rock. Clear them out and smash up the crates by the Checkpoint.

As Ratchet gets close to suck up the critters there, a new Deadgrove resident rears its head—the Grove Beetle. Hop onto the glowing spring pads to go flying up to a higher vantage point that overlooks the waiting beetle.

BUGGING OUT

Falling isn't what the foursome should be worried about here, though—a pack of deadly Dreadgrubs waits directly in the path. Clear a safe landing area by eliminating the first Dreadgrub and jumping across.

Grove Beetles boast impervious armored shells that resist all known weapons. However, their soft underbelly combines with an aggressive temperament to make them their own worst enemy.

As soon as one spots a potential meal, it charges full speed ahead. The key is to jump over it so that it runs headlong into the wall and stuns itself. While stunned, the Grove Beetle flips on its back and leaves its belly vulnerable to attack. A single slam attack is all that's needed to squash this giant bug.

BUGGING OUT

If every member of the team successfully avoids being barreled over by a Grove Beetle in the Deadgrove, the "El Matador" Trophy is awarded for the impressive feat.

ZERO TO SIXTY

The Grove Beetle gives no warning it's about to charge and moves at full speed from a complete standstill. Pay careful attention and be ready to jump at a moment's notice.

It hurriedly scurries over to its post and mans the turret. The Proton Turret is heavily shielded from the front where its cannon is located but its rear is completely exposed. Have one teammate draw its fire while another opens fire on the turret's exposed rear to make short work of it. Reload at the Ammo Pad and then hop up towards the Checkpoint by a tunnel entrance.

PLAYING HOOKIE

The safest way to trick a Grove Beetle is by having one teammate drop down to catch its attention and then immediately hookshot back to safety.

A gap in the rock bridge impedes progress past the Grove Beetle's remains. Although a target pad is conveniently placed on the other side, it sits directly in front of more Dreadgrubs. Fortunately, they are still well within range of the Combuster. Clear the way then launch a teammate over before hookshotting to them. Once across, drop down to the next Checkpoint where a Nanotech crate makes a welcome sight. Launch a teammate across a gap to the target pad.

LEADING FROM THE REAR

As President, it's important to demonstrate you stand behind your teammates, far behind your teammates. A Grove Beetle waits on the other side and while you could defeat it, why hog the glory? Wait until your teammate clears the way before hookshotting over.

HAMMERING THE POINT

Follow a descending series of rock piles that are dotted with a Nanotech crate and several critters. Before reaching the bottom plateau, the gang attracts the attention of a Proton Turret robot on its water break.

WATER BREAK'S OVER

Smash the robot's water cooler before leaving to acquire the "Back to Work" Skill Point.

A few feet ahead are Quakehammers for all. These heavy-duty pieces of mining equipment are used by the Tharpods to prospect for treasure amid the rocks. Use the right stick to open the weapon wheel and press **R1** to switch pages to the utility wheel where the Quakehammer can be found on the right.

GREY GOLD

The reflective grey rocks ahead are susceptible to the might of the Quakehammer. Shatter them at every opportunity for additional bolts.

To clear the debris blocking the tunnel, the gang needs to work together by combining the might of their Quakehammers. Hold **R1** while standing atop the weak point marked with the glowing red X. As the Quakehammer loosens the rock additional X's appear for Ratchet's teammates to target with their Quakehammers. When all the weak points are hammered simultaneously, a Mega-Quake shatters the barrier. Every player receives 5 Co-op points for their efforts.

On the other side of the tunnel, a row of spring pads sits on the edge of the sheer drop. Bounce off them to get launched onto the sloping rock ramp ahead.

REWARDING UPHILL HIKE

Before going with the flow and heading downhill, backtrack up the ramp to the right. There are several crates and a Co-op Crates for you and your favorite teammate where it meets the gorge wall.

The ramp leads down to a flat plateau where another Proton Turret robot stands idly by its post. Split its attention and destroy it with ease, but be ready to quickly wipe out the Dreadgrubs that descend from above after. Reload at the Ammo Pad, and then take the launch pad on the left over to the next gorge-spanning bridge.

A voracious Grove Beetle is waiting for a quick bite. As soon as the team touches down, get ready to jump over it and strike mercilessly. Take the launch pad on the left onto a lengthy root tendril the foursome grinds down.

UP FOR GRABS

Land with both hands swinging after the grind to acquire the Bolt Grabber at its terminus. Add to the presidential coffers all the bolts in the crates ahead. Of course, there are also critters and a Nanotech crate.

After reloading at the Ammo Pad, proceed to the left across the top of more tipsy rock piles—stopping to liberate a Co-op Crate of its contents—and hop past a Checkpoint before landing on more stable ground.

Suddenly, another tri-armed robot swoops in overhead to trap the quartet in an energy shield. Ratchet and his allies must battle successive waves of Rift-Jumper Minions, Cleaner Minions, Scout Minions, and a single ornery Gravoid Brute. Don't hesitate to use the Ammo Pad to restock the most powerful weapons to fend off this tide of foes.

Take a hard-earned break to thoroughly explore this particular rocky expanse covered in crates and critters. Having cleaned out the place, use the Vac-U to shoot a teammate across the gap ahead towards the target pad by the Checkpoint and two Nanotech crates. Although it rests right below two Proton Turrets, they aren't immediately aware of the team's presence.

CAUGHT IN THE CROSSFIRE

At first two Proton Turrets seems like a troublesome prospect, but their increased number is actually an advantage. Draw their fire so that one Proton Turret stands directly between Ratchet and the other Proton Turret. They're so caught up in firing that they don't stop—not even when they are firing directly at the exposed side of their ally. Tricking one into the destroying the other nets the "Have You Two Met?" Skill Point.

Explore the area for the scattered crates and various critters roaming before ascending via the launch pad. Team up to open the Co-op Crate and head up the naturally forming rock steps to the left. Explore the ledge to the right to find Hero Bolts for the entire team. Next, head into the tunnel and use the Quakehammer to break through the obstruction to reach the next Checkpoint.

ROOT CAVERN

March forward towards a gap in the ground. In the distance, light filters through the network of intertwining roots stretching as far as the eye can see. Running through their twisting tendrils is a rail system. The gang is getting closer to finding a way to Ephemeris.

Send a teammate across the gap to the target pad and hookshot behind. Sprint ahead once on the other side and be the first to find a Bolt Grabber.

After gathering everything, use Quakehammer to break through the weak rock surrounded by safety lights. The heroes land directly beside a native plant species that produces explosive blast bulbs.

POLLEN PACKS A POWERFUL PUNCH

Use the Vac-U to suck up one and then head to the left. Fire it at the root covered metal gate to blast it open to reach the Co-op Crate and crates on the other side. Backtrack and pick up another blast bulb to destroy the metal gate on the right. Only a few short paces ahead there is another gate, so repeat the process to move onward.

Past the next Checkpoint is another weak section of rock flooring. Reload from the Ammo Pad on the opposite side before teaming up to use the Quakehammer, plowing further down with a Mega-Quake.

The gang bounces along a series of springy mushroom tops to land safely before a Nanotech crate. The platform directly above is home to Hero Bolts for the team. To access them, suck up a teammate with the Vac-U and fire them at the giant mushroom to the right. Hookshot right behind them as they bounce up to join them atop the platform and claim the Hero Bolt. Drop back down and advance to the right, blasting the Dreadgrubs that roll up on the team.

Upon reaching the gap, shoot a teammate at the target pad and then hookshot to cross.

There's an X marking a Quakehammer target here. But rather than break through the rock, it actually shakes loose a blast bulb from above. Use the Vac-U to suck it up and fire it at the metal gate to the right.

The other side slopes down to a Checkpoint and an Ammo Pad. However, don't be too eager to deploy the Quakehammer again on the glowing X marked by the safety-light. Instead, backtrack and use the Quakehammer to retrieve another blast bulb. Return to the Checkpoint then fire it high and to the right to destroy the metal gate there.

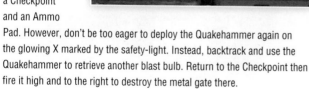

Double jump up there but be ready to Hookshot immediately after them. There's a modest but valuable collection of crates found there. Return to the safety lights and burst through the weak rock with a Mega-Quake. The team lands in the path of a none-too-happy Grove Beetle. Nimbly avoid its attack and squash it safely.

To the left of the target pad is another Quakehammer site. But first it's necessary to send a teammate across the gap to the target pad on the right. Use the Quakehammer to drop another blast bulb and then fire it with the Vac-U across the gap to the teammate's waiting Vac-U. They can then use the bulb to blast a path through the metal gate there.

Smash the Nanotech crate there before swinging from the Hookshot anchor points above to the right. Upon landing, a Proton Turret robot rushes to its position. Double jump safely across to the metal platform above the Proton Turret. Head to the other side of the Proton Turret to flank it with the help of a teammate to blast it to pieces.

Particularly dexterous teammates can pick up the blast bulb below even before the Proton Turret is taken out. Use it to blow open the metal gate on the right to proceed onward where a Co-op Crate sits by the Checkpoint there.

Head down the slope to the right until you reach the gap. Launch a teammate across the gap at the target pad, hookshot behind, Quakehammer the X, catch the blast bulb, and break open the metal gate on the right.

On the other side, a Proton Turret stands at the ready on a metal platform while a Grove Beetle roams below. Drop down by the spring pad and let the Grove Beetle knock itself out against the metal lip of the platform. After clearing the lower level pest, it's easy enough to flank the topside Proton Turret with teammates using the spring pads.

The only way forward is by swinging between Hookshot anchor points. While mid-air, a large subterranean creature known as a Wigwump makes its first ugly appearance. It peeks out from the roots to lap up several of the transports running along the rail system.

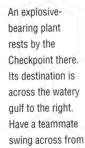

The foursome lands on an old metal walkway that begins to shudder under their weight before it starts to collapse. Sprint ahead of the disintegrating ramp to the right and then bounce safely across several mushroom tops to solid ground.

An explosive-bearing plant rests by the Checkpoint there. Its destination is across the watery gulf to the right. Have a teammate swing across from the Hookshot anchor and then use the Vac-U to pass them the blast bulb to break the metal gate there.

Past the Ammo Pad on the other side is a Grove Beetle patiently waiting for its next meal. Dealing with it is once again a matter of dropping down to trigger its charge then hopping back up and waiting for it to flip over before smashing it.

Team up to use the Quakehammers on the rightmost X marked on the ground and break through. The quartet drops only briefly before being shot back up by a large spring that puts them atop a metal platform. From here, shoot a teammate at the target pad to the left and then hookshot behind to claim a Hero Bolt.

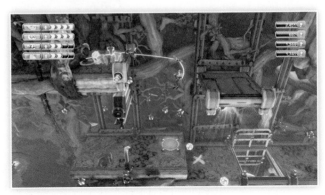

Drop back down and use the Quakehammer on the remaining X marking to drop an blast bulb to destroy the metal gate on the right. Head down the ramp and past several stacks of crates to reach another Proton Turret. Take the spring pad up and flank it with a teammate to put it out of its misery quickly. Before moving on, heal using the Nanotech crate on the elevated metal platform.

Where the turret once stood, perform a Mega-Quake to break through the marked rock by the safety lights. It drops the foursome down a series of metal pipes that send them grinding further and further down until they land on a metal platform.

ACCESS SHAFT

The team's destination is still further below. Suck up the critters on the platform and heal using the Nanotech crate before moving left and dropping down. There's a Co-op Crate on the left and even more critters to collect. Head right to collect the crates and Nanotech crates before deploying a Mega-Quake by the safety lights to burrow down.

The quartet lands on a lengthy metal pipe by a Checkpoint and grinds down through some conveniently placed jet packs left behind by the Tharpods. It allows them to gently land on a small metal platform in the center of a metal access shaft with a Checkpoint. Drop off the platform and the jet packs automatically deploy. To activate the jet pack's thrusters for a boost, press ✕.

ACE PILOTS

Carefully navigate the area ahead while flying the jet pack. Every player must avoid touching all the hazards for any one of them to acquire the "Jetpack Master" Skill Point.

Continue down and avoid the spinning blades along the left that have been left running as well as the flame vents along the walls. In addition to stationary blades, there are also those that run along tracks.

Avoid the encroaching flames emanating from the left wall before landing on the next level. Collect the critter before teaming up for a Mega-Quake to break through the rock by the safety lights to reach the rest of the shaft.

Land at the next Checkpoint's platform and make good use of the two Nanotech crates there to heal any wounds sustained from the idle mining equipment. Continue on by taking the spring pad on the left side to get airborne and automatically redeploy the jet pack.

PEPPERED WITH PODS AND PITFALLS

As the foursome descends, note the glass-enclosed pod on the left side. These little supply storage areas were left behind by the Tharpod miners and frequently contain both crates and Nanotech crates. To liberate its contents, press **R1** to perform a Wall Slam with the jet pack. These emergency supply pods are plentiful and scattered throughout the access shaft. Keep on the lookout for them to replenish any health lost to out of control mining equipment.

PARTNER UP ON PLUNGERS

Lead your favorite teammate to a landing on the right side where a Co-op Crate sits.

Team up and free its contents for bolts and Co-op Points.

WINDOW OF OPPORTUNITY

Wall slam the large pane of glass on the right side of the shaft. Collect the Hero Bolts which were hidden inside.

Unmonitored mining equipment isn't the team's only concern. Robotic minions of Ephemeris have mounted Proton Excavators. These pods are equipped with mining-grade lasers that cut people to pieces, but never any slack. Coordinate multiple wall slams with teammates to break open the control pods and end the threat.

AIMING HIGH

Proton Excavator beams cut across the width of the shaft and can aim at upward angles. When lining up a wall slam, stay close and above the maximum height of the beam to avoid taking damage.

After surviving a series of Proton Excavators, the quartet lands briefly at another Checkpoint. There's nothing to see here so break out the Quakehammers to break through the soft rock. More Proton Excavators wait on the other side. Be especially wary when dealing with the pair facing each other from opposite walls—their deadly lasers cross and leave little room to maneuver.

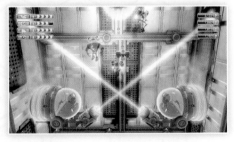

Continue a careful, controlled descent past the spinning blades of death. Deal with the sporadic Proton Excavators along the way and a landing on the left offers up a Nanotech crate for those in need. The shaft dead-ends with a row of impassable blades. Wall slam the pane of glass on the right as it's the only way to proceed.

On the other side, wait for the spinning blade moving vertically to pass before dropping down to the next Checkpoint. Smash the two Nanotech crates there before bouncing off the left spring pad.

The foursome continues their downward trajectory past many more blades and Proton Excavators. After surviving the grueling ordeal, a Nanotech crate and Checkpoint can be found on a landing along the left side.

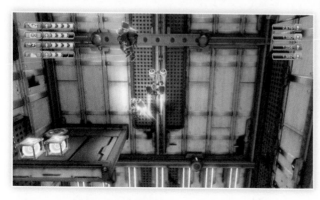

SQUEEZING THE SIDES

Enjoy the brief break while it lasts. As soon as the quartet continues, a row of blades stretching the width of the shaft follow hot on their tail. Navigate carefully until the shaft opens up on the right but don't confuse it with safety—a wall of spinning blades encroaches unrelentingly from the left.

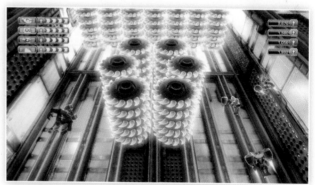

Both the ceiling and floor are lined with flame vents and spinning blades with plenty more directly in the team's route ahead. Be especially cautious about avoiding damage as Nanotech crates are few and far between here. Fly through the columns of suspended crates for bolts and wall slam through glass panes to forge onward to the next Checkpoint.

SMASHING GOOD TIME

Break all the floating crates in this section of the level to score the "Crate Hater" Skill Point.

PANE-FULLY OVERSHOOTING

Don't overdo wall slams by starting them too close to the glass panes. The momentum can carry your character directly into spinning blades on the other side. Either begin wall slams from a safe distance or use melee attacks on the glass panes to break them.

AHEAD OF THE CURVE

A deadly spinning blade runs along a track exactly where the team needs to fly. Instead of timidly following close behind it, take control of the situation and fly around it, leaving the lethal threat in the dust.

Past two more Proton Excavators, and to the right, is the next Checkpoint. The two Nanotech crates here are sure to come in handy before the foursome breaks through the marked weak points in the rock to access the last stretch of the access shaft.

After descending past the last of the deadly machinery and Proton Excavators, the foursome finally arrives in the significantly more grounded mining camp.

MINING CAMP

Despite the extreme depth, and having been abandoned long ago, GrummelNet can still deliver its products to the mining camp without a problem. Head to the Apogee pod on the left to upgrade before exploring the abandoned camp. The Blitzer weapon is now available for those who like to take down their enemies with a personal touch.

Stroll through the camp and sweep up the numerous critters wandering about as well as heal with the two Nanotech crates. Once the site has been properly cleaned out, head onwards in the direction of the launch pad ahead.

A LITTLE TO THE LEFT

There's a Bolt Grabber along the left side of the camp. Help balance the intergalactic budget one crateful of bolts at a time.

SECRET LAB #3

Before taking the launch pad deeper into the camp, drop down from the ledge to its right. Aside from the Hero Bolts here, it also features the entrance to the next Secret Lab which requires 48 critters to enter.

Another Mortar Toss greets the team. Using the Mortar Slam on it lowers a barrier to grant access to a series of Hookshot anchor points. Swing between them until you can attach to a Spinshot.

SECRET LAB #3

Before starting, propel a teammate onto the target pad to the right of the starting area. They must then activate the power plunger to flip the Slambot back on the left side.

Slam attack the Slambot to lower the first section of tube and its Slambot partner flips up on the other side. Have the teammate there slam attack that Slambot to lower the first tube section. Immediately team up to perform a Mortar Slam on the Mortar Toss to extend the bridge.

The Spinshot propels the entire foursome ahead where three Slambots on two different levels must be activated quickly and in sequence. The critter has really picked up the pace to catch up with the quartet despite their speedy hookshot acrobatics, so act fast.

With the critter safely among its own kind, the Checkpoint activates, a teleport pad appears, and the entire team gets an additional RYNO part.

After defeating them, several waves of Cleaner Minions fly in. Don't let their large numbers allow them to flank the foursome. Focus fire on the same targets to eliminate them efficiently. The last wave of enemies to cope with consists of just two Scout Minions. The shield falls when they are destroyed.

BACK IN CAMP

Take the launch pad to the rock bridge ahead and head down it with guns blazing to clear out the Dreadgrubs. At the Ammo Pad below there are several critters to suck up.

Their arrival does not go unnoticed by the Mortar Minion ahead that immediately begins opening fire. Similar in appearance to the Scout Minion, it fires arcing explosive rounds from a distance. After it's broken down for spare parts, another one drops into take its place for the few moments it takes to blast it to pieces.

Once the minions have been turned to scrap, take the launch pad to head onward. It deposits the foursome right in front of two more Mortar Minions while a tri-armed robot traps them in an energy shield. Toss an ally across the gap to the platform where the Mortar Minions are located. In addition, a large posse of Rift-Jumper Minions crosses the shield's threshold to attack. Luckily, the Ammo Pad falls within the boundaries of the shield.

Move past the Checkpoint and across the bridge to the railway cars. Collect the critters encountered en route before heading up the metal ramp to a waiting Nanotech crate. Dreadgrubs try to bite off more they can chew and attack fruitlessly. After putting down the pests, Clank notes the railway platform should lead to Commander Spog.

As the cart passes through to the Checkpoint on the other side of the tunnel, the Wigwump suddenly bursts through the wall and tears a chunk out of the rails with its mighty jaws. Unable to hit the brakes and with no rail left, the team's transport tumbles end over end through the air.

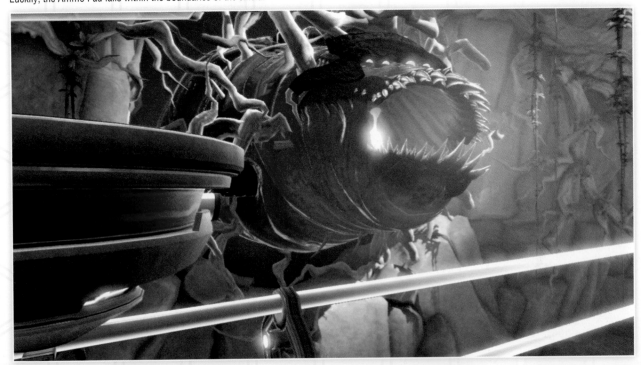

ABYSS

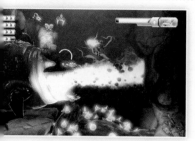

Fortunately, the foursome's jet packs kick in to save their hides. The only way out now is the subterranean railway station somewhere in the depths below. Avoid the spewing flames while claiming the domed contents on the way down.

HEALTHIER TO WAIT

A supply dome on the right can be a lifesaver or a lifetaker: it lies close to where the Wigwump's jaws are about to strike. Don't lose health rushing to regain it and instead wait for the Wigwump to move on before claiming it.

Without warning, the Wigwump reappears from the left and spews molten rock and magma from its mouth. Slam attack its face while avoiding the arc of its attack to scare it off temporarily.

A THORNY SITUATION

Be wary of the bright yellow thorns growing on the roots that wind through these dark depths and avoid losing any health to their prickly presence. Avoiding the thorns on the left, keep a ready finger on the jet pack thrusters—the Wigwump marches through from the left and is not about to stop for any fliers in its way.

After that close call, touch down on a small rocky outcropping on the right where a Checkpoint and two Nanotech crates brighten up this dark area just a tad.

Continue the descent past the thorns and be ready for the Wigwump to stick in its unwanted nose from the right. Avoid its unpleasant upchuck and use wall slams to knock it in the noggin back where it came from. Once it retreats, the path is now cleared on the right to pass by the thorns.

Below this encounter is another safe landing spot where the team can visit the Checkpoint, reload at the Ammo Pad, and heal with the Nanotech crate. And not a moment too soon, as the route ahead remains narrow and twisting.

Keep heading down, dodging both thorns and the Wigwump's appearances. The path soon opens up and Nanotech crates can be liberated from domes on both sides of the shaft as Ratchet and his allies drift down past the next Checkpoint.

This open space only encourages the Wigwump who tires of its hit-and-run tactics. As the foursome passes a Checkpoint, it comes barreling straight down the shaft from above.

DEATH FROM ABOVE

There's little margin for error when outrunning the Wigwump and hesitation is a luxury the team can't afford. If the Wigwump manages to catch up to any team members, they are as good as dead—literally. The ferocity of the Wigwump's downward velocity kills on contact, so stay ahead of it at all times.

THE EYES HAVE IT

Dark niches and corners abound ahead and it is important to peer into that seemingly unfathomable darkness. The Wigwump's yellow eyes foretell an imminent intrusion by the nosy ne'er-do-well. Avoid being caught in the chompers by steering clear of spots where evil eyes gaze at the team.

The team needs to hastily navigate past the thorns and carefully weigh the delay required to break the domes they pass on the way down. Upon reaching the bottom, look for a spot to wall slam the glass on the right to reach safety. From this alcove, witness the Wigwump continue on and shatter the rock below.

BOSS WIGWUMP

The foursome is fighting on the Wigwump's home turf, so it naturally has a significant tactical advantage. It is capable of moving at great speed throughout the burrow and striking suddenly. Long-range weapons are an absolute necessity to take on this beast.

The Wigwump relies primarily on its ability to spew volumes of molten lava and rock from its massive mouth. It targets the ground in front of it in three sections. Simply standing on the superheated rock in the path of its putrid plumes inflicts damage.

After knocking the Wigwump around a little to show Ratchet and his allies aren't such easy prey, it withdraws only to poke its head out of a side tunnel to spit more lava. It's soon emboldened enough to draw near again and open itself up to further firepower to the face.

Once the team has dealt the Wigwump some additional punishment, it realizes the need for some assistance in this battle. Consequently, it summons Dreadgrubs that drop in from above. These nuisances should be ignored. Focus the team's attention on the launch pad that becomes active on the left or right. Any hero hopping on it is flung into the air where his jet pack gives him excellent maneuverability.

Wall slam the Wigwump in its cranium repeatedly to stun it. When it collapses to the ground, the Dreadgrubs are taken out by the impact. While it's vulnerable (it takes more damage when stunned), switch to your most powerful weapons (while the Wigwump is stunned, the Ammo Pad recharges).

PENNIES FROM HEAVEN

As the Wigwump roughly traverses the burrow, its passage shakes loose crates from above periodically. Among them are Nanotech crates that should be claimed immediately.

Regaining its composure, the Wigwump isn't done yet. It summons more Dreadgrubs to assist it in its assault. The Wigwump takes no chances and canvasses two of the three tracts of ground in front of it with each punishing emission. Move laterally in the opposite direction when the Wigwump readies itself. As it grows more desperate, it brings more Dreadgrubs into the fray and activates the launch pads along with them. Take to the skies at every opportunity to give the Wigwump a raging headache with the help of Ratchet's teammates, bashing its temples from both sides. It's only a matter of time before the Wigwump succumbs to the punishment and collapses in a heap.

A CRYPTIC CLUE

With the Wigwump slain and a way out just ahead, things are starting to look up for the gang. Jump across the boiling waters towards the tunnel on the right where a Scanner Bot assesses the area following the fierce fight that just occurred.

As they venture on, Clank discovers an old holo-diary on the ground. It recounts an attack by Ephemeris, led by Commander Spog, that devastated Uzo City. Alluding to a mysterious enemy whose motives and plans are unknown, Dr. Croid fears the worst may come from the ark and that the tragic fate of Magnus is merely the first step. Cryptically shouldering responsibility, the recording comes to a close before any more is revealed.

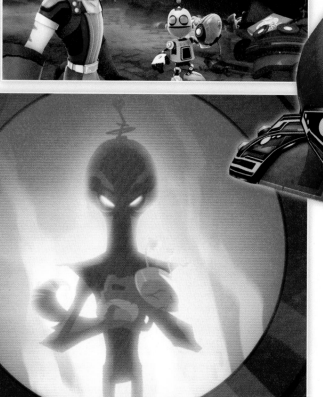

Clank has a bad feeling and urges the group to find Commander Spog at once. Together, they ride the rail system out of the Deadgrove and back into daylight.

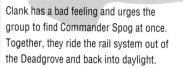

PLANET MAGNUS
N.E.S.T.

OBJECTIVES

ELEROX PASS
- Defeat Narbot

MOKTOR OUTPOST
- Defend Moktor Outpost
- Find a Way Inside the N.E.S.T.
- Grind the Power Conduit into N.E.S.T.

VERTIGUS CLIFFS
- Infiltrate the Sorting Facility

N.E.S.T. ENTRANCE
- Search the Facility for Commander Spog
- Descend the Security Tower
- Defeat Mr. Perkins

REHABITATION CENTER
- Track Down Commander Spog
- Defeat Commander Spog

The transport comes to a stop at the edge of the Northern Extraterrestrial Sorting Terminal (a.k.a. N.E.S.T.). Commander Spog tags and redistributes all manner of creatures from this facility.

Although the foursome is free from the lurking threats in the Deadgrove, they must still keep their wits about them as they attempt to infiltrate the facility. While the number of wild creatures has diminished, the minion presence is sure to increase as they draw nearer.

HERO BOLTS

✓	**ELEROX PASS**
	On the ledge after the pulley lift immediately before Vertigus Cliffs
	VERTIGUS CLIFFS
	Following the pulley lift
	N.E.S.T. ENTRANCE
	To the left after exiting wind tunnel elevator shaft fans
	On the right in the first room after re-entering the facility on the rail system
	REHABITATION CENTER
	On the right after descending the elevator following the Commander Spog fight

NEW ENEMIES DEFEATED

ELEROX PASS

 Weevoid

Hunter Minion

REHABITATION CENTER

 Commander Spog

VERTIGUS CLIFFS

 Bouncer Minion

 Turret Minion

N.E.S.T. ENTRANCE

 Sentry Minion

 Tank Minion

 Mr. Perkins

NEW WEAPONS PURCHASED

ELEROX PASS

- [ ] Mr. Zurkon
- [ ] Pyro Blaster
- [ ] Critter Strike

REHABITATION CENTER

- [ ] Darkstar Fission Tether

ELEROX **PASS**

The target is the villainous warbot, Commander Spog, lurking somewhere in the facility, so now's a good time to make use of the weapons vendor just ahead. The flamethrowing Pyro Blaster, aggressively protective Mr. Zurkon, and transmogrifying Critterstrike are all now available for purchase. After claiming the new weapons, suck up the critters in the rocky terrain nearby as well as any crates scattered about.

4
MISSION

The only way to proceed is up, calling for the use of Hookshots at the anchor points overhead. This leads to a series of narrow ledges. The critters to collect here don't seem too concerned about the drop though.

Once the team scales the ledges to the top, they discover one bridge out of commission and another suspended overhead. Bust out the Glob Lobber at the flashing Glob target to lower the still-intact bridge.

Displaced Tharpod refugees populate a makeshift encampment on the other side. Collect the critters that mosey about and claim the crates spread throughout. After cracking open the plunger box in the center of the area, head to the right where a heavy metal gate is secured by two heavy stones. Target the Glob targets on either side to lower the counter-weights and raise the gate.

There is another Glob target on a panel to the left. Lob Globs at it to lower the panel and reveal a bell. A well-placed throw attack rings the bell to release the boulder blocking the bridge.

BRIDGE BATTLING

PARALYZING POISON

The foursome only makes it a few paces onto the bridge when Rift-Jumper Minions appear along their route. Deal with them quickly by sucking them up with the Vac-U.

Critters rest on the rocky stretch between bridges. More Rift-Jumper Minions appear on the next bridge and are easily dealt with. The bridge ends on another rocky platform. Beside the idle critter there is a barrier blocking access to the next bridge.

Backtrack to the bridge and equip the Glob Lobber to lower the panel to expose the bell behind it. Ringing the bell releases a nearby boulder from its perch to send it barreling across the bridge and into the barrier. To avoid

being flattened like a pancake, immediately sprint back to the barrier after ringing the bell and sidestep the rolling rock's path.

On the far side of the next bridge, the quartet discovers the ground littered with pulsating puddles of dangerous Weevoid toxin. Touching the toxin causes the victim

to become temporarily paralyzed while it encapsulates them. It eventually dissolves, but it's faster to have teammates knock the victim free of their gooey prison.

Free one trapped critter there and suck up a second. Visit the Ammo Pad before turning towards a Glob Lobber target panel to its right. Lower it and ring the bell to lower a catapult platform.

Once every team member has gotten into position on the pads there, press ● to drop a boulder that flings the foursome through the air to the next bridge.

Upon landing at the next Checkpoint, the group is confronted by the source of the toxin: a vicious Weevoid. These predatory pests spit their projectile toxin to paralyze victims before striking with their spiked tails. Their rock-like shells allow them to curl up into small, protected cocoons that resist all attack. Avoid the toxin, freeing teammates who fall victim to it, and do as much damage as possible while the Weevoid's vulnerable flesh is exposed.

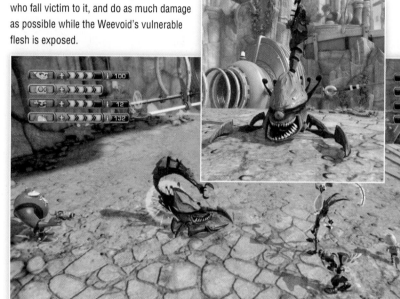

After defeating the ruthless creature, head across the bridge to the right. The aged wood planks creak under the team's weight and it shatters to pieces as soon as they've crossed. At the Checkpoint on the other side, the foursome must deal with a swarm of Rift-Jumper Minions that materialize.

Smash the crates and open the plunger box in the center of the stone circle before hopping off to the right. A series of mushroom tops bounce the

quartet safely to a small rock column with a critter and a Nanotech crate for the taking.

Continue bouncing along mushrooms until a pair of ornery Weevoids appears. Don't get caught in the crossfire of their toxin and conserve ammo by switching targets as soon as one curls up.

When the diabolical duo are defeated, head to the right where a floating rock platform rests just out of reach above. Deploy the Glob Lobber on the flashing target to bring the platform down.

GET A FLYSWATTER

Hop across the platform to reach the next Checkpoint. Search the nearby area for critters, a Nanotech crate, and an Ammo Pad. Clean out the place then hookshot to the overhead anchors that lead up to the next Checkpoint. Hunter Minions, a new enemy type, make their first appearance at this point.

These flying fiends attack by focusing their individual laser beams on one target. Luckily they are poorly armored and can be taken out with little effort. Even better, they are susceptible to the Vac-U and can be plucked right out of the sky.

CRATE SECURITY

While everyone else focuses on swatting the flying robots, try to snag the Bolt Grabber here.

Head to the left near the edge of the pooling water that cascades into a waterfall. Launch a teammate across it to the waiting target pad on the other side then hookshot after. In a flash, three more Weevoids burst out of the water to confront the foursome. Coordinate with teammates to eliminate them one at a time rather than giving the Weevoids time to curl up and draw out the fight.

CRATE SECURITY

Normally the President isn't the first to scout a new area but make an exception in this case. The first player across gets the first crack at the Bolt Grabber there.

Continue on to the left and shoot a teammate across to the target pad. After hookshotting to their position, collect all the critters, Nanotech crate, and plunger box. Proceed up the ledges, and cope with the Rift-Jumper Minions and Robot Minions that arrive on the scene, ready to attack.

Once all the enemies are defeated, four metal platforms are lowered. Hop onboard and press △, then follow the on-screen prompt to rotate the analog stick to raise it up to the next Checkpoint.

MOKTOR OUTPOST

Ratchet and his allies are now getting closer to the N.E.S.T. facility as evidenced by the increased presence of high-tech equipment amid the natural setting. Don't forget to collect the Hero Bolts here. Suck up a teammate and aim high to shoot them at the target pad the next level up. The foursome arrives at the Moktor Outpost where a merciless raid by robotic minions is underway. On the other side of the cobbled together barricade, Scout Minions are laying waste.

Reload at the Ammo Pad but don't simply rush out to defend the outpost against these invaders. The Scout Minions are hiding behind cover but can still be reached by well-aimed Plasmabombs. Even better, the barriers by the team are indestructible but the ones the minions are hiding behind are not.

Next up are four more Mortar Minions who drop in to stack the odds. Ignore the temptation to face them head-on and switch to the Glob Lobber. Fire at the flashing target on the right to bring a massive tower crashing down on the Mortar Minions, wiping them out in one fell swoop.

Continuing past the oppressed Tharpod deeper into the outpost, a pack of Rift-Jumper Minions teleports in to harass the team but don't put up much of a fight. Immediately to the left, a Mortar Minion acquires them as targets and

opens fire. Hang back and take out the lone robotic aggressor, as it is no match for the combined forces of the team and quickly falls. Two teammates should head to the right for a plunger box.

As the foursome approaches the next Ammo Pad, they catch the attention of another Mortar Minion. This one foolishly fires from behind destructible cover. Heal using the Nanotech crate there if necessary. Head to the left where two more Mortar Minions appear. Make short work of them and then head on to the next Checkpoint. In the distance there is an Ammo Pad behind destructible cover, as well as two Mortar Minions even further away.

The tower also broke through the barrier to open a new passage. Hop up the steps to the next Checkpoint. Aside from the plunger box directly ahead by the Ammo Pad there are several critters, a Bolt Grabber, and a Nanotech crate to the right.

OUT OF THE OUTPOST AND INTO THE FIRE

Moving forward triggers the arrival of several Rift-Jumper Minions. Further ahead, a few Scout Minions, accompanied by two Mortar Minions, wait for some action. Destructible cover litters the field, so use it while it lasts and fire Plasmabombs from safety.

After eliminating them, the coast is clear to collect the critters, and Nanotech crate by the liberated Tharpods. A Checkpoint and an Ammo Pad flank the bridge directly ahead. As soon as the team sets foot on the bridge, it starts to crumble. Ratchet and his teammates need to sprint ahead to avoid dropping to their doom.

Two waves of Rift-Jumper Minions and two waves of Hunter Minions appear on the other side—all easily dealt with using the Vac-U. These are followed by Gravoid Brutes that put up a little more of a fight.

Blasts a hole in the makeshift walls penning in the group. On the other side of the barriers is another Checkpoint, an Ammo Pad, critters, and a Nanotech crate. At the edge of the rocky cliff is a series of Hookshot anchor points. Swing between them and then spin from the Hookshot ring to draw closer to the crate factory. Mount the four platforms and raise the team up the cliffside.

This peaceful break gives the team the opportunity to collect Hero Bolts, critters, and a plunger box. The next Checkpoint is to the left by the launch pad.

Gather the team on the launch pad and activate it to be flung through the air and onto a large metal conduit. As the quartet grinds along it, jump to avoid the rings of electrical death that threaten to interrupt their zippy travels.

Don't let the brief glimpse of Commander Spog distract you from the jump ahead. Sideways jumps are necessary to switch conduits before the current one reaches a dead end.

The conduit eventually leads the team directly to the bustling metal platforms adjacent to N.E.S.T.

VERTIGUS CLIFFS

Beyond the metal platforms, an Apogee pod appears before the quartet. Take this opportunity to upgrade and acquire weapons after smashing up the many crates lying around the platform area.

The metal walkway comes to an end not far from the plunger box. Send a teammate across to the target pad then hookshot right behind them. On the other side, Rift-Jumper Minions idly rove on the left side of the metal walkway. Reload at the Ammo Pad before rushing off to meet them, then proceed to the right where more minions wait a short distance away.

TACTICAL RETREAT

Look for the Bolt Grabber on the other side of the dangerous vents in the opposite direction of the robotic enemies.

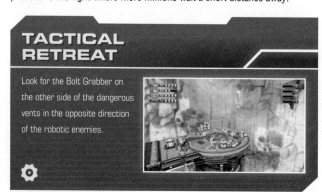

 The bridge the team needs to cross is currently retracted. To activate it, suck up the nearby Voltergeist and deposit it into the waiting receptacle to the left of the bridge. Don't pass up the Nanotech crate by the Voltergeist if healing is necessary.

Cross the bridge to the next Checkpoint where another Nanotech, a critter and many more stacks of crates are waiting. As the foursome approaches the end of the platform, the bridge ahead extends and a wave of Rift-Jumper Minions materializes. As the team fights through the morass of robotic opponents, more keep showing up. Keep blasting away and pressing forward across the extending bridges.

The last bridge ends just short of the next platform, so launch a teammate to the target pad and follow close behind with a hookshot. The elevator needed to ascend is deactivated and requires a Voltergeist. Use the Vac-U to send a teammate ahead to claim the Voltergeist from the small ledge protruding from the cliff. Shoot the Voltergeist across the gap to a waiting teammate who can then deposit it in its proper receptacle.

The elevator quickly moves into position and it's a matter of sending one teammate over using the Vac-U then following close behind with the Hookshot.

BOUNCER BRAWLS

The elevator comes to a stop by an Ammo Pad and a rocky slope leading upwards. As they proceed up it, the team encounters a hardy new adversary: the Bouncer Minion.

These beefy robots are close-range brawlers that use their oversized arms to throw punches and slam the ground with supercharged strikes. It's easy to keep a safe distance and whittle away their armor with ranged weapon attacks.

Move past the next Checkpoint where the path splits. Take the lower path to claim some more critters and pick up a Bolt Grabber among the crates down there, but be ready to quickly dispatch the two Rift-Jumper Minions that seem to have accidentally wandered into the wrong place at the wrong time.

Hookshot up to the overhead anchor point and then swing to the right. Two more Bouncer Minions appear along the rocky path. After dispatching the bruisers, keep going forward and deal with the swarm of Hunter Minions flitting about. After thinning their numbers, several more Bouncer Minions appear to harass the quartet.

Only after all the minions have been defeated will the first switch robot get the courage to stick his green head up. Slam attack him right back down and do the same to the remaining two switch robots to lower the energy shield to the right.

Replenish any health lost in combat with the Nanotech crate by the cliff edge and then proceed to the Cluster Cannon. The next Checkpoint is there along with a critter to collect.

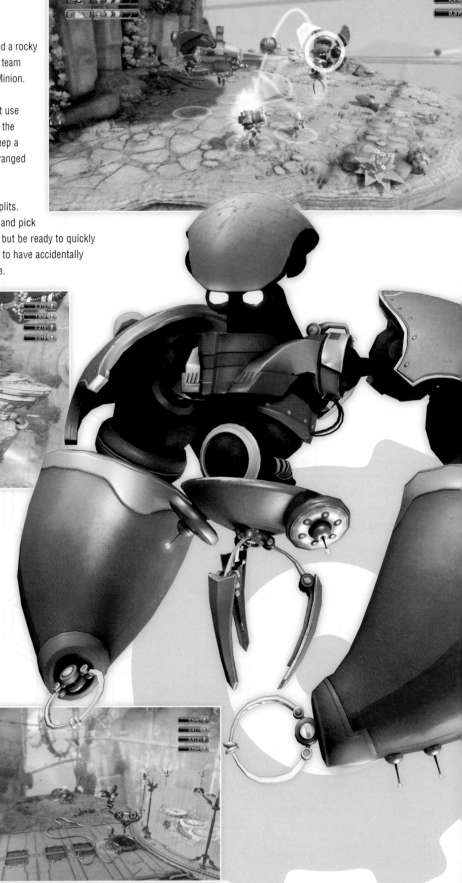

SKEDADDLE TO SAFETY

Reassemble the team on the next Cluster Cannon and have it send them through the sky to an unstable metal walkway. The impact of their landing immediately causes it to collapse. Sprint away from the crumbling metal pieces and reach the final Cluster Cannon. The team safely escapes—albeit briefly—onto another haphazardly assembled walkway.

Unsurprisingly, this metal platform starts to disintegrate as well. As the quartet continues to sprint away from danger, Rift-Jumper Minions appear. Ignore them and head to the next Cluster Cannon that propels them to safety and the next Checkpoint.

Move along the metal platforms to the left past the plunger box and critter. It ends right before a series of Hookshot anchor points. Swing from them to reach greater heights and the next Checkpoint. Smash the two Nanotech crates there before proceeding along the path ahead.

Reload at the Ammo Pad by the cliff's edge before sending a teammate up to the target pad upon the rocky ledge overhead. Their arrival triggers the Turret Minion, a well-armed, stationary defensive robot that can fire in all directions. A circle of shields that that foils any incoming attacks protects it.

The key to defeating the Turret Minion is waiting for it to pause between attacks. During this time, the pilot sticks its head up and is vulnerable to attack. Suck up a teammate with the Vac-U and launch them at the pilot so they can perform a mid-air slam attack. After three mortar slam attacks, the Turret Minion is reduced to spare parts.

Continue onward to the next Checkpoint where several critters frolick by the stacks of crates.

Use the Hookshot to attach to the robot overhead that transforms into a Hookshot helicopter and sweeps the team to the next Checkpoint.

N.E.S.T. ENTRANCE

Use the Apogee pod that just landed to upgrade and acquire some new weapons. Once everyone has made the necessary additions to their arsenal, it's time to knock on the front door. As they approach, a welcome party of Rift-Jumper Minions greets them.

Smash through the dense pack of robots, making use of the Ammo Pad to the left if it's needed. Smash up the crates nearby and open up the plunger box on the metal platform protruding to the right.

After claiming all the goodies, have one teammate pick up the Voltergeist to the right of the entrance. Another teammate must then use their Vac-U on the power plunger to the left of the entrance. This exposes the receptacle for the Voltergeist. Depositing the Voltergeist there activates the entrance, granting the team access to the facility.

MILITARY-INDUSTRIAL COMPLEX

Move toward the next Checkpoint and be prepared for a deadly new enemy: the Sentry Minion. These robots possess their own personal shields and sweep the area with an unforgiving blue light. Even the Nanotech crate here can't save those who get caught in the Sentry Minion's cold gaze. Get spotted by one and it's lights out—Sentry Minions kill with a single shot.

Luckily, they aren't very well constructed. All it takes is a single blow to bust it to pieces. The ideal weapon to tackle these foes is the Plasmabomb Launcher, since it can fire over their shields with ease.

Take cover behind the convenient panel that rises up directly in front of the minion or sprint safely to behind the row of panels to the left. Fire a single Plasmabomb from here and rest easy.

Another Sentry Minion waits just around the bend but a protective series of panels stands between it and the team. Eliminate it easily with a Plasmabomb before smashing the heavy crate on the left. Shoot a teammate across to target pad on the next platform and hookshot right behind them. Repeat the process by aiming for the target pad to the left that places the team directly in front of two more Sentry Minions. Blast them with Plasmabombs then use the Vac-U to send a teammate to the target pad near their smoldering remains and hookshot after them.

Heal using the two Nanotech crates here and reload at the Ammo Pad before proceeding across the bridge through the imposing metal doors to the next Checkpoint.

TANK MINION THROWDOWN

On the other side, the foursome encounters a towering, fierce warbot: the Tank Minion. This death-dealing machine is equipped with laser arms that sweep from side-to-side and mortar launchers on its back.

The Tank Minion has a good deal of armor, requiring the team members to exhaust most of their arsenal. Continuously fire while jumping over the laser beams as they sweep in from the sides. When the Tank Minion switches to mortars, avoid the red crosshairs on the ground and move into position where mortars have just landed, as those are the safest positions.

After expending a significant quantity of ammunition, the Tank Minion finally succumbs to the fierce foursome. Upon its demise, a target pad appears where it once stood. Use the Vac-U to send a teammate over and hookshot behind.

DEADLY DETOUR

On the other side, activate the power plungers to raise the tram platform leading deeper into the factory. Unfortunately, the computer detects their

unauthorized presence and Commander Spog has them diverted through the steam channel.

Lethal green fumes spew from various vents and the team's platform is destined for one in particular. Leap to safety between the many moving platforms to reach the safety of the stationary platform in the left corner of the chamber.

Team up to open the plunger box there before mounting the nearby elevator pad. It takes the team a short distance up to the next Checkpoint. The walkway also boasts an Ammo Pad and a Nanotech crate. Move to the right to find another Nanotech crate. When the computer informs Commander Spog of the quartet's survival, he summons more reinforcements in the form of Rift-Jumper Minions that materialize to thwart the team.

After dismantling them, the assembly line adjacent kicks into gear. As it does so, metal platforms periodically extend and retract. Wait for each platform to light up blue and extend. Then, move together as a unit and time each jump well to avoid dropping into the grinding gears below and reach the elevator pad on the other side.

HELPING HANDS

Gather together on the elevator pad and activate it to descend. It doesn't get far before Commander Spog orders the pad to self-destruct, dropping the quartet into a freefall. To survive, the group links hands and you must maneuver them over the heavy-duty fans below. The powerful wave of air pressure they produce keeps the gang aloft so they don't find themselves splattered at the bottom.

Only one of the four fans is active at a given moment, requiring coordinated mid-air movement over the active one. The colored circles over the group's hands indicate how centered they are on the currently activated fan.

Riding each fan in succession eventually launches them out of the top of the elevator shaft and back outdoors. A number of critters along with a Bolt

Grabber are wandering around an area filled of crates. More importantly, Hero Bolts are found immediately to the left of the top of the shaft.

Head towards the metal bridge leading to an archway. Pass the Checkpoint and heal up with the help of the two Nanotech crates. The next room is full of Sentry Minions.

Two Rift-Jumper Minions teleport in when the team enters the room. After dealing with them, use a well-placed Plasmabomb to deal with each pair of Sentry Minions.

With the coast clear for now, head across the room to the other side where there are two Nanotech crates and a plunger box. Two more unimpressive

Rift-Jumper Minions make a late appearance. Approach the large turbine and press ◉ to activate the Vac-U to spin it up. Once it reaches maximum speed, it retracts into the floor.

Head back to the center of the room where a manual release has risen from the floor. Press ⬤ to rotate it and manually descend on the elevator to the next Checkpoint.

Similar to the Tank Minion, Mr. Perkins retains the former's arsenal but also benefits from an impenetrable shield that draws on nearby power. Rather than swinging a single laser arm, he brings his arms together for a double-beam that sweeps side-to-side.

As the platform settles one floor below in front of three Sentry Minions, a shield rises up from the floor. However, this shield moves left and right, so its protection from the searchlights of the Sentry Minions is not guaranteed.

Keep behind it and fire off Plasmabombs to eliminate the watchful robots. Collect the three Nanotech crates found here before activating this floor's turbine to reactivate the manual controls.

TOO CLOSE FOR COMFORT

Don't get too close to Mr. Perkins. This causes him to deploy an expanding wave of deadly blue energy that knocks anyone off their feet.

POUND MR. PERKINS

Take the elevator down another floor to the next Checkpoint where three Bouncer Minions lie in wait. After seeing them reduced to scrap metal, Commander Spog becomes frustrated. He sends in a more reliable subordinate: Mr. Perkins.

To defeat Mr. Perkins, the team must coordinate to slam attack the Mortar Tosses flanking his position. Once both are smacked down, Mr. Perkins' shield lowers temporarily to allow incoming attacks to land. It's only when his shields are down that Mr. Perkins uses his back-mounted mortar launchers.

CONSERVATION IS KEY

Don't get anywhere near the Ammo Pad on the right until absolutely necessary—and definitely not before Mr. Perkins shows up. His heavy armor requires a great deal of ammo to shatter and the Ammo Pad doesn't reset upon his arrival.

REHABITATION CENTER

The reward for taking down Mr. Perkins is an Apogee pod on the platform ahead. Advance towards it and the nearby Checkpoint, sucking up the critters hopping about. The Darkstar Fission Tether, a devastating electrical weapon that automatically locks onto its targets, is available here. Use the Nanotech crate to heal up after the grueling battle and claim all the bolts from the crates in the area.

Cross the bridge to the rail transport. Once every team member is onboard, they are whisked back indoors to the next Checkpoint. Head up the ramp to the Ammo Pad and then cross the walkway into the next room.

The doors open to reveal a group of Cleaner Minions poised to attack. After defeating them, Bouncer Minions arrive on the scene followed by Hunter Minions. Once they are defeated, a power plunger rises up. Check the right side of the room for Hero Bolts before moving on.

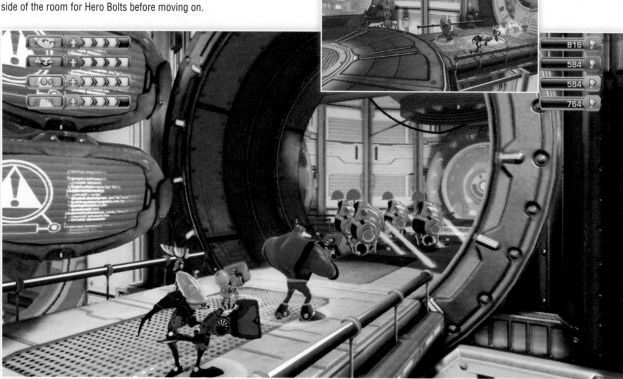

One teammate must activate it with the Vac-U to open the door to the next room. There, another team member must use their Vac-U on the power plunger on the other side to permanently keep the door open so that everyone may pass.

Reload using the Ammo Pad and heal with the Nanotech crate before proceeding. In the next area, the team faces two Bouncer Minions followed by repeated waves of Cleaner Minions. Defeating the final wave of Cleaner Minions raises up another power plunger. Activating it with the Vac-U flips up the nearby

robot switch. Have a teammate slam attack the robot switch back down to open the door behind it to the next room.

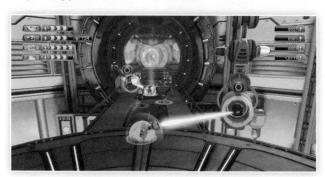

Look for a Bolt Grabber and Nanotech crate beside the Checkpoint. After healing and collecting, step onto the elevator pad ahead. It raises the team up several levels and rotates them to face a thick metal conduit. Leap onto it and proceed to the left.

LIKE DREADGRUBS IN A BARREL

The Dreadgrubs seen dangling from mechanical pinchers can be targeted and shot for bolts.

The conduit leads the team to an area guarded by two Mortar Minions located behind cover. They aren't paying much attention though, so the team can safely reload at the Ammo Pad without drawing their attention. However, as soon as they step onto the circular platform with the incinerator at its center, the robots start unleashing their explosive payloads. Take them out quickly by firing arcing Plasmabombs over their destructible cover.

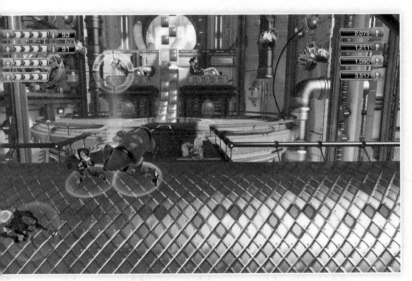

After wiping them out, a power plunger opens up on the left side of the chute leading to the incinerator. Activate it with the Vac-U to reveal another power plunger on the opposite side. Keep the Vac-U going while a teammate heads to activate the other. Once both are activated, the rapid flow of materials destined for the incinerator comes to a stop. It's now safe to climb up the ramp.

Head through the tunnel ahead past the Nanotech crate to the next Checkpoint. Look for critters and another Nanotech crate in the vicinity.

After everyone has had a chance to heal and fight over the bolts, swing from the Hookshot anchor points ahead to reach the Hookshot ring. The centrifugal force

of it whips them straight through a giant glass wall and onto a heavy-duty metal pipe outside.

SLIDING PAST SPOG

Commander Spog is displeased and has decided to intervene personally. In addition to jumping over the electrified rings that intermittently appear in the way and jumping between unfinished pipes, the foursome must now contend with bombs dropped in their path by the wrathful Commander Spog.

Near the end of the line, Spog briefly unleashes motorized saw blades that come rushing at the quartet in trios. Jump over them to avoid their sharp edges and keep on grinding until arriving at the next Checkpoint.

There's no time for a breather because an aggressive Scout Minion is waiting. Reload at the Ammo Pad and duck behind the panels for cover. Use Plasmabombs to safely eliminate the Scout Minion, and then press forward to do the same for the next Scout Minion farther down the walkway.

At the end of the walkway a third Scout Minion drops in, backed by a Mortar Minion on the next level up behind it. Keep a safe distance to eliminate the Scout Minion first without also drawing the Mortar Minion's fire. The Nanotech crate on the walkway is sure to come in handy.

When the third Scout Minion is downed, sprint up the ramp to the left and toward the next Ammo Pad to reload. Now re-equipped, make short work of the Mortar Minion.

MOVING ON UP

With the other enemies eliminated, two Voltergeists rise up into position. Suck up the Voltergeists with the Vac-U and deposit them in their proper receptacles on either side of the platform. This causes the platform to rise up before Commander Spog brings it to an abrupt halt.

He has his robotic minions drop in a trio of Weevoids onto the platform. Once they are defeated, Spog sends in Bouncer Minions to deal with the quartet. Once the minions are reduced to gears and copper wiring, a Gravoid Brute swoops in and launches its mortars. After this last threat is eliminated, the elevator continues on its way up uninterrupted.

The group appears at the next Checkpoint inside an observation room high atop the complex. Make use of the two Nanotech crates here if necessary. Once the room has been stripped of its valuables, step onto the elevator pad.

BOSS COMMANDER SPOG

The elevator takes the team up to the very top of the tower where they finally face Commander Spog for an epic showdown. The old warbot is equipped with laser beams on his arms that he uses to sweep the field of battle. His arms also convert into massive pounding surfaces he uses to strike either the left, right, or center of the ground with.

From his pseudo-wings, he deploys bombs—each has their own individual timed fuses. Fortunately, these explosives are powerful enough to damage their maker. Suck them up with the Vac-U and toss them right back in Commander Spog's face to save on ammunition.

Commander Spog also unleashes spinning saw blades from his arms that cut along straight lines in random directions.

After the Bouncer Minions' defeat, he returns with a new trick up his robotic sleeve: he now deploys both laser beam arms at the same time requiring agile jumping to avoid as they move across the screen. The Ammo Pad is also reactivated upon his return.

Once Spog's primary systems have been compromised, he again circles to a new position where a new Ammo Pad waits for the quartet. After suffering even more damage, he retreats once again and summons several Bouncer Minions to deal with the team. The Ammo Pad reactivates in anticipation of their arrival.

After the minions are taken out, Spog has no choice but to return again. The Ammo Pad reactivates so reload and continue to hammer away at the warbot. When he's almost on his last legs, Spog retreats for the last time and sends in more Bouncer Minions. Reload at the reactivated Ammo Pad to deal with them quickly and force Spog to return to the fight. Upon his return the Ammo Pad reactivates, all but guaranteeing sufficient ammunition to put the Commander down for good this time.

HOT POTATO

Don't hold onto Spog's bombs for too long. Even while swept up in the Vac-U, their fuses keep counting down and can blow up right in your character's face.

After the team inflicts enough damage to slightly compromise his systems, Spog swings around to the side by a new Ammo Pad to renew his attacks. Further compromising his system sends him into retreat. In his place, he sends in Bouncer Minions to do his dirty work. Luckily, their arrival coincides with the reactivation of the Ammo Pad.

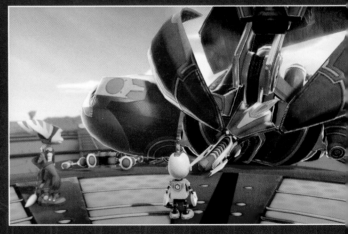

GETTING DOWN AND FUNKY

Spog has been bested and lies broken before the team. Clank manages to cut a deal with him after convincing Nefarious to lend his mechanical expertise. Honoring the bargain, Spog instructs them to seek out the architect at the lighthouse to learn how to destroy Ephemeris. With the deal complete, the former Commander flies off to greener pastures.

Head forward through the arch and activate the elevator pad. It descends to ground level, depositing the team before a locked doorway. Collect the Hero Bolts on the right and then trigger the two Mortar Tosses flanking the doorway to open it. A Scanner Minion swoops through to ascertain the status of the gang following the defeat of Commander Spog.

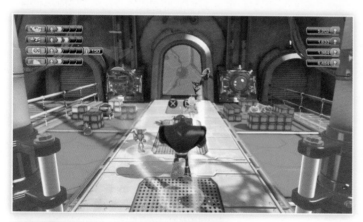

Another holo-diary emerges from the doorway, an earlier entry from Dr. Croid—his first—plays back. He describes how critters are a rite of passage on Magnus, their presence seeming to augment and enrich the lives of the Tharpods. Collaborating with Nevo Binklemeyer, Dr. Croid sought to understand the effect of creatures on their owners. Under the vectomorphic triscilloscope, they detected a strange radiation. He eagerly anticipates their attempt to separate the energy with the protomorphic extractor. The diary ends before the results of the experiment are revealed.

87

PLANET MAGNUS
OCTONOK CAY

OBJECTIVES

COVE
- Head into the Tharpod Fishing Village
- Ask a Tharpod for Directions to Terawatt Forest

W.A.S.P.
- Use the Feeding Cannon to Reach the W.A.S.P.
- Destroy Charging Dock Alpha
- Destroy Charging Dock Beta
- Destroy Charging Dock Gamma
- Destroy the W.A.S.P.

REEF SHALLOWS
- Navigate the Reef with Your Escape Raft
- Cross the Ship Graveyard

OCTONOC LIGHTHOUSE
- Go to the Octonoc Lighthouse
- Use the Shock Towers Against the King Sepiad
- Defeat the King Sepiad

TOP OF LIGHTHOUSE
- Access the Lighthouse Railway Station

HERO BOLTS

✓	**COVE**
	Just after first swingshot section
	Just after second swingshot section
	W.A.S.P.
	After the first wind fan
	REEF SHALLOWS
	On the left before the first turn
	TOP OF LIGHTHOUSE
	Beside the fallen King Sepiad

The N.E.S.T. has been infiltrated and Commander Spog has been overthrown. For once, it seems the unlikely band of galactic saviors may actually be picking up some momentum. As the holo-diaries describe, there is something innately special about Magnus: the adorable critters inhabiting the planet are not mere cuddly pets, they seem to imbue those they are around with enhanced abilities, leading to an age of unprecedented Tharpod innovation and paradoxological discovery.

But if that is true, then why are the Tharpods relegated to time-forgotten villages instead of towering modern-age skyscrapers? How could a machine as massive and powerful as Ephemeris exist here? Something is afoot. Ratchet and crew must head to the Terawatt Forest to find Dr. Frumpus Croid—hopefully to get off this rock and back home. But getting to the Forest is going to be as difficult as traversing the forest itself…

NEW ENEMIES DEFEATED

COVE

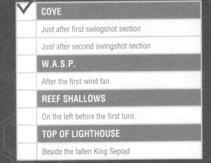 Flabberfish

Armored Slorg

 Sepiad

W.A.S.P.

 Slorg

 Bomber Minion

 Missile Minion

NEW WEAPONS PURCHASED

COVE

☐ Omegatech Frost Cannon

OCTONOC LIGHTHOUSE

King Sepiad ☐

TOP OF LIGHTHOUSE

King Sepiad (Again!) ☐

A short boat ride deposits the heroes onto a rather rickety looking series of docks. Though the Critters here are plentiful, they seem to be the only source of non-aquatic life left—mysterious given Octonok Cay is supposed to be a bustling fishing village. Setting off in search of a Tharpod that can offer some clear direction to the Terawatt Forest, Ratchet and pals quickly discover that the Cay is still quite populated, but not with the denizens they were hoping for.

5
MISSION

COVE

The Cove exhibits signs of a once-prolific fishing operation; thick rope lashes beams to undulating plank walkways that seem to end almost as soon as they begin over gently gurgling waterways. Though picturesque, navigating the Cay will require even more unconventional means of traversal.

WHAT A MOUTHFUL: TORTEMOTHS, FLABBERFISH, AND SLORGS

A weapons pod waits for the heroes, offering up upgrades to familiar weapons and a new weapon that promises some chilling results: the Omegatech Frost Cannon. Scoop up this valuable sub-zero temperature delivery system as soon as possible; when upgraded, its ability to instantly target enemies in range and heavy payload potential, especially when multiple heroes are using it, provides an extremely efficient way to deal with smaller enemies. Even without upgrades, its ability to freeze enemies in their tracks is formidable. Once enemies are frozen, a single shot or melee strike shatters them.

After stocking up on supplies and any available upgrades that bolt stores allow, Ratchet and his comrades head down to the dock to encounter an interesting sight: a Tortemoth sitting languidly in the water. Though it gives a curious head-turn as the party moves across its back to another series of planks, it makes no effort to actively reject this means of impromptu aquatic traversal. Handy as none of this foursome can swim.

FLABBERFISH HO!

With their flappy beaks and purplish-blue coloring, these little creatures hardly seem much of a threat, but Flabberfish overcome their fairly slow movement on land with sheer numbers and the unfortunate ability to latch onto a target with little notice. Should Ratchet or one of his cohorts find that a Flabberfish has glommed onto their dome, look for a telltale exclamation point and ⊗ button prompt. Hammer that button to escape the beaky maw.

Otherwise, Flabberfish are relatively harmless, and can be quickly dispensed via simple melee strikes or VAC-U inhales/exhales if one needs to conserve ammo. Weapons like the Critterstrike, Fission Tether or Frost Cannon also make short work of unarmored enemies such as these. Simply hold down the trigger and watch the auto-targeting system do its thing.

A small encounter with a gaggle of Flabberfish immediately after jumping off the Tortemoth leads to another scuffle to the right, near a slam crate. After taking care of them, the team continues onward, around a curving dock platform next to a familiar sight: a sonic pylon eerily similar to the one used in Luminopolis to hail a cab. Hop on the Tortemoth and swing across a pair of swingshot targets to land on another zig-zagging set of dockworks.

FIRST ON, FIRST OFF

Familiarity (or this guide) with the number of swingshot targets in a sequence can actually set up non-squishy-minded players with a serious advantage. In this first swinging section, there are only two swingshot targets, which means the first person to jump on becomes the first to jump off. Granted, there's more jostling for position when there are three or four players at the same time, but being the first back onto dry land here means an opportunity to quickly suck up a Bolt Grabber and a few Critters nearby, but keep in mind that there's another Bolt Grabber just a little farther up the dock.

The Creatures are so plentiful most of the time that they aren't a huge deal, but instantly sucking up and doubling bolt reserves means a faster path to new or upgraded weapons—and sniping both Bolt Grabbers is just too tempting to pass up. Make the most of the opportunity by attaching to the grapple point first, then jump quickly to the last part of the chain. Some insolent dolt beat you to it? Try reeling yourself in after they've landed for a chance at early collection.

Regardless of who lands first, everyone can benefit from the Hero Bolt sitting to the far left of the landing platform. Everyone should suck one up before moving on—unless some greedy friend/enemy/frenemy has already made a dash for the second Bolt Grabber.

YOU'RE CUT OFF!

So what if some bolt-hungry so-called buddy has scampered off ahead? In *Ratchet & Clank: All 4 One*, the majority (usually) rules, meaning the camera moves with the bulk of the group. Make greedier players pay by moving quickly away from the Hero Bolt stash, and don't let them head back by quickly moving on. After all, if you can't partake in early spoils, why should anyone else? It's how intergalactic justice is served: Qwark-style—quickly, by mob rule and with no time to worry about the consequences.

SLORG? SLORG!

Rarely do the fauna on Magnus present such an interesting dichotomy. Slorgs are brimming with electrical energy and can only be killed with the Frost Cannon. Thankfully, they can be kept at a distance with weapons that deliver a constant output such as the Critterstrike. The ability to "push" Slorgs out of the way is crucial to earning the "On Some Planets They're a Delicacy" Trophy. Give a Slorg a light push to start things in a direction, then help them over the edge of the docks. Not all Slorg disposals go as easily as these first two; keep an eye out for bouncy railings that can send one of the electrified quasi-threats your way. Put the Slorg between your character and open water, then unload.

After giving the Slorgs the heave-ho, another group of Flabberfish arrives to make things more annoying. Deal with them quickly, and then move onward toward a hookshot target ahead. A couple jumps over gaps and a quick tether deposits everyone near another Slorg—this one illustrating why just firing at one while its back is to something solid can end poorly. Instead, unload with plenty of Critterstrike oomph to push it to the right, down near the waiting Ammo Pad.

A waiting Creature and Slam Attack Crate are the more obvious targets after leaping from the Ammo Pad dock, but remember that bolts and

Creatures aren't the only criteria being judged at the end of a level. Co-Op Points are important too, which is why a quick VAC-U suck on the goody reels to the left yields not just a crate filled with goods, but those precious cooperative bonus points.

Regardless of your choice, the group must cross another series of swingshot targets, this time three-wide. Quick math may help advantageous players to hold off in hopes of being the first one to the landing, but all that waits here is another bunch of Hero Bolts to the bottom-right and a few crates to break up a short Flabberfish scuffle upon arrival.

Another choice waits up ahead: a VAC-U-powered bit of fishing to the right or a Creature and bounce pad to the left. Once the party has split the spoils, continue onward past another set of bounce pads leading to more Slorgs. Rather than attacking head-on, sweep around to the left of them and give them a Critterstrike-fueled nudge off the docks to the right. With them and the Bomb Crates dealt with, a platform drops, allowing everyone to ring the sonic pylon and move upward.

SLORGS OF A DIFFERENT COLOR

The path pitches sharply down to the right, littered with Critters. A small scuffle ensues, first with a smattering of melee-friendly threats, then a few more packing a some firepower. Deal with the group, scoop up another crate with the goody reel before everyone hops on the waiting platform and rings yet another sonic pylon.

SLORG? ARMORED SLORG?!

Though they may look more menacing than their non-plated electrified brethren, Armored Slorgs are little more than a minor threat—provided Ratchet and crew have been making use of the Critterstrike. It quickly punches through the armor plating and leave the Slorgs open to the same handy nudge as before, all without letting go of the trigger. In fact, the Strike's explosive jettisoning of the armor can give a Slorg even more of a push in whatever direction the team deems prudent.

Is there anything that rainbow-beamed weapon can't do? No, no there isn't, which is why it should be one of the first weapons to be upgraded as fully as possible. Even without extensive powering-up, the Critterstrike pushes the Slorg off to a watery end either to the far right, near a set of various crates, a VAC-U suction co-op opportunity and an Ammo Pad. Be wary of the rolling bumpers along the bulk of the initial walkway, as they have a tendency to keep the Slorg bouncing around instead of sailing gracefully off the elevated platform. Scooting quickly below the creature and blasting it upwards, then quickly getting out of the way is the easiest means of dealing with it.

CATCH AND RELEASE

Those little goody reels are handy for scoring a few Co-Op Points and whatever spoils they haul up, but you rightly earned those spoils by applying your VAC-U with authority. Why not show other players who is in charge by continuing to suck after the crate has been hoisted. With a little luck (and more than a little jockeying for a position early that makes them want to jump over you), you can suck up your one-time partner and give them a long flight off a short pier.

The view as the foursome move closer to a possible Tharpod still living nearby is disturbing. A massive, constant vortex is doing something to the sea nearby, and may just have been the reason for the recent desertion of the Cay. Time to move on to find out for sure.

More Slogs in Armored and non-Armored flavors await the rainbow kiss of the Critterstrike. Dispose of them quickly while moving along the zig-zagging docks, remembering to establish proper angles for bouncing them off the docks rather than toward an unsuspecting team member.

A tentacled threat appears after the first batch of Slorgs, but it provides little in the way of real danger. Wait for the business end to slap down through the docks, and then jump over the gaps toward another group of all-Armored Slorgs. Thankfully, the circular platform they're on is scarcely protected at the edges, making a Critterstrike barrage a quick and easy disposal job.

A curious set of bubbles near another sonic pylon reveals a submerged Toremoth. Ring the pylon to raise the slumbering beast, cross over, and deal with more Slorgs. Nearby stores of Nanotech, crates and an Ammo Pad can help beef up any struggling teammates, but the real goal is down the docks, past the Slorgs.

There's a Co-Op Point opportunity after another brief tentacle encounter and a sea of Slorgs bustling with electric cast-off. Guide the Slorgs gently (or otherwise) toward a waiting well at the top of the screen. With four of them deposited, the red meters on either side glow blue, allowing for a VAC-U assisted escape through a door to the left and all the sweet Co-Op Points that come with it.

Another set of tentacle-hewn gaps and more Slorgs bookend a smallish landing with crates and Nanotech. Deal with them like the others, pushing them not upward, but to the left into another well that uses their juice to power up a pair of power plungers that lower another door.

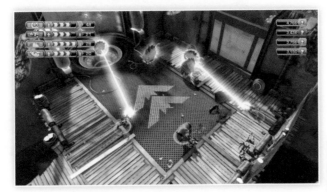

BOUNCY BOUNCY

Have any teammates become a little uppity lately? Show them who's really in charge by unleashing a storm of fire on one of these Slorg groups. The more of them that are hit and caroming around their relatively small pens, the harder it is for the other squishy "friends" to avoid their electrical embrace. Sure, it might mean a few shocks of your own, but you have to break a few eggs to put an omelet in its place, right?

After a few criss-crossing bounce pads, a platform holds a few Creatures, co-op opportunities, and Nanotech as well as a view of additional Slorg encounters. Scoop up the spoils, then head down to confront the Slorgs, this time sending them into the nearby well rather than over the edge of the platform.

Don't fret if they accidentally spill off the platform; more jump in until the meters above the well turn blue. At which point, all remaining Slorgs are destroyed.

HEROES ON THE MOVE

With so much apparent volume when the Cay is humming along at peak capacity, it's not surprising that conveyor belts have been constructed. These provide a slight impediment when moving against your character, but quickly jumping against the flow can help speed things up (as can using **L3** to sprint for a bit). Proceed across the walkways, stopping to scoop up any lingering Creatures and crates while taking note of the appetite of whatever is attached to those tentacles. A platform and sonic pylon combo raises the group to an upper level filled with more walkways and a small alcove with a Creature and Slam Attack Crate.

THE EASY WAY TO FLY

The moving walkways are a cunning and devious foe, but should a persistent Lombax, a power-mad mechanized despot or a tiny robot pal take the lead, make the most of their gumption and pluck by simply pressing ● at regular intervals to catch up. Their pain is your gain—all the better to be ever-vigilant in the battle against all manner of do-baddery. A quick approach from the rear means one's blaster always runs hot.

A wide platform just past the conveyor belts offers plenty of space, but little in the way of goodies. Tag-team the goody reel, scoop up loose crates and pocketing a few Creatures and/or Nanotech. The team encounters them all on the way to a nearby Ammo Pad. It's prudent to continue the collection on the other side of the bounce pad. But before heading on past a door, the team must first overcome a new threat.

BOMBS AWAY

Bomber Minions like the other Minions in the employ of Ephemeris are aptly named. They spit out a stream of projectiles that head slowly earthward. Though this first introduction doesn't offer much in the way of latitude, longitudinal movement isn't quite so dangerous. Use the ability to side strafe as all teammates unload on the Bombers with the same weapon for maximum effect, leaping sideways when shots near your character. Four of the new threats must be contained before opening the door to the right.

Proceed through the door and down the walkway to a pair of VAC-U-ready goody reels and a few crates. Farther down the path waits a double-jump-worthy gap and an Ammo Pad, as well as a view of a decidedly crowded platform teeming with Slorgs.

MORE THAN JUST BOLTS

It is never a bad thing to help out an ally in need, especially when a few Co-op Points can be gathered in the process. But, hauling up these goody reels is not just an opportunity to team up with a friend for bolts, the crates also may contain Creatures. These slightly longer crates offer a valuable reward for applying expeditious use of the VAC-U.

WALK THE PLANK

Teamwork and quick reflexes are required when facing the sparking, bumbling group of Slorgs ahead. Since the conveyor belt that brings the heroes down to this landing retracts after depositing them, there's precious little room to maneuver the Slorgs into the well at the center. Use careful guided bursts of the Critterstrike to push one at time into the well, concentrating on the slightly faster un-Armored variety first when possible. After clearing them out and sending another waiting Slorg off the edge, suck

up a teammate with the VAC-U and fire them onto the landing pad across the gap, then have everyone zip to the waiting buddy before continuing on.

A long pier extends off into the distance with little in the way of things to collect—a sure sign that things will be all business going forward. Sure enough, the tentacles return, slamming into the dock and creating gaps that must be crossed. The smaller ones can be easily traversed with a normal jump, but the wider ones encourage double-jumping. Go with the ol' gut here; a double-jump is nearly always safer than a single one anyway. After a small bolt cache and a series of bouncy stairs, the team arrives at a sonic pylon that summons yet another Tortemoth for a short pylon-powered ride.

Maneuver the docile creature first toward a small platform littered with crates and Nanotech, then again across a bigger expanse of water in view of the weather manipulating W.A.S.P.—the creation of Dr. Croid's partner, and a possible insight into who is pulling the strings of Ephemeris.

Extend the team's own strings to cross a series of swingshot targets to land on a platform with little in the way of spoils, but plenty of more dangerous threats. A group of Bomb Minions crashes the party; they can be easily dealt with using concentrated weapons fire. As there's an Ammo

Pad nearby, unload with the biggest and baddest of the arsenal (so long as everyone's using the same one; combined firepower is key).

A conveyor belt pushes against a bigger platform to the left holding a stash of bolts, another pair of ggody reels, and plenty of Nanotech to heal any

wounds taken in the last few fights. Scoop it all up before bouncing up to the higher level and an enclosed tussle against some familiar minions. Pour on the combined firepower to overcome them and lift the energy bubble containing the group before scooping up any spare crates and heading down the walkway to—gasp—an actual Tharpod!

DINNER TIME

So Ephemeris did have something to do with the W.A.S.P. As the foursome nears the raging vortex meant to provide a hospitable domain for the Sepiads (don't forget to grab any spare Critters or crates lying around), an ominous form patrols the water. A quick series of swings across to a platform reveals the Sepiads in all their fury (or hunger).

TENTACLE TROUBLE

Behold, the Sepiad! Finally the group encounter the source of the tentacles wreaking havoc on the docks for so long. Amazingly, this Sepiad isn't even the biggest of the species. It seems to be a herald seeking out food and delivering it for the Sepiad King. Unfortunately, a Lombax, a pair of robotic taggers-on and some kind of hulking lummox makes a tasty meal for the King, so the Sepiad quickly goes to work subduing the heroes with powerful tentacle slams.

Cronk and Zephyr are really no help here. When the creature brings its tentacles together, it slams the middle of the platform. When they're apart, it covers the outer edges. A third attack is a little less obvious; repeated slams sweep from one side of the platform to the other in quick succession, but again these can be avoided fairly easily.

The key to taking the creature out is ceaseless firepower (as always, with the same weapon whenever possible). After hitting the creature with enough attacks, it slips back into the water and must be coaxed out by ringing the nearby sonic pylon. The creature stays fixated on the bait for a fairly long time. If you do not use the sonic pylon, the Sepiad still emerges but isn't as vulnerable. Use the opportunity to close the gap and switch to a short-range weapon like the Arc Lasher or Fission Tether to hold the creature in place. With enough concentrated firepower, it can be brought down quickly, but don't forget to move back if it scoops up the bait; a powerful body slam injures anyone nearby.

Pummel the beast, repeating the same basic actions each time to avoid tentacles, call it back from the briny deep with the pylon, and then unload at close range until it's defeated. Your reward is a one-way ticket to the W.A.S.P. by way of the feeding cannon and another lengthy bit of exposition explaining Croid and Nevo's relationship.

W.A.S.P.

Ring a pair of sonic pylons to gain access (by way of a couple Tortemoths) to a platform just past the Sepiad. Good news! It is loaded with goodies: a Creature roams the left side, crates are stacked high and a long-awaited return of the GrummelNet kiosk all greet the heroes after Dr. Croid's holo-diary. Take the time to load up on supplies; upgrade any weapons that can use it (the Critterstrike and trusty Combuster are great go-to Elite upgrades if the bolts are there), then proceed to the food cannon and get ready for one heck of a ride.

The sight that greets the group when they finally make it up the vortex and into the W.A.S.P. itself is chilling. The machine is simply gigantic and crackles with unimaginable power. Thankfully, that power is the only thing keeping the weather-rending monstrosity aloft, so the group heads toward the first of three charging docks, which keep the generator powered-up.

Fire a member of the team across the way to a landing pad, then have the rest of the team zip across. Multiple Minions descend, first offering some melee-heavy competition, then advancing with a wave of flying snipers, which should be dealt with post-haste before tackling any remaining ground forces. As always, concentrated fire with identical weapons is the key to cleaning up. If everyone has been playing together for a while and has had the chance to upgrade the same weapons, default to those, however weak they may seem. A two-, three-, or especially four-way assault with the same weapon is superior to a mix of different weapons. Should they be needed, multiple Nanotech crates are waiting near a pair of barriers straddling the only path forward. When all enemies have been felled, head down this path.

THAR SHE BLOWS

The W.A.S.P. is well equipped to handle any intruders. In addition to the scores of enemies that converge on the foursome as they make their way to the charging docks, great fans threaten to blow one or all of the team off the narrow platforms that must be traversed. Move slowly, paying close attention to the power up/down cycles of the fans.

The first fan offers no real challenge other than pushing back. Wait for it to die, then move on, letting one player take the lead and then holding ⬆ to zip alongside them when the coast is clear. Behind the first fan are Hero Bolts, some Creatures, more Nanotech and a few crates that can be looted as needed. A moving wall blocks the thrust of a trio of fans. Be patient and move slowly to get past them.

YOUR BIGGEST FAN

Just past the moving wall and fan triplet are an even bigger fan and a challenge of coordination. To deactivate the fan the foursome must hit four pads. Each of the pads must be slammed in this sequence: lower-left, upper-right, upper-left, and finally the lower-right. The problem is that fan's powerful push; should a team member jump while it's on, the force is enough to easily push them off to their doom. Instead, wait for the fan's cycle to almost end, then attempt as many of the buttons as possible before it starts up.

Don't fret if things can't be completed on the first or even second attempts. With slow, steady progress, part of the sequence can be completed far enough that when the fan begins blowing again, it won't completely revert back to the first target. Take things slowly here; rushing only leads to death and greater setbacks.

When the sequence is completed, loot the remaining crates and Nanotech, then hop onto the platform to rise up to the level of the first charging dock.

Charging Dock Alpha is relatively unguarded. A handful of melee-friendly threats appear to impede the team, complemented a few moments later by beefier threats. Get into the habit of concentrating fire as heavily and quickly on a single bigger threat; it's not as important here as it is farther ahead but this is a great time to practice.

Once the threats have been removed, concentrate Glob Lobber fire on one of two key points on the cylinder holding the charging dock up. Lower the wall that covers a melee attack target, strike the target, and then repeat with the other wall and weak point. Charging Dock Alpha explodes and tumbles down into the waiting vortex below in a hail of debris.

FEELING SPARKS

A set of conductor panels acts as a portent for challenges to come. Harmless when the static electricity in the air has dissipated, they glow white and absorb a small lightning strike as the electricity gathers. Needless to say, being zapped isn't a pleasant experience, so take note of the amount of time it takes for the pads to be fully powered up and struck. This information is invaluable later.

Just beyond the panels is a slight tweak on the three fan/moving wall challenge from earlier. This time, one teammate must power the wall with the VAC-U while another (or the rest) run along the safe zone to another panel that lets the first hero pass (though they can ⬆ over to their comrades once in range).

A series of moving platforms and yet another fan offer a limited threat to the group's march toward Charging Dock Beta. To proceed, simply leap when the platforms are moving from left to their farthest position on the right, then repeat all the way to the end. Take comfort in the ease of this challenge, as the next part isn't quite as simple.

As before, a swarm of smaller, easier enemies confronts the group first, then another group of stronger ones flies in. While tackling these threats, the ominously dark floor panels won't provide any real danger, but the second all the guards are taken out, they sputter to life and begin discharging lightning bolts. Use the timing learned earlier to scoot between adjacent, dark panels while lobbing Glob Lobber goo onto the familiar targets. A melee attack on both weak points brings the second charging dock back to earth. Before the foursome can move on, however, a new threat emerges.

MEDDLING MINIONS

The Missile Minion is one of the most imposing foes yet seen by the group, and its hulking size isn't just for show. Numerous missiles are launched skyward and then plummet straight down at high speed, with a red targeting reticule on the ground marking their impact point.

The missiles are launched in waves, necessitating constant movement, which can be difficult in more hectic firefights. Concentrate heavy weapons (the Warmonger works great) on the target to take it down before those missiles can find their target, and above all else, keep moving!

CORRIDORS OF FORCE

Up until now, getting to the charging docks has been relatively simple, but Charging Dock Gamma is anything but a cakewalk. Immediately after polishing off the Missile Minion and heading to the right, the gang is confronted by a massive fan down a long corridor, shut down only temporarily by a pair of familiar buttons. Slam Attack them in sequence, then quickly sprint down the corridor until a mortar strike is possible. Suck up a teammate, toss them at the target, and then repeat on the second button before the fan starts up again. If the fan does start to spin up while in the corridor, everyone is blown back to the start, though any slammed buttons stay slammed.

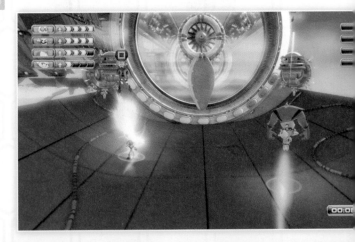

Up next is a series of blue waves, pulsing electrical energy every few seconds. These waves won't damage anyone when not electrified, but they 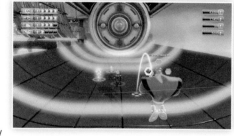 do push back anything in their path. This becomes an issue ahead.

There is a checkpoint and two more buttons ahead. Beyond them, the moving waves are back. Another pair of targets wait at the end of the corridor. You must slam them home before the clock expires. Instead of waiting until everyone is all the way down the corridor, VAC-U up a teammate. While carrying a teammate, jumps are strictly one-a-time affairs, so don't try to double-jump here. Deposit the payload at the end of the hall before repeating the tactic with the other target.

It's likely, if you're playing with fewer than three people, that this process can take a few tries. Take things slowly and methodically, taking out one  target at a time. Though the team has just passed a checkpoint, the next challenge doesn't come with the same kind of hand-holding, and this entire sequence must be repeated if the group perishes.

A trio of moving platforms and one stationary one with a tempting switch is just begging to be slammed. Use caution here, though; the platforms must be crossed in a specific order to maximize the effectiveness of that switch. Have one buddy jump onto the middle moving platform, then to the switch, then ⊕ over to meet them. VAC-U up one of the team members, fire them at the landing pad, and slam the button. A familiar power source is ejected onto the right moving platform, which must be sucked up and then shot into the waiting receptacle ahead. Once the doors are open, zip through the doorway to register at a much-needed checkpoint.

This last chamber combines nearly everything encountered on the W.A.S.P. thus far: moving platforms, conductor panels, buttons, Voltergeists and power receptacles and, most troubling of all, a constantly ticking clock.

Start by leaping over the conductor panels to the sporadically moving platforms. Either have a fellow hero slam the button while another waits in the middle platform for a Voltergeist, or supply the button bashing yourself. Smashing both buttons isn't necessary, but with three or more players, it can make the process go much more smoothly.

The timer is mercifully reset, and the next challenges requires no such coordination beyond simply ejecting someone from a VAC-U to hit the twin buttons that should seem quite familiar by now. Stay on the non-electrified green panels and tag both targets to move on.

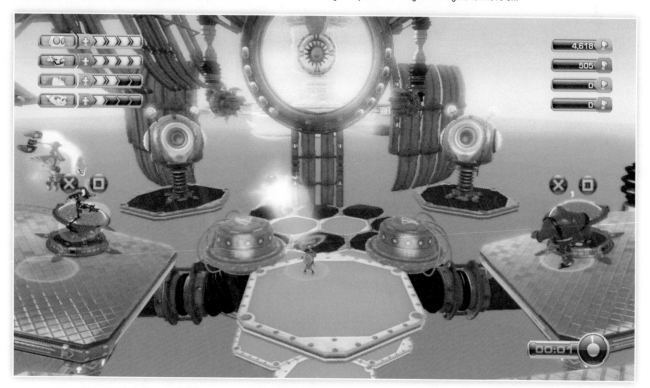

GAMMA BURST

The stores of Nanotech on the right and Ammo Pad on the left make it obvious things will heat up quickly when taking out Charging Dock Gamma. It's not so much the complement of weak but plentiful initial targets and inevitable second wave of heavier units, but the fact that almost the entire floor is made up of conductor panels. Quick movement to lower the walls with the Glob Lobber and attacking the exposed weak points is important, as is keeping on the move to safe, dark panels—though they won't stay that way for long. Use the Nanotech crates by the door to restore any health lost from the tussle.

If taking out the charging dock didn't feel risky, the Missile Minion that rises in its place should up the excitement level. Unload with the Warmonger or otherwise combined attacks to quickly remove the threat. Another minion rises, but once it's finished, a platform leading into the core of the W.A.S.P. appears. Have everyone head straight for this before the machine loses its lift—permanently. Inside the core are Nanotech and Ammo Pad rewards, though once scooped up, the emergency raft should be the priority.

REEF SHALLOWS

The crew's exploration of the inner sanctum of the W.A.S.P. isn't exactly a lengthy one. Almost immediately, the foursome are ejected into a shockingly tranquil underbelly, left to plummet in freefall with only the raft beneath them to cushion the ultimate belly flops they would otherwise feel. After landing, things quickly become a little clearer: the lighthouse ahead provides a clear objective—to say nothing of a route down to the train system that can carry the intrepid group to the Terawatt Forest.

A RAFT BUILT FOR FOUR

Navigating the raft takes more than a little coordination. With four points of VAC-U-assisted thrust available, it's all too easy to get the inflatable conveyance headed in the wrong direction. Early on, this isn't a big deal; after all, the group needs only proceed forward at first, and the gentle, bumpy barriers lining the narrow path won't harm the raft. Later, though, things aren't nearly as forgiving...

After proceeding through the first doorway, the group's next goal should actually be a brief diversion to the left of the partially submerged boat. A small platform is littered with crates for the bolt hungry among the team, but it also offers a peek at another platform just ahead—one studded with Hero Bolts (and, yes, a few more bolt-laden crates). Head to this next little outcropping before scooting back to the right and through the next gate.

Head right toward the sonic pylon next to some kind of spiny outcropping. As the team nears the infinitely dingable pylon, the true nature of the impediment is made obvious: a Tortemoth, covered in decidedly puncture-prone spines. Obviously a forceful rendezvous with the docile beast's back would be a bad thing, so ring the pylon and wait for it to sink before proceeding.

A checkpoint gives way to a set of blinking targets—pyrocidic sea mines, to be exact. Either a thrown melee strike or a ammo-plentiful shot causes a chain reaction that detonates all the mines, handy for clearing the way to the next target as guided by another spiny Tortemoth.

The waterway curves back to the left, revealing a row of spiky mines that the group would do well to avoid. Use small, deliberate movements to scoot the raft forward and then to the left, where another outcropping offers a short berth and a path upward. Scoop up the few crates along the path, then VAC-U someone up to a landing pad, following them up with a zip to a high platform dotted with various crates and otherwise vaccumable wildlife. Head back down to resume the voyage.

BOATING ACCIDENTS: MORE LIKELY THAN YOU THINK

Everyone loves boating. Sipping some bubbly beverage on the deck of a mega-yacht just makes a person feel alive. But even on this over-puffed slab of plastic, the vessel knows to obey the whims of a gallant seagoing Galactic President. Should the raft happen to slowly drift away while investigating some irresistible stockpile of bolts, just wait a bit. The undeniable magnetism of Qwark means it's only a matter of seconds before the boat drifts back on its own, waiting for a big, green hero to set sail again.

Resist the temptation to head toward the far-off crates and instead take the Tortemoth's lead. Detonate the mines standing in the group's way and travel up to the narrow corridor, busting crates along the way to a welcome (and until now, nigh-unseen) Laboratory requiring at least 120 Creatures spread out over the whole party's reserves. Hop in to inch ever-closer to the RYNO!

LABORATORY 3

It's been a while since the last Lab, but things are quickly starting to get more complicated. Attack the button with a slam attack while another hero scoops up the Voltergeist and deposits it into the receptacle above. Head quickly to the right, VAC-Uing anyone willing over the gap, and then following quickly behind. Slam the button, Vac-U the power source, and shoot it home. Have a team member do the same on the other side of the small barrier—preferably simultaneously, as time is at a premium here.

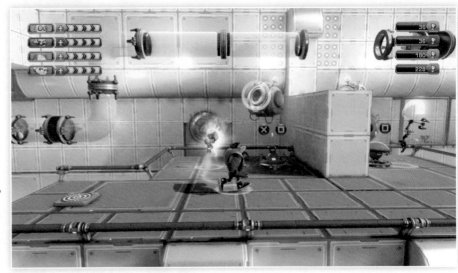

Proceed right, then tuck into a cannon that propels everyone across a huge chasm and to the next leg of the challenge. Here, one player should be shot over to the landing pad, wait for the Voltergeist to be spat out on that side, suck/shoot it back to another teammate across the gap who then plugs it into the power socket. The rest of the team simply zips over, vacuums the waiting socket to lower more of the tube, deals with a smattering of simple baddies and finally, tag teams a set of buttons and Voltergeist/socket objectives. Presto, one more piece of the ultimate weapon!

BY LAND OR BY SEA

With the Lab behind them, the team can concentrate on reaching that elusive lighthouse. For the especially bolt-hungry, the group can double back to the left to reach another set of floating crates, but the real path lies ahead to the left: a series of slowly rotating water wheels that fling the raft forward. By taking the left wheel rather than the right one, the raft is pushed into a set of crates, then scooted sideways to another group to the right, maximizing the water wheels' potential. Scoop up the crates and move forward to a checkpoint and a leftward-curving pathway.

When the flood gate lowers, another set of crates near more drums provides bolts and forward momentum out into a widening expanse of water. Farther ahead, the path is rimmed with mines, some of which can be detonated on either side to allow access to a few more crates if desired. Skirting a moving Tortemoth toward a sonic pylon, the group rings the bell and scoots into a narrow path formerly blocked by a stationary Tortemoth.

Follow the spine-backed creature forward, detonating the mines and proceeding with caution into another open waterway. A cluster of floating crates offers a brief view into a steady stream of Tortemoths with gaps between them just wide enough to fit a raft. Wait for a moment, then surge forward with a combined set of VAC-Us only to be greeted by more Bomber Minions

The small area of the raft makes the heroes rather easy targets, so if any Nanotech is lost, detonate the blocking mines to the left after taking out the bombers to soak up some health and crates, gathering more crates to the right if the mood hits. Another string of mines blocks a small collection of floating crates and, finally, a place to dock and move onto dry land.

The trip across land is a short one, providing a much-deserved Ammo Pad, GrummelNet vendor (now offering the mighty Thundersmack) and bounce pad up to a Critter, and an undulating path before an encounter with a final Bomber Minion. Dust the 'bot and enjoy a brief respite as the story of Dr. Croid, Mr. Dinkles and Nevo grows more provocative.

More warped walkways await—after firing a teammate across the nearby gap, zip over to them and proceed ahead to a strangely welcome sight, that of a few more Slorgs. Use the Critterstrike to "escort" them into the drink, scooping Nanotech and bolts where available. A bounce pad, more Slorgs and, finally a sonic pylon lead the way to another raft ride. VAC-U a compatriot to the pylon, zip over to them, and ride the Tortemoth by way of an additional pylon to an all too familiar ride.

WHAT'S YOURS IS MINE

The appearance of mine-dropping Minions should make it obvious this won't be the same leisurely romp. Almost immediately, they begin raining down bombs that quickly begin counting down and must be disposed of by way of the VAC-U—not especially easy when there are VAC-U-ready sources of propulsion dotting the raft. Resist the temptation to veer off course to pick up the few crates on the right and left unless the raft is already headed that way.

Dead ahead is another water wheel that flings the raft toward a kind of plunger that sends the raft soaring above a long line of mines (to the right of the area in front of the raft jump there is a quasi-secret area with some slam crates). Landing on the other side, the group can either daintily scoop up a few crates to the left of the landing or just make landfall as soon as possible—the mines won't stop falling until they do.

Stock up on Nanotech and pillage the few crates on this berth, then focus on the two sets of swingshot targets to the right, followed by a mandatory landing pad that necessitates the VAC-U. A series of smallish islands and barely-afloat ships provide some light platforming (and more than a few crates to break open), leading up to a short encounter with a few Flabberfish and more boat-hopping. A lone Nanotech crate and a cluster cannon are all that stand between the team and a trip to the lighthouse.

OCTONOK LIGHTHOUSE

Okay, so maybe that cluster cannon's aim was a little off. Thankfully, there's a path that leads directly to the lighthouse and past it, the hatch to the Terawatt Forest. Take the time to stock up on the supplies provided on this smallish landing: a GrummelNet vendor and a few Creatures that are just begging to be VAC-Ued.

The path to the right leads down a surprisingly sturdy platform, and the platform to a few swingshot targets. Upon landing, scoop up more Critters and crates, and then keep moving rightward for an encounter with your final foe in the Cay.

EXTREME WATERSKIING

The King Sepiad, not surprisingly, is much bigger than his smaller kin. Just as the group is about to be swallowed whole, a helpful Tharpod shows up to pull the crew out of danger by way of a little tether-powered water skiing.

What follows is rather straightforward: the Tharpod happily tows the heroes through the drink, offering plenty of opportunity to smash through crates littering the water. Watch for mines (easily jumped over) and electrical barriers (just scoot around them) while the King Sepiad tries to catch up.

Eventually, of course, it does, offering just a few simple attacks that must be avoided, lest the team attempt the whole rescue-turned-battle again. When its tentacles slam down on either side of the screen double-jump to avoid the sweeping motion, and when it tosses a boat into the drink, move to the sides. If the beast submerges, look for telltale bubbles indicating where it re-emerges—and make it snappy; one bite from the King Sepiad is all it takes.

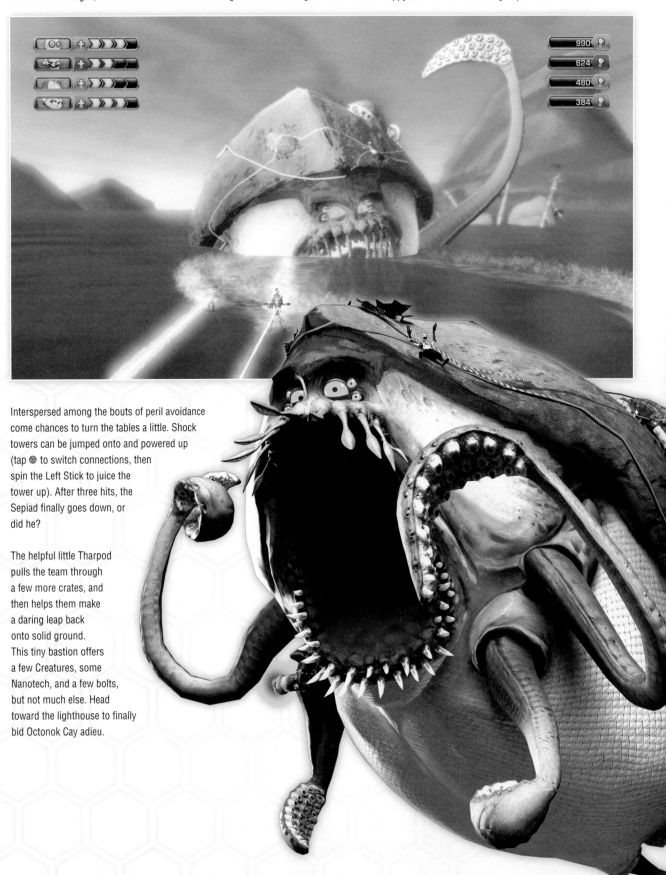

Interspersed among the bouts of peril avoidance come chances to turn the tables a little. Shock towers can be jumped onto and powered up (tap ⬆ to switch connections, then spin the Left Stick to juice the tower up). After three hits, the Sepiad finally goes down, or did he?

The helpful little Tharpod pulls the team through a few more crates, and then helps them make a daring leap back onto solid ground. This tiny bastion offers a few Creatures, some Nanotech, and a few bolts, but not much else. Head toward the lighthouse to finally bid Octonok Cay adieu.

NOT SO FAST...

Well of course it wouldn't be that easy. A few zaps aren't going to put down something that big, though it's done a bang-up job of invoking the beast's ire. Head toward the top of the lighthouse with haste, making sure to avoid the bits of the tower with slightly broken tiles, as that's where the King Sepiad likes to slap its tentacles down. Suck any missing bits of the tower into place with two teammates and get ready for another scuffle when everyone reaches the top.

Despite the size of the creature, it isn't terribly dangerous. Its tentacles snake up underneath the barrier to try to squish the heroes. Quickly run to the left or right side of the lighthouse when a tentacle is on the opposite side to avoid the attacks. Eventually, a tube door opens up, allowing a sleepy Slorg to walk into the open. Once the door in the center of the biogenerator slides open, guide the Slorg in with the Critterstrike and repeat with more Slorgs until the lighthouse's versa-crank reveals itself.

Turn the crank to activate the beacon and watch a massive predator turn into a harmless transfixed monstrosity. The plunger-enabled buoy stuck in his mouth is pulled down with the VAC-U, and from there it's simply a matter of shoving as many Slorgs into its maw as possible. After a few zaps, the process starts over again, only when the right versa-crank pops up, the King Sepiad tries to block it with a tentacle. Introduce it to the business end of some firepower and continue the process to show the big baddie why Dr. Heimlich was such a smart fellow.

Ratchet and pals have a clear path to the Terawatt Forest hatch. Guide them down the elevator to where the felled beast lies, and scoot around the platform to scoop up all the hard-earned treasure—particularly the Hero Bolts waiting to the right of the elevator.

FINDERS KEEPERS

While all the do-gooders rush off to combine their efforts to unlock a co-op crate, take the opportunity to jump ahead a bit and scoop up some of the Creatures that litter the leftmost parts of the landing. While they're stuck VAC-Uing a little box, you can partake of these valuable critters yourself, helping to clinch the bonus at the next checkpoint.

Better still, lead the way when everyone realizes what you've done; sprint ahead to grab more bolts and a Creature before the hapless saps can catch up.

A final cutscene guides the foursome deep underground to the Terawatt Forest transit system. Finally, a chance to dry off in an area that looks strangely familiar...

TERAWATT FOREST

OBJECTIVES

KALEERO TRAIL

- Search for Signs of Dr. Croid's Whereabouts
- Explore the Forest

ROSSA FIELDS

- Power up a Guardian
- Traverse Rossa Fields with the Comet Shard

GORTHON CRATER

- Cross Gorthon Crater

EXPLORATORIUM POWER STATION

- Restore Power to the Hall of Paradoxology

HALL OF PARADOXOLOGY

- Confront Dr. Croid in the Hall of Pardoxology

At long last, the team has reached Terawatt Forest and none too soon. Cronk and Zephyr's communications seem to be getting scrambled a bit by the forest's namesake energy-rich deposits. Electronics-razzing rocks, a naturally iridescent forest choked with purples and blues and greens, and wildlife all too eager to end the heroes' journey? Why does that sound so familiar? No matter, on to Dr. Croid!

HERO BOLTS

✓	**KALEERO TRAIL**
	After the shielded arena battle
	Near Guardian tractor beam
	ROSSA FIELDS
	After second Rossa Fields energy tower
	EXPLORATORIUM POWER STATION
	After deploying third cable cannon

NEW ENEMIES DEFEATED

KALEERO TRAIL

 Anthropods

 Croid Bot

 Shard Beast

 Razormoths

NEW WEAPONS PURCHASED

KALEERO TRAIL

Darkstar
Fission Tether

KALEERO **TRAIL**

The train system does its job ably, depositing the heroic pack deep in the heart of the forest. Thankfully, the trail ahead seems fairly straightforward, even inviting...

6
MISSION

FAST AS FAST CAN BE

Zip ahead of your dawdling cohorts to quickly soak up a Bolt Grabber and a handful of Critters. There's no telling what the rest of the forest has in store, but being well-stocked on valuables can only make the more eager members of the party that much richer.

It also happens to play host to an orb-o-matic, a device that encases the heroes in a shell allowing them not only to move across flat land at high speed, but also harness and redirect the flow of energy from the nearby tesla orbs. Complete the circuit by rolling up between the orbs to form a bridge between allies.

IT CAME FROM BELOW

Anthropods have a clever means of hiding from predators: they can burrow easily under the earth, rising in groups to attack their own prey at a moment's notice. Thing is, even in large numbers, they can't really do too much. Make sure they're dealt with swiftly, either by way of a rapid VAC-U suck/spit process or by simply clobbering them with melee attacks. Like all weak-but-plentiful enemies, auto-targeting weapons like the Fission Tether, Critterstrike, Plasmabomb Launcher and Frost Cannon abso-lutely decimate crowds—par-ticularly when powered up.

Just past the Anthropod encounter is a small place of refuge. The area includes a GrummelNet vendor (stocked with even more upgrades), plenty of crates and Critters, and some Nanotech.

SHARD TARGET

It's not just the rocks around the Terawatt Forest that have apparently developed high-energy properties. Shard Beasts have ingested so much they've been imbued with the same electric properties and can summon huge electric shards from the ground that help shield them in a protective electric bubble.

Without question, the shards should be taken out first. They sap the Beast's strength and leave it vulnerable to attacks—the only time at which this is possible. Crack the spikes (but don't get too close), then unload with the combined firepower of whatever weapon everyone has at the ready. It may well take a few phases of shard-cracking and full-bore unloading to fell the Beast, but eventually it will succumb to the com-bined might of the group.

Beyond the Shard Beast, there's nothing left for the group to do but venture off to the bouncy fungi to the right of the former battlefield. Past a Checkpoint littered with Critters, Nanotech and an Ammo Pad, the team ventures across a bridge to another Shard Beast encounter.

Deal with this one the same way as the last, peppering it with fire when it's vulnerable and shattering the shards as quickly as possible (if the group has invested in Mr. Zurkon—and who wouldn't?—the automated offense system can target and crack the spikes with deadly precision).

An ammo pad leads to another set of bouncy mushroom-looking platforms, which in turn spills right into a shielded encounter with some familiar robotic foes. Long range weapons can keep them all at bay, but of course concentrated firepower of the same weapons is really the core strategy here (a nicely upgraded flurry of Plasmabombs works wonders). After a few waves, the enclosure vanishes and opens the way to the spoils, which aren't numerous, but are certainly appreciated—namely Hero Bolts and Critters to the left of the checkpoint.

Another trip into another orb-o-matic opens the way to another launcher, this time offering a quick jump between sticky platforms. Hammer the ⊙ button to bounce from one brief perch to the next until everyone is safely on the other side of the chasm.

AN UNEXPECTED ALLY?

As the group traverses a series of elevated platforms, a Tank Minion slams down in front of them, all too ready to cut short the search for Dr. Croid. Instead of needing to face this twin-beamed menace, though, what appeared to be a bit of background clutter reveals itself to be one of the Forest's Guardians, a massive robot with significant tractor beam (not to mention crushing) skills.

The Guardian itself isn't exactly an enemy; it simply searches for and unceremoniously squashes anything that might present a hazard to the good doctor. Unfortunately for the heroes, they're seen as a threat and can just as easily be sucked up into the tractor beam as an enemy. If it happens, quickly VAC-U that ally away from the beam, but be careful that the rescuer doesn't end up in the beam along with their friend!

BOTS PILOTING BOTS

A diminutive threat waits for the party as they move across a few platforms away from the Guardian. This Croid Bot quickly enters, powers up, and opens fire.

Croid Bots are surprisingly adept at dishing out pain; they can suck up heroes that venture too close, firing them back as projectiles at their friends (jumping at the last second is the best way to avoid this sort of damage), and can unload with a single arm with accurate beams (side-jump to avoid them), or lash both arms together for a pair of beams.

Like most foes, quick application of concentrated firepower is the easiest way to make short work of these baddies. If

available, the Warmonger is a great choice, especially if it has been given its potent (and pricey) upgrades.

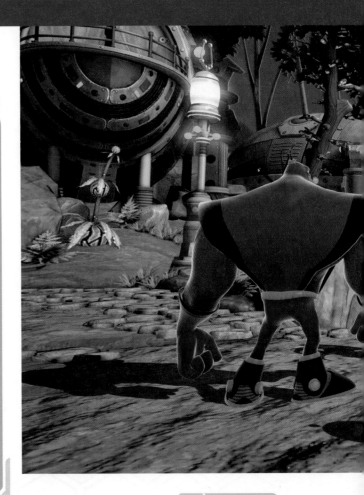

A few Critters and crates are to the left of three Slambots. Hit the switches in sequence to reveal an elevator that takes the team onward and upward. A series of natural steps lead up to an area littered with more Critters plus a Bolt Grabber. It's a good item to chase as the x2 bonus can come in handy for the few sets of crates here. A co-op crate at least gives those unlucky enough to have scooped up the Bolt Grabber something to busy themselves.

A HEAD START

Like so many of the Forest's inhabitants, the encroaching Razormoths that swarm into the following open area are plentiful, but weak overall. Unlike the others, they sport the ability to glom onto the heroes similarly to the Flabberfish of the preceding Cay. If this happens, mash ● to escape and then unload on them using auto-targeting weapons that do well against weaker enemies. An

upgraded Fission Tether is a joy to behold, zapping the Razormoths almost before they're even seen on screen.

After dealing with the threat, take the time to scoop up bolts before moving on (whichever hero manage to snag the Bolt Grabber may just have enough juice to make the most of the stacks of crates here before it finally runs out), as well as a few Critters near the VAC-U-necessary Hero toss target. Flush with cash, head down toward another Guardian in search threats.

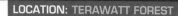

Another swarm of Razormoths descend, but they're easily dispatched with a little Fission Tether oomph (use the nearby Ammo Pad to restore any low ammo supplies before, during, or after the fight). Giving the nearby power plunger a suck with the VAC-U pulls the tesla orbs closer to shore (with a rather short timer), at which point everyone should quickly use the orb-o-matic to assume spheroid shape and connect the tesla orbs, revealing a launcher and path ever upward.

More Guardian-avoiding antics ensue, with a power plunger sucked open to extend a series of swingshot targets that drop down into a quick fight involving a Shard Beast in the distance and a group of slowly-emerging Anthropods. The latter can be scooted past to deal with the Beast first, but don't forget that they're approaching from the rear; a bunch of pesky melee-weak targets are not what one wants when trying to navigate a field of deadly, protective spikes. If it comes to that, then the Fission Tether can help subdue both targets with alacrity.

The Guardian oversees a valuable prize: Hero Bolts. The only problem? Its tractor beam sweeps dangerously close to the coveted currency. Either have the team sweep around the right side and sneak in one at a time to seize the treasure or confront the spawning Rift-Jumper Minions first from the relative safety outside the Guardian's sweep, then head out as a group.

As a reward for the harrowing Hero Bolt smash and grab, look for a Nanotech crate on a path heading upward to the right.

A Hero toss target allows a VAC-U-fired ally to serve as a hookshot target right into a Croid Bot scuffle. Unload with heavy weaponry to maximize damage, but make sure it's a long-range armament; becoming an impromptu projectile isn't exactly good for team unity. A lone stack of crates stands between the heroes and another VAC-U/tether opportunity up to a high ledge. If you go to the right there are some Critters in the Croid Bot area as well.

A series of bounce pads and close Critters herald the arrival of yet another Croid Bot. Lay down the heavy firepower first, then scoop up the Critters. Move forward to a perilously placed trio of Slambots, more Critters and a Nanotech crate.

Watch the pattern here carefully; the Guardian's tractor beam sweeps mostly back and forth, but the movement isn't always consistent, and knowing just how far it goes past the buttons is important. Wait for it to pass, and then slam as many buttons as possible before high-tailing it away. Another tactic is to sacrifice one ally to pull the tractor beam away from the buttons. Just remember to pull that character out of the beam's grip.

ROSSA FIELDS

Finally, a chance to take a breather and enjoy one of the most impressive sights on Magnus. A friendly Tharpod plays tour guide for a bit, explaining the once-majestic past that came from the Croid and Nevo's partnership and Critter-fueled technological advancement. Meant to be as much educational tool as tourist attraction, the Frumpus Croid Exploratorium of Scientific Wonderment stands now as a dilapidated and dangerous place the foursome must approach. Take the time to use the Ammo Pad, and collect the crates, Nanotech and GrummelNet offerings before stepping onto the tour cart introduced by the Tharpod.

ROSSA FIELDS

The tour cart shows how time has changed a former edutainment tool into a rickety, dangerous trip toward the dark and deadly Rossa Fields. Use the Fission Tether to zap pesky Razormoths before they're a threat. Enjoy the (relatively) easy ride, because things are about to become much more heated.

UNHEEDED ADVICE

Rossa Fields are dark; their once-bright lights long since drained of power. The group must tow a shard to power up the Guardian and to provide enough light to keep the otherwise lethal flora at bay. The only problem? The shard constantly loses energy and must be bolstered by spare shard fragments littering the path to the Gorthon Crater. To complicate matters, the normally shard-filling energy repositories that power up floodlights can't be used if your goal is to earn the "Night Lights Are For Wimps" Trophy. Make the decision on how the adventurers are to proceed now, as it's an all or nothing proposition. No checkpoints are set until the end of the segment if you don't use the recharge stations (making this a hard trophy to earn on the first go).

Explore the area around the shard for Critters and some bolts (look for a Bolt Grabber just after leaving the tram) before embarking on the quest. Assign one team member to hauling the shard around, with everyone else on support duty. Razormoths and Anthropods crop up from time to time, attempting to feast on the shard's energy stores, but they're easily dealt with using the trusty Fission Tether. Otherwise, hunt for shard fragments and valuables while constantly pulling the shard carrier.

The journey across Rossa Fields is straightforward. Whether you're chasing the Trophy or not determines how much venturing off the beaten path to discover crates, Nanotech and Critters are hiding in the dark the team will do. Spare shard fragments remain the priority, with Hero Bolts being a close second. Stick close to the shard, tugging it with VAC-U's through the meandering course while keeping an eye on the ever-dwindling energy meter in the bottom-right of the screen.

At about the three-quarters point, the shard is scooped and carried slowly to another resting point. Follow the light slowly, letting it spill over the staircase and frightening away the otherwise deadly plant life. Duck into orb-o-matic form to raise a few platforms, then resume towing the shard toward a platform dotted with Croid- and Nevo-boasting screens. At the final destination, the shard becomes a means to activate the essential Guardian to cross Gorthon Crater.

Hero Bolts are to the far left of the first energy repository outside the starting point. They're tucked into an alcove near a slam crate.

EXPLORATORIUM POWER STATION

The site of a massive asteroid impact some time in Magnus' past, Gorthon Crater is the home to Dr. Croid's Exploratorium, which sits over the remnants of the asteroid in a towering display of Tharpod ingenuity. Before the Exploratorium can be accessed, however, the Crater itself must be traversed, and the only way to do that is with a handy little Guardian—preferably one that isn't in Murder Mode.

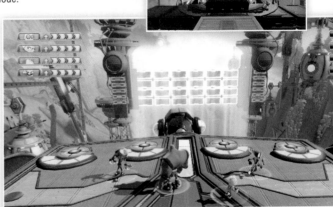

EARMUFFS!

Cronk and Zephyr come through at the last possible second, transforming the murderous Guardian into a lumbering but incredibly powerful ally. As the team leaps up onto its shoulders, a quartet of cannons becomes available, turning this next segment into something of an on-rails shooter. Quick acquisition of targets is important, as only the combined firepower of the cannons can take out threats before they sap the Guardian's energy.

KEEP FIRING, MORON!

There's little in the way of strategy here beyond shooting everything that moves. If you're attempting the "It Was Like That When We Got Here" Trophy, assign one ally to taking out the sunflower-like towers that litter the landscape. That's not to say there aren't lulls where everyone can open fire on the towers (particularly the twin towers straddling the elevated platform before the Guardian makes a huge leap to another area below) but many of them crop up during heated firefights. Splitting up concentrated fire is a quick way to say bye-bye to the lumbering Guardian.

For maximum Co-op points, those on defensive duty must learn how to prioritize targets. Designate one ally as the spotter, following their reticule and unloading as quickly as possible with the right kinds of shots. Airborne enemies and turrets should be taken down with rockets **L1**, while other targets like towers powering barriers and, later, other Guardians should suffer under normal energy blasts **R1**. Follow the leader, combining firepower on their target before moving to the next. Teamwork here is critical.

After squaring off against a handful of enemy Guardians, the team's friendly robotic pal pushes an eject button and jettisons the foursome up to a path leading directly to the Exploratorium Powerstation. Another holo-diary catches up with everyone and spills its secrets, revealing a terrible outcome for Dr. Croid, Nevo and, tragically, Mr. Dinkles. Next, the team heads toward the Exploratorium Powerstation with a newfound determination.

POWERING UP

As Ratchet and pals head to the right, stop to stock up on GrimmelNet upgrades and weapons as needed. There's also a peek into what Nevo had cooked up. The Steward, an AI system capable of managing all the power station duties, should have kept things humming. Unfortunately, after years of neglect, it seems the team must restore its power.

Head to the right—past the bank of screens explaining the power station—to find a handful of Critters and plenty of bolt crates. Double back and head toward the massive structure. A quick bounce between perches in orb form deposits the heroes at the start of a rather helpful tutorial. The Steward explains the basics of restoring power all along the surrounding lattice of power sockets, turbines and the like. Follow the Steward's lead, using the

VAC-U to drag the ion conduit into the power socket, then VAC-U the turbine to left to breathe life into the tired power lines.

The restored system reveals a versa-crank, lowering everyone down to a more complex set of objectives. As before, VAC-U the loose power elements (this time a power director that must be rotated until the arrows at the base line up with the power lines). Bolt-hungry teammates can suck up the crates by the elevator and in slam crates on either side. Once all the nodes are in their sockets, turn the VAC-U's on the central turbine to move things along.

With a walkway extended, the next phase of restoration can begin. VAC-U an ally and deposit them on the other side near the turbine where they can feed power to a power plunger across the gap. VAC-U this while another teammate scoots around to grab the ion conduit and places it in the power plunger. Greedy teammates may grab the Critter to the left at any time, but the co-op crate requires two people. Crank up the turbine again and ride a new elevator upward.

Up until now, things have been mostly puzzle-driven—and fairly simple at that. The introduction of a quartet of Croid Bots seeks to put an end to that, but they can be dealt with as before: heavy firepower concentrated on a singular foe. Slam crates populate the sides of the fairly open area with Critters appearing on the left. After collecting everything, choose an ally to launch at the elevated button on the right side of the area. There's another orb-o-matic bouncing adventure once the barrier is down.

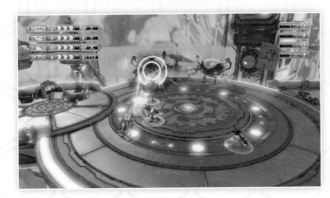

After bouncing to an isolated platform, the team need only VAC-U someone across the gap to the right, then tether over to combine forces in reconnecting the versa-plugs a little farther up. There's nothing in the way of spoils here, so all that remains is to activate a power plunger with the VAC-U to extend a series of platforms, jump up, and continue to a versa-crank that raises everyone up to the next phase.

Blessedly enemy-free (at least for now), the next challenge is rather spread out. There's an ion conduit near the crates in the upper right, and it must be dragged down to the middle of the area before an ally applies the VAC-U to the turbine on the lower left. This activates another power plunger which must be powered up while another teammate uses the VAC-U to send someone up to the upper platform. One ally must keep their VAC-U trained on the power plunger at all times while the hero above pulls down a power director that is socketed and rotated back in the middle.

A cable cannon is activated, allowing for the first major injection of energy directly into the station itself. As soon as this is done, a Croid Bot crashes the party. Deal with it quickly. Nanotech is at a premium here, and as soon as the group orb-launches themselves to the new platform ahead, things heat up.

As soon as the group lands, a flock of Razormoths appear. So long as teammates aren't being greedy about the crates nearby, dispatch these minor threats using the reliable Fission Tether. Once they're dealt with, Orb up for another bouncy trip.

Next, the team encounters another light brain teaser. The turbine ahead raises shields around a pair of tesla orbs. Use the orb-o-matic to get spherical and juice up the electrified towers before dealing with the spoils nearby.

HASTE MAKES BOOM!

Spare bolts are harder to find in this maze of power conduits, but you can punish greedy teammates for their lack of generosity. Turn the VAC-U on the explosive red crates as someone makes a dash for the other surrounding crates to detonate them, leaving the Slam Attack crate all for you.

With the versa-crank all juiced up, there's just a bit of bolt wrangling and some cranking before rising up to the next part of the power restoration. A power director

in the upper-left must be brought down to the center and aligned before smashing the buttons in sequence. Nearby Nanotech can help top off health reserves, and a few crates and a co-op opportunities near the raised walls are there for teammates quick enough on the draw. Use the VAC-U to connect the versa-cables, and witness the emergence of a cable cannon. After it's fired, another pair of Croid Bots shows up to spoil the progress, and like their earlier brethren, should be dealt with as quickly and painlessly as possible.

FOE BECOMES FRIEND

A powered-up Critterstrike is an amazing thing. Not only can it reduce enemies to harmless animals, but when upgraded to its Elite version, the Strike creates animals that actively attack enemies. Since enemies are transformed faster with multiple Critterstrike streams, it's possible to earn co-op points and another ally all in one easy move.

Another orb-o-matic launch ends immediately in an attack from all sides. The tiny platform offers little in the way of movement, but everything helps as a Croid Bot opens fire instantly and the skies are filled with Razormoths. Use the Critterstrike here to lay down concentrated fire on the Bot, then quickly switch to seek-and-make-adorable for the airborne targets. There's another series of bounces afterward, though no Nanotech is available at the end, which is a good reason to end the scuffle on this small platform as quickly as possible.

The orb-o-matic helps power up the tesla orbs in the back, releasing a turbine that can work its magic. Apply VAC-U suction to the turbine while another teammate

administers theirs on the power plunger above the turbine. This diverts the power flow to a complete circuit that raises another source of power. Unfortunately, there's another problem. There's no complete circuit to the to the ion conduit! To fix this, have one teammate apply the VAC-U to the turbine while another sends the power director into the socket and arranges it to point to the right, opening up another socket. Quickly switch to the now-available power plunger to complete the circuit and raise a platform upward.

Rising to the next part of the power restoration attempt, the team encounters the same ion conduit that needs moving from the middle to upper-right side of the area. Properly socketed, the team need only connect the versa-plugs on either side to lower another elevator. Make note of the Ammo Pad before moving on to restore reserves.

The elevator not only helps the crew ascend, but raises the ion conduit as well, linking the lower and upper parts of this challenge. Though the crates nearby are tempting, there are also a few Critters in the lower-left part of this platform. Scoop up everything before giving the power plunger in the upper-left a tug to bring a versa-plug in range of its mate. Attach the two to unveil the third and final cable cannon, then drive it home and prepare for the inevitable wave of enemies.

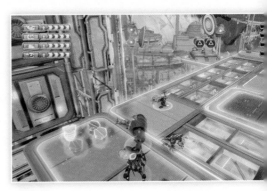

Three Croid Bots try their best to stop the foursome from advancing any farther into the Exploratorium. Put an end to their meddling with a heavy weapon or one that has an area of effect bonus like the Critterstrike. Take care of the four remaining Slam Attack crates and move left to capture hard-earned Hero Bolts before jumping on the last orb-o-matic launchers and perches.

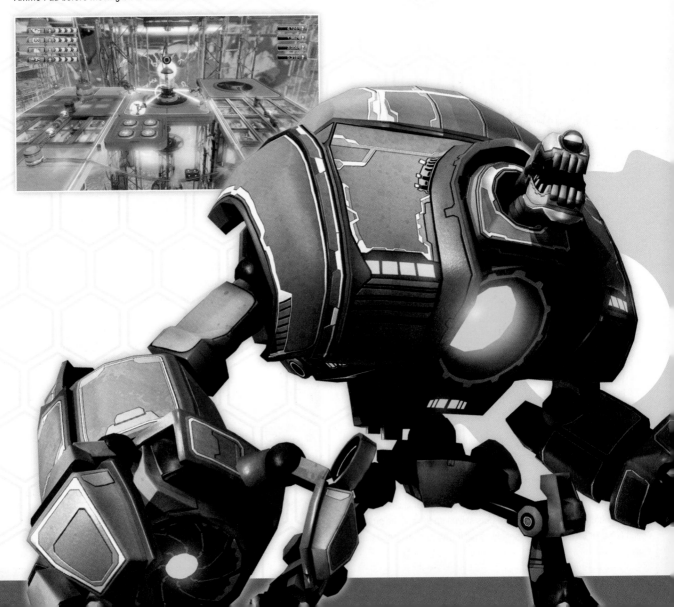

IT'S QUIET, TOO QUIET

After caroming down to a little nook, the team is able to scoop up some much-needed crates and even a Bolt Grabber if someone can get to the left fast enough. Heeding an automated warning (and response from Zephyr), the group heads onto an elevator into a disarmingly enemy-free area. A GrummelNet vendor with more upgrades and any remaining weapons still left to be purchased is to the left of the buttons. To the right are more crates that need extra elbow grease to open, and a few Critters just hanging out. Return to the center and activate the buttons in sequence, then prepare for a big fight.

EVERYTHING BUT THE KITCHEN SINK

There's no proper "boss" fight in this part of the heroes' journey, but that doesn't mean things aren't about to get extremely difficult. The security system has been restored, and every creature collector minion is making a beeline toward the quartet. Proper management of threats here is important for the crew to finish off the seemingly endless waves. There's no Ammo Pad to fall back on, so every shot must count.

Begin by taking out the Pyromites and the Bouncer Minions with a quick zap of the Fission Tether. Linking two or more allies together helps chain the zaps between the closely-grouped enemies, and the speed at which the zaps can be dispensed keeps the threat level low—at least until the next wave of Missile Minions arrives. Take them out with weapons that offer an area effect bonus, such as Critterstrike, Frost Cannon, or whatever's available.

A third wave begins with Scout Minions followed by Bouncer Minions. Employ area effect explosions to take out multiple enemies at once to save ammo, and to spare the team from errant crossfire of multiple foes. Circle-strafe the group, laying down as much concentrated fire as possible. Even by using L1 to lock onto a single enemy, most of these melee-happy combatants tend to block beam-based weapons. Just keep on them until either a big area effect detonation can hit the group, or the arrival of an old friend takes care of things for you.

Hooray, it's the Guardian! Not just content to blast away the last of the security forces, it also raises a bridge to the inner sanctum of the closed-off Hall of Paradoxology and helps the crew enter—but not before being called back into action elsewhere.

HALL OF PARADOXOLOGY

There's almost nothing in the way of collectables during the dash down a narrow corridor. There is, however, a painful truth: Dr. Croid isn't here. Apparently the good doctor was so paranoid about Nevo breaking in and sabotaging the lab that he moved the entire operation to the nearby moon of Phonica. After an unlikely bit of bonding, the foursome prepare to finally leave Magnus and confront Dr. Croid at his new, secret base of operations.

PHONICA MOON

OBJECTIVES

ORNITHOPTER ASCENT
- Pilot Ornithopter through the Asteroid Field

SECURITY TUNNELS
- Bypass Dr. Croid's Defenses

DR. CROID'S SECRET LAB
- Infiltrate Dr. Croid's Secret Lab

Magnus no more! Even without finding Dr. Croid, the fearless foursome has a means of inching closer to his position thanks to the Ornithopter. The tri-engine rocket tears out of the Hall of Paradoxology headed straight for the troposphere—incidentally where a certain pair of old-time robots have been stranded for most of the heroes' adventure. As the rocket kicks off the last of its payload a low-gravity pod is ejected and the crew inside slowly make their way toward Phonica Moon.

HERO BOLTS

✓	**PHONICA CRATERS**
	Bottom-left of landing pad
	SECURITY TUNNELS
	Behind Ion Turret at first rotating platform
	DR. CROID'S SECRET LAB
	Bottom-left of elevator platform after escaping Security Tunnels

NEW ENEMIES DEFEATED

PHONICA CRATERS

Craterpede

Lurker

Ion Turret

ORNITHOPTER ASCENT

The situation at present isn't dire, exactly, but it's not exactly as smooth sailing—or boosting—as the situation could stand to be. Gelatonium reserves are scarce, but Zephyr reckons the crew can find spare tanks floating around the asteroid field. The only catch? They must find them first.

7
MISSION

ALL 4 ONE

If your heroes have any hope of making it to Phonica Moon, everyone must learn to work together. Teamwork here is paramount, meaning most navigation decisions should be relegated to just one hero with the rest following in line. Nominate someone early, then be clear and consistent with using boost. Four heroes, each with their own thrusters could end up spending needless amounts of fuel boosting in every direction. Coordinated efforts are necessary for everyone to reach the destination in one piece.

ALARMING ASCENT, DANGEROUS DESCENT

Start by heading straight up to the first gel tank. Once it's banked, continue upward and scoot left, then right, skirting the bigger asteroids while avoiding the smaller, more mobile ones. A narrow squeeze through some close rocks is rewarded with another gel tank, ripe for the plucking.

Make a hard right after picking up the second tank, scooting around the large asteroid before smoothly steering left around more rocks. When an opening appears to head straight up, take it. There's another gel tank and a stranded pair of allies in that direction.

Continue past Cronk and Zephyr, up and around a large asteroid to the left. Continue to left, letting gravity tug the craft down to another gel canister. Nudge the craft a bit up, then left, up over a large asteroid and then down. Use quick boosts to keep from slamming into any slow-moving debris. The planet's perigee is reached after just a few moments, meaning Phonica itself looms directly below. Let the moon's gravity guide the ship in the rest of the way.

PHONICA CRATERS

It's almost immediately obvious why Dr. Croid would pick this crater-pocked outpost as the site for his secret lab. There's bound to be some resistance on this hunk of rock, so set out now and begin exploring.

TREASURES AND TERRORS

Directly down and to the right of the landing site is a set of Hero Bolts—consider them a 'congratulations' for surviving the harrowing journey. Look for a healthy smattering of Critters and crates just above the Bolts, with more found up ahead. Scoop them up, pausing to investigate the arriving GrummelNet vendor's new upgraded wares. Buy everything you can, then climb the stairs above.

MULTI-SEGMENTED, ULTRA-DANGEROUS

Here comes the welcoming party. The Craterpede doesn't have much in the way of actual attacks; it simply marches toward the heroes and can turn on a dime thanks to its many-segmented body. Worse, though, is the fact that a frontal assault does absolutely nothing until the rear segments have been destroyed.

Locking on with L1 is a must here, as is avoiding the Critter. Its ability to quickly turn to face enemies approaching from the side makes it tough. Use double-jumps liberally to get behind the Critter, then unload with everything available. The individual segments themselves aren't too tough (at least not if the team has been steadily upgrading their arsenal), but their strength is in numbers. Whittle away the segments, staying behind the lengthy threat as much as possible until only the head remains. Take it down and the path beyond is opened.

There's another Craterpede atop the ram, but this time it's not alone. A group of Anthropods come bursting from the ground to offer their help to the Craterpede. Deal with them with a quick-targeting weapon like the Fission Tether. It chews through them, leaving the space more open for taking down the Craterpede.

Evidently Dr. Croid is fond of airborne travel. A set of spinshots rise from the chasm below. By now, you should be more than familiar with the ins and out of them. ○ up, spin the Right Stick and bounce over to the next, keeping an eye out for the ○ prompt. Another leap and the team lands on an outcropping littered with an Ammo Pad, Nanotech, Critters and precious crates. Suck up what's needed, then proceed up the ramp to face a pair of Craterpedes. Give the beasts a wide berth, concentrating fire on one until attention can be turned on the other. As reward, a few crates and some Nanotech are in the smallish craters nearby.

THE EYES HAVE IT

The pools of green goop ahead look uninhabited, but a five-eyed threat is already locking onto the heroes. A Lurker emerges, using the nearby pools to move invisibly between bits of refuse. When it emerges, unload on the menace while watching for it to spit green globs. Locking on with L1 isn't just a good way to keep shots headed in the right direction, it actually notifies the team as to where the beast should emerge next (as if the investigative eye didn't give it away enough). Concentrate any and all heavy weapons fire on the Lurker. Keep in mind that while the Lurker can live in the green muck, Ratchet and company cannot.

Collect the Nanotech to the left of the entrance to the next bridge; it comes in handy for the next encounter. Multiple Craterpedes and Anthropods again swarm your characters, but at least this time defeating them is becoming routine. Clear the Anthropods first, then navigate carefully around the toxic pools of green sludge to get behind a Craterpede and unload on it. High-powered weapons are recommended, as an Ammo Pad sits at the top of the area. Stock up, then swing across the gap and prep for yet another encounter.

If one Lurker is annoying two can be downright infuriating. The numerous pools allow them to travel freely and get the drop on the team quickly. Use the combined firepower of the heavy hitters as fast as possible; the sooner one is gone, the sooner the incoming sniper-like volleys are cut in half. Defeat the pair, then sweep the perimeter for Critters and crates before continuing.

A hop, swing and a jump brings the gang to a platform with a pair of Croid Bots. After all the natural enemies, a few robotic ones feel like a breath of fresh air. Concentrate fire on one target at a time to take them down quickly. With multiple Nanotech reserves available and an Ammo Pad (plus a few handy crates of bolts), there's no reason not to go all out here to finish off the encounter as painlessly as possible. There's a nice reward here: the ultra-valuable Reflector, which is put to ample use going forward.

ENGAGE REFLECTORS!

Though the path toward Dr. Croid's lab is fairly straightforward, actually arriving there in more than a smoldering heap is difficult to say the least.

The little guys powering the Ion Turrets would probably be considered adorable if their stomps didn't unleash eight separate beams of pain at a time. Thankfully, the Reflectors that were just picked up can completely nullify the danger posed by the beams. Still, getting them up in time takes a bit of practice, so learn the length of the beams' stay and use the down time to move upward.

The first Ion Turret isn't even much of a threat. The wall on the left side of the walkway provides infinite cover even without the Reflector, allowing Ratchet and crew to pause, wait for the lull, then charge forward and around the wall to take care of the operator with a few melee attacks.

The second set isn't quite so simple. After picking up some bolts from the crates in the center, pick a path and have everyone charge down the line. The hero in front can deploy the Reflector while everyone else simply stands behind it. Inch toward the operator, sprinting as necessary, and flank the threat. Look for Nanotech behind the Ion Turrets. Stock up before tackling the large wave of enemies coming up.

The beams may be double-wide, but the tactic for moving past them is exactly the same: Reflector, sprint, then smash. There are Nanotech stores, bolts, checkpoint and an Ammo Pad on the other side of these Turrets.

There's one more bank of lasers to cross. Once the group is past them, take out the Ion Turret as soon as possible. A swarm of Anthropods and a Lurker combine to form a busy set of targets. Thin the Anthropod herd before concentrating fire on the Lurker.

Just past the seemingly non-stop barrage of Ion Turrets, is a Craterpod encounter. Lure it into the open and attack it from behind. Stock up on Nanotech if it's needed, collect any bolts before one of your allies can, and get ready to face a different kind of ionic threat.

The first set of lasers is nothing, really. Deploy a Reflector, crowd behind it and move to the next walkway. The second, on the other hand, requires more pre-planning. Getting past the beams is simple enough, but one teammate must engage their VAC-U, another must hop in and be launched over to the landing pad where everyone can zip in behind them—no easy task when the platform offers precious little time to re-deploy a Reflector. Thankfully, this is only a major concern when playing with two people (or you're going solo). Move quickly and the threat is bypassed

Dispose of the Ion Turret, then skirt the perimeter of this circular landing to collect an impressive number of Critters. Nanotech and bolts make up the rest of the spoils. Once everything has been scooped up, a simple Reflector challenge awaits. A central beam cuts straight down, but can be redirected toward the four green generators flanking the beam. Sweep the Reflector from one side to the next to quickly and easily overcome this obstacle, then descend closer to Croid's secret abode.

I'VE SEEN BETTER DAYS...

The bottom drops out from under the heroes, forcing them to switch to jetpacks quickly. The ensuing descent should feel familiar, but doesn't require too much in the way of quick movements. Just take things slowly, scooting around the lasers and smashing into the pods lining the walls to free up bolts and Nanotech; there's plenty of both.

MINE, MINE, MINE!

While all the insects that claim to be comrades delicately navigate the maze of Ion Turrets, you know the real score here: bolts, and lots of them—so long as you can get the jump on everyone else. The key is to hug the bottom of the screen, tapping the boost button just enough to slow your decent without moving upward. Watch the background for the telltale muzzles of Ion Turrets but monitor the sides of the tube even more closely. By hammering the **L1** button and pointing toward the bolts, you can claim the prize before the others can even react.

Eventually, they might catch on, which is why it's important to mix things up. Went left last time? Go right this time, then go right again at the next opportunity to steal their thunder (and bolts).

When the gang finally touches down, there are a few spoils waiting for them: a few Critters, some Nanotech, a little bolt action and an oh-so-handy Ammo Pad. Race for what's most needed, then regroup for another bout of tag team Ion Turret reflection.

SECURITY TUNNELS

The search for Dr. Croid remains far from over even after navigating many difficult challenges. The next few areas test coordination, resolve and reflexes like few places thus far. Steel yourselves; this won't be easy.

UPON REFLECTION

The first two Ion Turrets are easily skirted with just one deployed Reflector, but the third is a bit trickier. One teammate must drop their Reflector (pointed right, of course) parallel to another teammate manning the VAC-U-friendly socket to help pull the platform forward. Once they're on the other side, someone quick to move can hop over and scoop up the crates to the left, becoming a simple ⬤ point for everyone else. VAC-U someone across the gap and ⬤ to them and everyone can move on to more Ion Turrets.

The Ion Turrets ahead are joined by a new wrinkle: a series of rotating discs that serve as walkways. The first requires only that one stand with the Reflector pointed toward the beams, adjusting as the rotation of the disc slowly changes the heroes' position. There's a further challenge here, however: Hero Bolts.

The Hero Bolts are beyond the never-ending wall of Ion beams, but getting to them requires a sacrifice. Have everyone equip the Reflector, then leapfrog, with double-jumps, up the beams, deploying the Reflector on the way down. Even if an ally is hit, there's a brief window where they can re-deploy and allow others to move up from behind. Jump out and around the Ion Turret and destroy it to claim this hard-earned prize for all.

After scooping up some Nanotech and a few crates, head to the second laser reflector puzzle, where their rotation offers an opening that, with patience, can help the beams bounce back toward the green generators all at once.

131

THE RIGHT PLACE...

The next beam that lances out toward the group calls for a little teamwork. Position an ally on one of the blue neon-rimmed platforms (or on both if more companions are around), then bounce the beam toward them, where they can angle the beam a second time to destroy the generators. It might take a little re-positioning, but the result should be explosive!

If none of the heroes have seized the crates on the right platform, scoop them up quickly before heading toward the waiting Croid Bot. Their weaknesses (at this point, it might well be everything depending on how powered-up the team's arsenal is) means a tag-team barrage quickly overpowers the threat and lets everyone address the real challenge: a beam and two power plungers. Aim the beam at the center (look for the circle) of the two bigger stationary reflectors on the right and left before commencing VAC-U operation to tag the green generators without breaking a sweat.

Tackle the next set of beams the same as in Clank's recommendation; prop up allies on the left/right platforms, then VAC-U the left and right points to bring down the walls blocking the beams. Finally, point those beams toward the waiting Reflector-deployed buddies. The towers are toast and the way forward is opened.

LABORATORY 4

It must seem as though these Critter challenge rooms are getting farther and farther apart, but in truth they're just waiting for a fully-prepared group of highly-trained heroes to conquer them. Even still, this Lab (requiring a whopping 250 combined Critters) is the most devious yet, requiring plenty of razor-sharp coordination to acquire the RYNO piece.

Begin by VAC-Uing the nearby port. As soon as the Critter starts moving, immediately suck up a companion with the VAC-U, then sprint right, and launch them over the gap. ⬤ over (or have them jump up) and begin VAC-Uing the port above while the rest of the team takes care of the Rift-Jumper Minions spawning nearby.

With the Lab trial completed, head back to the left and through the now-open doorway, scooping up crates as quickly as possible. An Ammo Pad offers a refill for weapons, and a pad waits patiently for all to ready-up.

GOING UP

Another jetpack sequence ensues, this time a bit more dangerous than the last. Boost upward around the spinning blades, keeping an eye out for any pods that can be smashed, but especially for beams sweeping upward from Proton Excavators. Hold out until the target is vulnerable, then smash through them on the way back up.

VAC-U a nearby teammate and toss them across the gap, then Slam Attack the button to kick-start the cascade of subsequent slams. ⬤ over the gap

as needed, aiding in button slams before bouncing up and onto the nearby platforms. VAC-U an ally, mortar toss them onto the button and bounce up to the next phase.

Time and teamwork are critical here. Assign someone to slam the button, and another to fire the Glob Lobber at the nearby port, then suck up the Voltergeist and deposit it into its home behind the Glob Lobber target. A spinshot rises into view. Quickly tether to it, eject and prep for position with the VAC-U. Watch out for a trio of Motar Toss targets, and the Critter's speedy approach. Hit them in sequence if possible, but definitely opt for the left-most target first. With enough speed, the Critter finally finds its way home, unlocking another RYNO part. The first to bounce up to the final platform has a chance at the Bolt Collector and the lion's share of the spoils.

After the second Proton Excavator, a window appears on the left side. Smash through it and then immediately begin boosting upward; a grid of lasers is nipping at the heroes' heels. A series of fiery platforms impedes a trip back through another window to the left, at which point the ascent continues, hampered by falling rocks. Look for a stream of debris and slip between them to avoid the plummeting hazards. Continue upward, smashing through a third window to the right, then take out the four pods blocking the escape from these cluttered tunnels. A series of springs, a spinshot and a bounce pad leads to a versa-crank, which finally leads to safety—and much more.

DR. CROID'S SECRET LAB

Dr. Croid's secret lab lies beyond! Round up the nearby bolts (including Hero Bolts to the right), Nanotech and Critters before moving on toward the sealed door ahead. Position an ally in front of the beam, then have another use the Glob Lobber to lower a small window where the beam can pass through on either side to destroy the green generators that would be otherwise protected. Hit up the Ammo Pad nearby, then sally forth toward the secret laboratory.

AN UNWELCOME RECEPTION

Just beyond the door is an unpleasant—but easily overcome—surprise. Anthropods pop out from the rock beneath, but can be quickly zapped into oblivion, leaving only a race to be the first to suck up the nearby crates and harvest the bolts within. A few more crates surround a versa-crank and a warning from Zephyr. The good doctor has been cooped up, riddled with paranoia, for more than a few years. Rotate the crank to head downward, cross the bridge and go through the front door of the lab.

The threat ahead is obvious. An Ammo Pad and Nanotech crates offer all the advice needed: stock up, and fast. After grabbing a few crates' worth of bolts, the battle with a trio of Croid Bots is on. Take them out quickly (that strategy should be hard-wired by now—something about pumping a single target full of the most explosive payloads available), then move on to more crates flanking a dizzying 16-fold blanket of Ion Turret fire.

The key here is to think ahead. Voltergeists are provided near the rightmost barrier, but why? The answer is near the top of the screen: a receptacle for the adorable little blob waits patiently for its soul mate.

Thankfully, the Ion Turrets here know how to take a break, which is precisely when one ally should move in, deploying a Reflector for everyone else. Move slowly, waiting for ebbs in the ionic carpet, then inch forward until your character is in range. Send the Voltergeist sailing home and enjoy the chain reaction.

With the door open, there's only one option left: enjoy a tally of your heroes' valiant efforts to punch into the core of the secret lab, and finally a meeting with the seemingly mad genius himself. When the cinematic ends, head out to the escape pod to get back to Magnus.

OBJECTIVES

MIDDLE OF NOWHERE

- Investigate Collector Encampment

POLAR ICE FLOES

- Locate a Railway Station

So, after all that trouble, the quixotic quartet has ended up almost where it started, back on Magnus. What was supposed to be a quick trip to the Vilerog Plateau instead has stranded the heroes in an icy world far from the original target. Still, there are signs of technology here—a doleful indicator that even in these chilly climes, the Tharpods in their tireless quest to serve as collectors for all the species on Magnus may have built one of their sprawling railway stations that could lead back to Ephemeris' Charging Dock. No choice now but to continue forward...

HERO BOLTS

✓	MIDDLE OF NOWHERE
	Below GrummelNet vendor at crash site

NEW ENEMIES DEFEATED

MIDDLE OF NOWHERE

Groundpounder

POLAR ICE FLOES

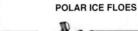

Scorch Minion

Grungoth

MIDDLE **OF NOWHERE**

Croid's escape pod is useless and the group has no recourse but to seek out a possible means of transport closer to Uzo City and the home base of Ephemeris.

8
MISSION

BRIDGES THROUGH NOWHERE

This landing is, if nothing else, rife with opportunities for a little selfish plunder. Scads of Creatures roam freely between more than a few crates rife with bolts. Divide and conquer what you can, then come together for the Hero Bolts just below the GrummelNet vendor to the far right of the icy expanse.

The ice bridges ahead make for a slippery slope. Thankfully, they're also dotted with opportunities to earn a few bolts. Think back to the old spiny mammal days of gaming; line up with a string of crates to pocket the bolts within, but stay agile. There are mines, pitfalls and an indigenous beast that has zero problem with scaling the towering ice structures seen throughout the Polar Sea.

As soon as the heroes find a place to slow down for a bit, things become dicey quickly. A shielded bubble locks them into place, pitting at first a few swarms of smaller enemies, then increasingly potent combatants against the group. Expect ground forces (take them down with heavy weaponry), then airborne enemies, and finally a familiar but unwelcome final combatant that requires heavy-handed use of the Critterstrike. Use the nearby Ammo Pad to reload the especially powerful, but ammo-starved, weapons.

GRAVITY, HOW WE LOVE THEE

Flying enemies are formidable opponents, sure, but they are all too susceptible to gravity. Use the Omegatech Frost Cannon to overload their fragile airborne bodies and send them crashing back down to where the heroes tread. Of course, if they're encased in an icy shell, they merely shatter upon impact, freeing the would-be galactic saviors to concentrate on more important matters—stuff like which weapon makes the best Magnusian shave ice, the perfect frozen treat to ward off sub-zero temperatures.

If this snow-driven no-man's land was so terrible, why would it be so littered with so many valuable treasures? Bolt-rich crates and Creatures aplenty lead the way to yet another rallying point beyond additional ice bridges.

If the next sliding section induces déjà vu, just wait a bit. Mines begin exploding, creating pits in the ice bridges, and things aren't helped by the re-appearance of a certain formerly-caged monstrosity. After leaping over a few gaps and scooping up some precious bolts, the beast actually has the gall to add snowballs to the mix. Navigate the giant rolling threats by scooting left and right. Though the initial tumbling wrecking balls arrive with little warning, the rest are fairly easy to avoid.

A few more crates offer additional bolts, but the wider expanse of the ice bridges quickly gives way to something a little more confined. Protruding ribs of ice force deft dodges around weirdly contrasting spurts of fire. Transition between ice tracks the same way as you would any other grind rail: hold left or right on the Left Stick, then jump when an adjacent ice track becomes available. The ice tracks are more thrilling than dangerous, and eventually the group ends on a platform with a hulking menace in the background.

Scoop up any supplies nearby, including bolts and Creatures, and send everyone to the Ammo Pad. Cross the crumbling ice to the three more stable floes and get ready for a rumble.

AN ALL-TOO FITTING TITLE

The Groundpounder possesses twin, gargantuan mallets for hands, and their singular purpose should be obvious: they smash stuff; specifically, smashing the stuff floating on water with the intent to sink it. What isn't immediately obvious is how much of a comparative cakewalk this mid-boss encounter is when placed alongside the rest of what the Polar Sea has to offer. There's no strategy here other than avoid getting crushed by the well-telegraphed targets on the ice floes.

That's not to say there isn't some challenge. The machine is resilient, requiring frequent jumps between safe spots that slows any combined Overload attacks. Still, keep pouring them on—the more concentrated and heavy-hitting the weapons, the faster the mechanized foe falls. Tools like a fully-upgraded Warmonger or Plasmabomb Launcher tear through its defenses.

What the heroes don't want to do is to run out of ranged attack weapons. There's no Ammo Pad here to restock, so conserve ammo where possible, make every hit count, and eventually the menacing machination topples. Remember the fundamentals: everyone uses the same weapon, concentrate on Overloads and bank those Co-Op Points. This thing goes down fairly easily, and nothing about the next few encounters share that property.

Take a breather after this fight to soak up the nearby Creatures and bolts; things only get harder from here on out. Activate the jump pad to get boosted up to another platform littered with bolt crates and Creatures, but keep an eye on the encroaching enemies headed the heroes' way. The threats start out simply (almost nostalgically), but quickly ramp up as more enemies appear.

Harken back to the original videos of the Plasmabomb Launcher and let loose with combined flurry of explosive arcs that completely remove any semblance of cover—just make sure everyone hangs back to deliver their salvoes.

Another boost to another slippery slide rife with mines and falling icy stalactites and your heroes are deposited onto another platform thick with bolts, Creatures and likely long-overdue Nanotech. Claim whatever prizes haven't been sucked up by friends and head toward a new threat.

POLAR ICE FLOES

The name of this section of the Polar Sea comes from an obvious source. Even just ahead of the last big deposit of goodies lies a few floes that serve as platforms, leading right smack dab into a brand new threat.

FIRE AND ICE

The group barely has time to enjoy their tally of deeds done before a Scorch Minion introduces itself. Igniting a line of fire that all but precludes the use of short-ranged weaponry, this fire-spewing threat is outfitted with twin cannons that can either punch out slow bursts of flame or concentrate them into twin beams of fire that must be avoided while in between them.

Here's the thing, though: it's actually a pushover—provided everyone took the time to fully upgrade the Critterstrike. The Strike's payload is used here to hilarious effectiveness. Pour on the rainbow-tinted streams to quickly overpower the threat and leave it nothing more than a friendly, adorable buddy that, sadly, must be left behind for bigger and badder threats.

What's that? Didn't heed the advice offered a while back? No matter, this baddie isn't any more daunting than most bigger foes. Unleash whatever packs the most punch from your arsenal (again, everyone should use the same weapon here) to overwhelm the Scorch Minion and move on. Don't worry, this isn't the last of his kind the heroes are bound to see.

Cross a few more ice floes, partaking of the Creatures and bolt stores here before pressing onward. The Ammo Pad nearby should be used regardless of whether everyone feels it's necessary.

As Ratchet and friends cross the floes here, a few more threats drop in to interrupt the view. Though the apparent cover they sport is indeed effective, it discounts the application of the Plasmabomb Launcher. Educate these poor bots with a few well-placed explosions and they might just see the light. Speed is a factor here, as there's limited room to avoid shots, so pile on the damage and make it quick. If the first encounter seemed too easy, rest assured that a second helps add to the peril.

As the comically-united commandoes storm the next bit of stable ice shelving, an adorably inept set of Flabberfish decide they want in on the fun. Kindly explain, through the use of quick-disposal weaponry like the Fission Tether, that they should head back to warmer waters. A few Bomb Minions show up, but quickly learn the same lesson as their friends— particularly when lit up by the area effect of something like a Critterstrike or Frost Cannon. Yet again, more adorably ineffective enemies arrive, while even more Flabberfish try to complicate things. The blast radius of the Plasmabomb Launcher makes it an effective weapon choice here.

Finally, a Missile Minion shows up to complicate things, but as it's airborne, the Frost Cannon seems a fitting way to end this encounter. Though the camera pitches counter-clockwise to show the next route, it's not a bad idea to scoot around this icy platform to grab any crates that weren't blown open by all those explosions. Bolts securely banked, it's time to head toward a real challenge.

A co-op crate, some Nanotech, a few Critters and a smattering of bolts from nearby crates comprise the whole of what's waiting after a short ride across an ice floe. Follow it up with another jaunt over the hypothermic liquid to a new rest area.

There's a great deal of goodies here for the taking. Take the hint and stock up, grabbing Creatures, bolts and Nanotech. Everyone needs to be stocked up on supplies. An Ammo Pad near more crates completes the fortification, and the group heads across more ice floes.

NOT BIGGER, NOT BADDER, JUST MORE

The ice blocks ahead are a rickety path and immediately available Nanotech crates indicate that the road ahead is perilous. This is an all-out assault with no chance of restocking ammunition. Take out the weaker enemies that appear as soon as everyone arrives on the platform with melee attacks or VAC-U use. Avoid the use of conventional weapons so as to conserve ammunition.

Once the smaller enemies have been dispatched, focus on the larger foes which appear. The Plasmabomb Launcher does a great job of not just arcing over cover, but helping to destroy it—an essential element in the coming waves of enemies. Lay out the targets on the periphery with concentrated fire to remove them and their crossfire as fast as possible. More soon drop in, along with Bomb Minions looking to soften up the group. Drop the fliers with Frost Cannon fire, removing the need for a finisher, then quickly switch to taking out the side threats. Hopefully by now, the Plasmabombs have removed any semblance of cover these machines might have, because every shot needs to hit home.

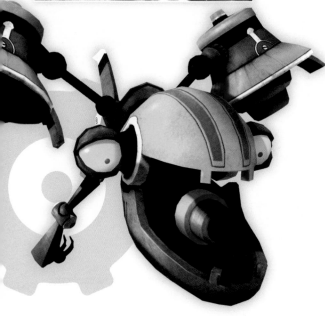

There's a brief (but doubtlessly needed) break after this, allowing for a checkpoint floe and another jump to a shaky sheet of ice. Make the most of the Ammo Pad, Creatures and Nanotech here to restock before encountering another bout of enemy attack.

Paired Fission Tethers can help spread the damage among nearby targets—helpful since the onslaught hits from both ground and air, though neither is especially well-armored. The combination of ground targets and elevated sniping ones can be lethal, so stay on the move and try to pile on the cumulative effect of the Tether where it's possible. Again, one weapon, all heroes, single targets. Pick a spotter to identify and unload on targets if need be; the Tether loves joining in and only bolsters the attacks.

Watch out as more side threats slam down, creating an opportunity for more Plasmabomb Launcher fire. In a pinch, the Warmonger can really help lighten things here, but the key is single targets being hit by identical weapons. The onslaught of arriving, ranged targets seems downright relentless, but an Ammo Pad should have restocked everyone. When ammunition for one weapon runs out (and it will considering the sheer number of enemies), swap to weapons that everyone can use at the same time. Overall firepower is less important than concentrating all of it on single targets.

Keep moving, and above all else, let the spotter call out who needs to go down first. This takes a dedicated, coordinated, unified effort to pass, and even then it's easily the most trying challenge thus far. When friends fall, be quick to scoop them up and revive them out of the lines of fire; it does none of the team any good to see a would-be medic gunned down right next to their friend.

More and more side threats drop in. Continue to work the fundamentals of combat: one target, everyone using the same weapon, and plenty of movement. As the battle rages on, the crumbling footing around the team makes it clear that things need to be executed with the utmost regard for time. A pair of flying threats tries to use the limited lack of maneuvering room by launching missiles. Retort with any remaining Frost Cannon beams if they're available. If not, switch to something like the Critterstrike in the hopes of catching both in the blast.

The encounter culminates in another Missile Minion finale that likely ends up chipping away at the available ice beneath the group. Look for shuddering sections and get away from them. Keep on the move and unload with Frost Cannon ammo to send the airborne threats plummeting.

Eventually another ice floe bobs to the surface, offering a path to a tenuous platform for grabbing Nanotech leading to another, more resilient platform to take a proper, well-earned breather before moving on. Creatures, bolt crates (some on crumbling ice) and an Ammo Pad offer some relief—but not before a Scorch Minion tries to ruin everything. Show him the power of the Critterstrike to remove the threat in just a few seconds.

QUICK-FIRE CHALLENGE

The Ammo Pad ahead might seem like a welcome respite, but in truth it's merely a chance to stock up for another withering fight. This time, the loose group of ice blocks that serves as a boat is more brittle and subject to damage than any previous landing. The last battle may have had multitudes of targets, but this one is even worse.

FIRE FOR EFFECT

This next section is littered with missile-spewing, heavily armored, auto-target-distracting threats. Obviously above all else, the source of those missles must be taken out as soon as possible—especially because your heroes are floating on a bunch of ice chunks that would probably disintegrate even without a bunch of missiles raining down on them. Incoming fire chips away at the platform and the only question is how your heroes can slow the degradation.

UNITY THROUGH FIREPOWER

Captain Qwark may not be the smartest cog in the gearbox, but he has the right idea about overcoming odds like these. A unified approach is the only way to float through these arduous aquatic areas without finding out what near-freezing liquid does to one's servos.

Employ a dual approach to the overcoming the following trials. Dedicate at least one ally to swatting down the incoming bombs with the Darkstar Fission Tether, zapping incoming threats before they can weaken the ice structure we must all ride. Let another friend tackle the source of the bombs with heavy firepower—perhaps the Warmonger or, if in range, the Plasmabomb Launcher.

To soften the target, a long-range weapon like the Combuster provides enough ammunition to attack from long range. Given that sensors detect no less than six core threats and innumerable potential ejections of extraneous targeting data, it would seem necessary to turn as much firepower toward the base targets with **L1** as it would to pick incoming threats out of the air with the strongest multi-targeting dispersal weaponry as possible.

Do not let up until all party members have lept off the ice boat and onto the quickly crumbling ice at the end of the voyage. ⬤ toward the person in the lead if necessary, but get to the checkpoint before attemping to collect any Nanotech or restocking at the Ammo Pad.

ENTER THE GRUNGOTH

Finally the beast from earlier presents itself properly. As the Grungoth slams down into combat, it's likely that at least one hero will succumb to the lashing attack. An Ammo Pad is present, but resist the temptation to restock just yet. As the Critterstrike would have had no real effect on the pods disgorging bombs prior, it's likely everyone has a fairly full stock of ammo. Put it to use immediately, unloading until there's nothing left on the

Grungoth, pausing only when the creature leaps into the air. Employ heavy **L1** lock-on to ensure every last bit of juice helps, then enjoy the results for now.

One Grungoth begets another, and after that another, and again still another, culminating in the arrival of what must be a kind of king Grungoth. If Critterstrike ammo is gone (even with the Ammo Pad's help), switch instead to heavy payload weapons. Concentrated Warmonger shots inflict massive amounts of damage.

Regardless of the weapon used, the key here is movement. Lock on and circle strafe around the target, pulling back when it leaps into the air, avoiding its shadow. When the beasts return to the ice platform, unload with everything possible. These are the final obstacles between the foursome and a trip directly to the home of Ephemeris.

VAC-U an ally across the frigid gap, then zip over to them, allowing for welcome rewards from the last few battles. Bask briefly in the awards bestowed, then scoop up any nearby crates and Creatures on the way to the GrummelNet vendor who no doubt offers a plethora of ways to spends those bolts—namely a means to upgrade even more weapons to Elite status.

Gather the lingering Creatures and bolt-laden crates ahead and get ready for a blast from the past—or is it? Regardless, the group is finally on its way to Uzo City, and therein Ephemeris' home base. Hope those bolts went to good use!

PLANET MAGNUS
UZO CITY

OBJECTIVES

CITY RUINS

- Trek through the Ruins of Uzo City

VILEROG PLATEAU

- Infiltrate Ephemeris and Defeat Nevo Binklemeyer
- Ride the Tracks to Reach Ephemeris
- Fight Through Ephemeris' Defenses

EPHEMERIS

- Proceed to Nevo's Inner Sanctum
- Defeat the Loki Master

There was indeed a train system built by the collectors, and after a little help from a suspiciously familiar bearded handyman, the gang is well on their way to slipping aboard Ephemeris and putting an end to Nevo's diabolical machinations. If he isn't stopped here, the entire galaxy will almost surely fall to the misguided over-collective efforts of the massive sphere. Coasting into the outer ruins of Uzo City with an ominous round shape on the horizon, the foursome steel themselves for what is sure to be a herculean task.

HERO BOLTS

✓	CITY RUINS
	Right side of rightmost platform after leaving train
	On side-scrolling bounce pads
	Upper-left corner of area with spinning turret
	EPHEMERIS
	Last hallway before core

NEW ENEMIES DEFEATED

CITY RUINS

Swarm Beacon

EPHEMERIS

Grivelnox

Toranaux Spirit

CITY **RUINS**

If the gang can infiltrate deeper into the city and up to the Vilerog Pleateu where Ephemeris is being charged, they have a chance at breaking in and breaking down whatever Nevo has started.

EVERYBODY OFF!

After the train's final stop, the group hits paydirt. There's a clear view of a nearby set of Hero Bolts and what looks like a surprisingly tranquil route through the old city splays out before them.

YOU SNOOZE, YOU LOSE

No time to dawdle! Make a quick dash toward the nearby Bolt Grabber. Either charge ahead with L3 or, more cunningly, get ready for a quick melee throw toward the blue box, snapping it up before anyone else can. Next, dash toward the numerous crates ahead to soak up the 2x bonus before anyone else has a chance to blink or dance or whatever it is squishy-two-shoes do. If you're lucky, you can even double back to the left and pocket a few Creatures to boot!

Once everyone has sated their hankering for bolts, Creatures or GrummelNet upgrades, have one teammate VAC-U another across the gap to the right and zip over to them to continue exploring what's left of the outskirts of Uzo City.

More Creatures and bolts are available to the quickest among the team, but everyone should head to the rightmost part of the platform to claim an easy Hero Bolt. Double back, slam the button and deposit the ejected Voltergeist in its proper receptacle and extend a walkway.

THE COMING SWARM

Swarm Beacons present a nagging problem for the gang. Impervious to normal weapons fire, they must be taken out—and quickly— by the concerted effort of two team members who can VAC-U suck the whole thing to smithereens. Until that happens, it continues to attract drones at a dizzying pace.

Clear a path through nearby automatons if the team must, but make sucking the life out of the Beacon the top priority. Like most threats during the adventure, this one won't show up in such isolated fashion in subsequent appearances.

IT'S LIKE AN ATM! WITH LASERS!

Pop quiz, Qwarkophiles! What does your favorite green hero hate most in this world? If you said 'vanilla soft serve—but only with rainbow sprinkles', give yourself an official President Captain Qwark all-sugar cookie. A close second, however, is being forced to work for bolts. The endless minions that are called in by the Swarm Beacon cough up cold, hard bolts when thrown under the Justice Bus, so why not wait a bit and rank up some easy money? Sure, eventually guns run out of ammo, but you have a long time before that happens, right? Right!

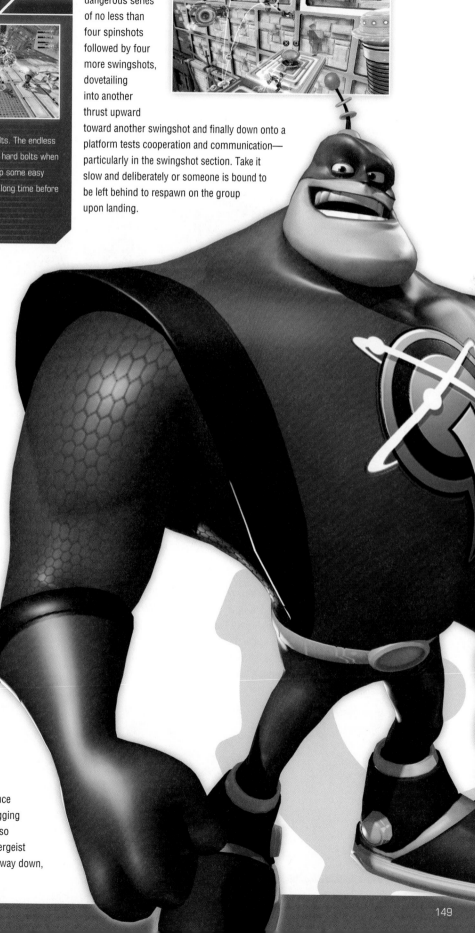

From here, a dangerous series of no less than four spinshots followed by four more swingshots, dovetailing into another thrust upward toward another swingshot and finally down onto a platform tests cooperation and communication—particularly in the swingshot section. Take it slow and deliberately or someone is bound to be left behind to respawn on the group upon landing.

After clearing out the area (including some plentiful crates), head to the right, but stop short of entering the blue targeting beam of the foe ahead. An easily aimed Plasmabomb arcs right over that puny shield and frees up someone on the team to grab the nearby Creature that served as bait. Make sure to keep that Plasmabomb Launcher at the ready; there's bound to me more of those guys around…

BOUNCES AND SWINGS

Immediately to the right are platforms with bolts and Creatures (in that order), then a quick spinshot ride over to a lengthy series of bounce pads. Bounce right slowly, quickly snapping the targeting reticule toward any more would-be snipers before they can draw a bead. Just past a checkpoint are some Hero Bolts, but don't be lured in just yet. Take out the threat nearby, grab the Bolts and move gently to the right, bouncing behind the wall for cover as needed to deploy a Plasmabomb right into the breadbasket of three more baddies. If upgraded fully, the Launcher eliminates all three in a single shot.

Another set of bounce pads and a brief trip skyward introduce a simple little test of coordination: a button and a target begging for some Glob Lobber shots. Give the bulbous icon what it so desperately craves, then slam the button and drive the Voltergeist home. The socket is only exposed when the panel is all the way down, so really unload on it with the Blob Lobber first.

The crates, Nanotech and Ammo Pad in this tiny area are a pretty obvious clue that more firepower is needed. Launch someone up to hit the button and prepare for battle.

Equip the heavy lifters—stuff like the Warmonger or better—to beat a path directly toward the twin blue searchlights that quickly become guards for a Swarm Beacon. Suck the life out of the machine before it can summon too many more reinforcements, then turn the team's attention toward the incoming waves of ground forces.

There's not a ton of room to jump over and around enemies, so continue to pour on the fundamentals of one target, same weapon to really tear through everything. Eventually a Missile Minion arrives, but by now it should be obvious that Elite versions of beam-type weapons like the Frost Cannon or Critterstrike can overpower these enemies quickly, sending them plummeting faster than almost any other weapon.

The appearance of twin VAC-U-ready points might make this little puzzle seem more complicated than it really is. Have one buddy VAC-U the right port to lower the back wall, exposing a Voltergeist dispenser, slam the button while bouncing, suck up the payload and have another teammate switch to the left port. Deposit the Voltergeist, then repeat on the second receptacle that appears nearby. A bridge extends offering a one-way trip deeper into the city.

CHAOS THEORY

After being deposited by the grind rail, all looks peaceful on this wide expanse of territory. The temptation to be the first to procure the Bolt Grabber to make the most of the crates nearby, coupled with an over-abundance of Creatures all around, almost makes it seem safe. That's when the dormant structure in the center and the twin wall-mounted eyes spring to life.

Ignore the Hero Bolts waiting in the upper left for a moment, concentrating the heaviest weaponry available on taking out the bomb dispersal bots along the wall. Their ability to cloud the air with hero-seeking targets is formidable, so getting to them before things get truly dicey is critical. Employing the same tactic as the ice floes can help here; clear the air with the Fission Tether while a Warmonger-equipped partner unloads on the eyes themselves. With the most immediate threat taken care of, the adorably ineffective turret in the middle can be dealt with.

TRUE POWER IN NUMBERS

Should you find your teammates in an agreeable mood, it might be possible to convince everyone to equip Darkstar Fission Tethers and simply charge the bomb-producing targets. The combined output of multiple Tethers quickly focuses on and leaps between the slow-moving bombs while making constant contact with their source when at close range. Since the eyes require multiple Over-drive charges, Co-Op Points here can be quite plentiful.

The turret itself has a hard time tracking multiple heroes despite all its barrels, so stay on the move (or just use this opportunity to go grab those Hero Bolts and any roaming Creatures) and wait for a kind of flower blossom-style discharge, at which point the driver pops out to catch its breath. Mortar toss a teammate up to attack the operator, then repeat three times to send the turret and driver alike packing.

As the team approaches the right side of the area, the camera pans over, revealing more threats and a fortuitous Ammo Pad. With full reserves, unload on these red menaces, scoop up stray crates, then move forward to deal with more flying enemies ahead. Their relative lack of armor and limited range means the flying foes are prime Frost Cannon targets—especially if multiple characters combine their firepower. As they begin to fall, more enemies drop in, including a pesky Swarm Beacon. Clear a path, suck the life out of it, and clean up before being presented with something a little more dangerous.

Well, dangerous might be giving the Scorch Minion a bit too much credit given how vulnerable it is to Critterstrike fire (use the nearby Ammo Pad top off everyone). Overdrive the fiery threat for a quick and easy end to the encounter almost before it could begin. A checkpoint signals the team's continued push into the heart of Uzo City.

CITY

This is a little more like it. Crumbling ruins have been exchanged for a little high technology, but of course that means more advanced forms of danger. Prepare to use every weapon in your heroes' arsenal to make it ever-closer to Ephemeris.

A swingshot point allows the team to grapple up and into decidedly more mechanical environs, but a Bolt Grabber and a few crates wait for those that want to jump out to the left or right. After scooping up the spoils, move on to a few more mixed crates and a warning from Zephyr, who apparently forgot about the dozens upon dozens of lasers the team has already overcome. Still, engage Reflectors!

There's not much to worry about here—aside from needing an Ammo Pad so soon after the last one. One teammate leads with the Reflector, while the others bring up the rear and unleash Plasmabombs on the two would-be assailants on either side of the narrow corridor. Keep moving up between breaks in Ion Turret fire until the clock strikes clobberin' time. VAC-U power the elevator for a brief peek at yet more enemies, but that's not where the group is headed. They're going left, over to the final Laboratory (requiring 280 Creatures in all) and the RYNO!

YIKES! AND AWAY!

Pay no heed to those swarms of enemies that appear. Ducking into the Lab has the added benefit of completely bypassing a wave of enemies and need to hit a switch at the far end of the area. Not only does the team get to finish the RYNO, but they can avoid a bit of pesky combat altogether, and all the spoils are still there for the taking! Now that's thinking like a true President Captain.

LABORATORY 6

This final challenge requires crackerjack timing. Don't be afraid to fail a particular section until everyone knows what their roles are, then execute them with precision. Have all but one of the team jump up to the orb-o-matic and assume orb form. The remaining teammate applies the VAC-U to raise the barriers on the tesla orbs and start the Creature on his way, then orb-o-matics themselves, joining the team in juicing up a launcher. Have everyone hop on and get ready for another speed challenge.

One teammate should immediately begin dragging the power director to the ion power socket, rotating it into position, while another begins VAC-

Uing the turbine below to expose a button. Suck up a teammate and deposit them on the button before the poor, mindless Creature falls to his doom.

A two-tiered set of platforms extends to the left. Quickly designate one person to stay below and power-up the turbine with their VAC-U, while the rest ⊕ up and assume orb form to spark up the tesla orbs. The lower teammate can then bounce up and everyone can crash the launcher, mashing ⊕ to bounce between perches and emerge into yet another challenge.

Once again, split up the team into two groups, one high, one low. Orb up and proceed forward in staggered groups, one juicing up tesla orbs to provide a walkway for the other half of the team (and the Creature, of course), repeating back and forth. A platform lowers when all the sections have been put into place, allowing everyone to come together for another tesla orb pow-wow and a resulting launch corkscrewing up a tower. The final leg of the challenge is to simply toss a teammate up to hit the button and claim the ultimate All 4 One prize.

With all the pieces now in place, there's only one course of action: take that bad boy for a test drive! In this chaotic shooting gallery, the RYNO suits never run out of ammo, so unload on any and everything with impunity. Savor the destruction; it doesn't come for free like this anywhere else.

BACK INTO THE FRAY

Deposited back into the tail end of the nearby conflict, your heroes need only thin out the remaining forces before moving on. There's an Ammo Pad at the far end of the combat zone, and plenty of crates (plus a Bolt Grabber

to make the most of them), and a few Creatures near the Lab entrance—though those are really only useful now for big checkpoint tallies for more bolts.

A wall of Ion Turret fire necessitates some Reflector use, but by now, you know exactly how to deal with these kinds of threats. The first leg of the path

offers easy cover, though the second is a bit more harrowing. Deploy Reflectors and play a little follow the leader, slipping behind a shielding ally as needed while meandering back and forth, inching closer to the Turrets themselves. Safe points with a Slam Attack crate and Ammo Pad offer chances to take a breather and regroup before moving on. Nobody gets left behind, now.

The third and final stretch offers the only real bit of challenge or necessary planning here. Block with a Deflector while another teammate VAC-Us a character up to the button (or just wait for the beams to subside and do it personally). The resulting explosion creates a sea of bolts and opens up the way to a proper challenge.

HERE WE GO AGAIN...

The wide expanse of these curiously gridded platforms at first seems like more than enough room to handle any incoming threats, but as the seemingly endless waves of enemies pour in, parts of the landing crumble away, reducing the team's movement. The single easiest way to avoid getting stuck with little to no room to actually dodge attacks is to open fire with beam weapons like the Frost Cannon and Critterstrike and don't let up until ammo runs out.

Those same beam weapons have the added benefit of acquiring and unloading on targets

from surprising range, mitigating many threats before they can even drop into the skirmish. There's even a steady stream of melee and flying units moving in individually. The key is speed in dispatching threats. Even with all teammates unloading with identical weapon on the same targets, the ground continues to crumble, so if cracks appear under the feet of your characters, there's precious little time to find another, stable square.

Keep lashing out with concentrated beam attacks and eventually a series of four trains glide in (meaning there's no need to jump on until they stop).

VAC-U friends across, then follow and repeat until everyone has made it to the end, stopping on the third and fourth trains to scoop up some Nanotech and bolts—the former of which is probably sorely needed by now.

A spinshot arrives when everyone's aboard the fourth hovering platform. It deposits the team on a platform with more crates and a Bolt Grabber for the first off the spinshot. Proceed forward for a welcome checkpoint, tally up the scores and then push ahead to watch an adorable cutscene with an old friend.

VILEROG **PLATEAU**

After giving Susie a pep talk and entrusting her friends with the perimeter, Ratchet's group looks over the bluff toward a massive show of industrialized chaos. In the shadow of Ephemeris itself, a constant storm of automated drones, equipment and machinery sorts and processes everything the sphere brings back from afar. Not even a pair of green cold feet will stop Nevo's operation from coming to an end.

NOT THE USUAL GRIND

Rallying everyone on the jump pad, the team is launched and deposited on one of the many grind rails snaking through Nevo's operation. With a little "help" from Cronk and Zephyr, the team can sit back, relax and dodge or jump for their lives.

There's really little to worry about despite the scale of the grind section. Keep an eye out for glowing pipes that scald on contact, be ready to leap to adjacent tracks when the current one is about to end and enjoy one of the most impressive views the crew has seen in their long and arduous travels. Eventually everyone is spat out into an area next to a GrummelNet vendor, an Ammo Pad, a few crates—and at the far end, two ominous eye-shaped structures.

Take Clank's earlier advice and whip out the Fission Tether to bring the electrical hurt to the wall-mounted annoyances. Overdrive them as quickly as possible to reduce the risk of damage before hitting the trio of buttons in sequence (that's right, center, left for the curious), then consider which of the team is to be VAC-U blasted out over the small walkway back to the left.

Once the group reaches the other side, a Scorch Minion tries to make things difficult on the narrow outcropping, but by now the Critterstrike should be the universal option for all players as soon as this blowhard shows up. Convert this threat into something more huggable, then move on scooping up bolts including a Bolt Grabber a little ways up for someone quick enough.

Yet another hero-seeking threat emerges along the back wall, and this time it's not alone. The red missile lobber on the perch has little trouble arcing his shots toward your heroes, so return the favor with some concerted Plasmabomb Launcher ammo (this also bypasses or outright destroys the cover the machine is hiding behind). Switch to the Fission Tether to tear through the missles no doubt nipping at the team's heels, then turn the

electrical goods on the remaining targets. Smash the trio of buttons, and it looks like another VAC-U trip across the gap is in order.

This is a tough, dangerous fight, so keep out of corners to avoid being surrounded, and be quick to rescue downed buddies. Remember: if their countdown clock hits zero, everyone must start all the way back at the start of this long, heavily defended slog.

The defeat of the bombers signals the end of this monumental wave, flicking one of the buttons nearby to green. Slam it and its twin to the right, then prep the Reflector to make short work of this beam-boasting threat. Sweep the reflected beam across both green towers to punch through shield and beam alike.

This next leg of the trip toward Ephemeris is no joke. Multiple heavies descend, and plenty more melee attackers head directly toward the heroes, trying to force them into the open. Don't fall for this strategy; instead, stay behind cover, concentrate on the closer, more persistent targets, then lob Plasmabombs over both the team's cover and the enemies' to keep things relatively safe. Stick to the sides when moving up if possible, but don't be afraid to employ heavy double-jump avoidance where necessary.

As the camera swoops back to the right, a former arch-enemy seems to have turned over a new leaf. Sharp eyes should also note the generous number of crates, Nanotech and a Bolt Grabber to the right of where the huge machine drops some kind of glass tube. Scoop up all the goods before jumping into Commander Sporg's unusual method of conveyance.

If this section beings to feel a little overwhelming, there's always the option of unleashing the RYNO for a ripping good time.

A breathtaking view of the full scale of Nevo's operation zooms by as Sporg explains just how impressive Ephemeris' collection efforts

Toward the end of the corridor, a Swarm Beacon makes landfall and starts adding even more targets to the chaos. By now, the team should know the drill: move in quickly, VAC-U the Beacon, then clean up the scraps. Keep pushing forward, toward the blue barriers, where (surprise, surprise) even more close-range fighters swoop in to wreck all that progress, followed by still more fliers (though a Qwark-approved introduction to gravity should make short work of them).

have become. With a fond-ish fairwell, the tube slides over to its final dock, the team is raised up to a massive corridor and a checkpoint is reached.

EPHEMERIS

This is it: the final leg of a journey that has seen countless enemies felled and every attempt at stopping your intrepid partnership overcome. Truly, if ever there was a time for back-patting and high-fives, this is it. Resist the temptation, however, for the core of Ephemeris holds the most challenging of all our heroes' tests.

FRICKIN' LASER BEAMS

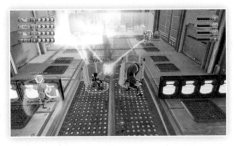

There's almost nothing to the approach into the core, but of course Ephemeris won't be completely unprotected. A pair of beams attempt to hone in on the team as they approach some bits of cover. Whip out the Reflector for a crash course re-education on why lasers are a bad idea, pop the green stacks on either side, then make a mad dash for all the spoils beyond. Hero Bolts wait for everyone, but near them is a Bolt Grabber that can turn this last bit of crate smashing into a truly valuable endeavor.

Stock up at the GrummelNet kiosk, as this is the last chance your heroes have to apply Elite status (or other, upgrades) to their arsenal. Ride the elevator up, Attach to the swingshot and get ready to shut down Nevo's operation once and for all.

WAIT, WHAT?

Yep, that just happened. All this time, it seemed Nevo was behind everything, but the truth was far more insidious. Mr. Dinkles, harboring the same dark energy carried with the asteroid impact ages ago, has some seriously twisted plans. Worse, he's co-opted Nevo into doing all the heavy lifting, leaving the formerly adorable Creature with a plan that seems ready to go off without a hitch.

Thankfully, there are four new hitches just itching to show just how well teamwork can get in the way of even the best-laid plans.

BOSS
MR. DINKLES

There's no sugar coating it; Mr. Dinkles is well prepared for the group, and this fight is going to be more challenging than his tiny size could

ever suggest. Not surprisingly, Mr. Dinkles is quick to dispense wave after wave of collector minions, starting with a handful of melee models, moving up to projectile-based versions and keeps ramping things up from there.

The first phase of the fight is just those two waves. The floor contracts, opening up the chance to restock at the Ammo Pads on the left and right. Mr. Dinkles drops a few bombs (easily dodged if you're watching the floor), then attempts a few laser blasts that must be bounced back with Reflectors. Overdrive these beams to lower the hoverthrone's shields, then let loose with the team's most powerful weapons while the Creature attempts some repairs.

After a few moments, Mr. Dinkles hops back in and starts lobbing bombs that explode with wide but slow shockwaves—including one that detonates in the air to keep the group grounded. Hop over them while unloading everything the team has, remembering to choose the same weapon for maximum effect and Co-Op Points.

After heaping enough damage on the hoverthrone, the shields eventually return, as do the laser attacks. Repeat the Overdrive process to take them down, and continue pelting the craft, using the Ammo Pads as needed.

At about the half-health mark, Phase two begins and more minions join the fray as the flooring spools outward again to aid in movement. Remember old lessons here: concentration of firepower is important, but when multiple melee enemies are together, it's often best to use an area effect Overdrive blast to consume all or most of them at once (saves ammo, too).

These enemies are more resilient and plentiful than the last, and can quickly overwhelm the group or break up their combined firepower, so stay agile and above all else, be ready for revives; there's no Nanotech here, so only allies can keep everyone in the fight.

When the floor retracts again, the shield/unload cycle gets just a bit busier. Smaller minions appear just to add annoyance. Finish them with quick fire weapons, but be ready to get back on the Reflector as needed. Reflector beams can be used to sweep across and hit the smaller minions, but could lead to the beams sneaking past the shield if a hero is careless enough, to say nothing of actually tagging a teammate.

Keep laying on the heavy firepower and eventually Mr. Dinkles decides to up the ante a little.

THE BEGINNING OF THE END—PART II

Well now thing are getting interesting. Mr. Dinkles calls in the Grivelnox, the beast seen earlier crammed into one of those tubes the team rode to Ephemeris in. If the Creature is allowed to possess something that big, things could get bad—fast.

The minions that storm in this time are far more powerful than before. Lay down heavy fire to dispose of them as soon as possible, particularly when a pair of twin, beam-sweeping threats descends. The Critterstrike does a wonderful job of reducing their effectiveness. Trying to take them on with anything less than combined Warmonger blasts leaves the team open to being caught in the beams that can sweep across the entire area. Bad idea.

When the two hulking monstrosities are taken down, the center of the floor rises, festooned with a Big, Scary Red Button. A cutscene shows a heroic effort on the part of Dr. Croid and Nevo, finally working together again after so many years apart. Unfortunately, it also shows the dark being inside Mr. Dinkles' body escaping right into the body of the Grivelnox. Uh oh.

BOSS
GRIVELNOX

The Grivelnox is an insanely huge creature, seemingly capable of swatting away your heroes with little to no effort. Even concentrated fire from weapons can only chip away at its health, and there are worse surprises in store.

Phase one opens with a simple straight-on encounter with the creature. It employs the same tentacle slap and sweep tactics seen in other monsters, such as the King Sepiad. Wait for it to hit one of the sides, then leap over the sweeping motion. Though it is strong, the nearby Ammo Pads can help refill the strongest weapons and keep them trained on the beast even while it tries to fight back. Don't stop firing, stick to the same weapons across the party. When about one-quarter of its health is gone, the Grivelnox attempts more drastic measures.

Getting even angrier, the Grivelnox turns to its natural ability to absorb other creatures' abilities, sucking down a fire creature that augments its previous attacks. Thankfully not much about the attack strategy has changed, despite the creature's knack for spitting out rolling pests that are, unfortunately, ablaze. These are more of a nuisance than anything else, quickly falling to even light weapons like the Combuster. Deal with them quickly while avoiding the same tentacle swipes as before.

Take things slowly and deliberately here; if a teammate falls and can't be revived, the whole Grivelnox fight must to be restarted from the beginning.

About halfway thought its health, the creature's strategy changes into a real phase two. A new strike plants one of the spiked tentacles in the ground on either the left or right side of the arena, releasing shockwaves that must jumped over. There's a small window of reaction time for the strike itself; a tentacle curls, then lashes out diagonally to the opposite side of the arena. Be prepared.

When the creature is down to about one-third of its life, phase three begins and another wrinkle develops: a massive fire beam is unleashed, sweeping across the whole arena. Double-jump over it while trying to stay in the middle in case the beam quickly reverses direction when it reaches an edge.

Further damage returns the monster to its shockwave attack, but mixes things up with more flame jets. Continue to pour on damage constantly, and when it moves around the arena, prep for a flame jet. With perseverance and quick jumping, eventually the monster loses its grip on the platform and drop out of sight.

THE BEGINNING OF THE END—PART III

Despite the beast disappearing from sight, more minions continue to attack your heroes. Grungoths (last seen near the end of the Polar Ice Floes) crash out of cages to attack. Deal with them like the original Gungroth fight: Critterstrike Overdrives all around. Don't forget the Ammo Pads if ammo dips too low.

BOSS GRIVELNOX (REDUX)

This next phase showcases just how huge this beast is. It returns, and the Z'Grute that was so much trouble at the start of this adventure is ingested, imbuing the Grivelnox with new electrical and regenerative powers. Yes, that means a completely full life bar again.

According to Zephyr, this also makes the creature invulnerable—a term that's not quite accurate as its health can still be chipped away at (even as swirling swarms of comet-like electrical energy chokes the arena). Leap over the swirling threats and continue to unload in the hopes that something might take the beast down.

When about-one-quarter of its health is shaved off, the monster starts to restore its own health. Again. Thankfully, Croid and Nevo devise a plan: if the Grivelnox's arms can be locked down, perhaps it dark spirit possessing the creature can be extracted.

Continue to pound the creature with everything the team has. Eventually it attempts the restore cycle for the billionth time, at which point the ball of energy in the center can be targeted. Overdrive it, and a button appears, allowing a teammate to be VAC-Ued up to slam it. The Grivelnox's arms are pinned!

Repeat the process on the other side, taking care to avoid an electrical beam spit from the monster's mouth. When both arms are pinned, two more buttons appear near the head. Slam both of them to lock down the Grivelnox's neck, and begin the extraction process.

Eventually, Croid and Nevo ask for help. Unleash the might of a combined VAC-U stream Overdrive to wrench the dark spirit out of the beast. Stuck in the open, the heroes need only unleash their strongest combined attacks. With no protective Grivelnox body, the spirit is finally taken down. Or is it?

Enraged, it heads straight for Qwark before being stopped by Nefarious, ending this nightmare once and for all. And with that, the adventure comes to an end. Croid and Nevo have reconciled, and there might even be a change of heart in ol' Dr. Nefari-nevermind. Oh well. Heroes do need villains, after all!

UP YOUR ARSENAL
THE WEAPONS

UNIVERSAL WEAPONS

The universe is rife with the tools of destruction, from a rocket launcher that buys heavily into the "more is better" mantra to whips made of electricity to weapons so powerful they are only referred to by code name.

The following weapons are usable no matter which character has been selected, and can be upgraded in a number of ways—so long as you have scoured the landscape for enough bolts to pay for them.

COMBUSTER

WEAPON COST
00000

The mainstay of heroes and villains alike, the Combuster combines a sleek, pocket-sized blaster with a propensity for delivering a staggering number of shots per second when pointed at the same target as another Combuster. In other words, the more people pew pewing, the bigger the resulting boom (not to mention a few handy Co-op Points for deluging a target from multiple angles).

The Combuster's ability to pile on damage is balanced by its need for multiple users to ramp up speed and firepower, so bear in mind that single shots don't carry nearly the same oomph as some of the bigger weapons. Thankfully, it is loaded with one of the biggest stores of ammo, and upgrading both the ammunition and the damage at a GrummelNet vendor will help make the Combuster one of the mainstays of any arsenal.

WEAPON STATS

Ammo Count	Ammo Upgrade Cost	Upgraded Ammo Count	Power Upgrade Cost
100	5000	150	10000

UNLOCKED AT:

Skyway
LUMINOPOLIS

Elite Upgrade Cost	Elite Ability
30000	Fires a 3 blast spread

UPGRADE

COMBUSTER

PLASMABOMB
LAUNCHER

ARC LASHER

WARMONGER

BLITZER

MR. ZURKON

PYRO BLASTER

CRITTER STRIKE

DARKSTAR FISSION
TETHER

OMEGATECH FROST
CANNON

THUNDERSMACK

PLASMABOMB LAUNCHER

WEAPON COST
00500

Plasmabombs are cool—so cool, in fact, that they fuse two of the most deadly words in galactic weaponry into one super-word sure to strike fear into the hearts of any poor targets on the receiving end. While the explosive spheres ejected at high velocity are handy in their own right, it's the fact that they're launched in an arc that makes them such handy tools—especially if an enemy happens to be taking shelter behind a bit of cover that would block normal frontal assaults. Simply lock onto a target and fire to propel the payload up and over anything providing supposed protection for a foe.

WEAPON STATS

Ammo Count	Ammo Upgrade Cost	Upgraded Ammo Count	Power Upgrade Cost
18	5000	30	10000

UNLOCKED AT:
Power Station Exit
LUMINOPOLIS

Elite Upgrade Cost	Elite Ability	
30000	Each plasmabomb breaks apart into 3 secondary explosives	UPGRADE!

ARC LASHER

WEAPON COST
04500

Taking the best parts of the analog and digital worlds, the Arc Lasher is a highly advanced kinetic energy whip. Each crack of the Arc Lasher sends thousands of volts coursing through its target. Hold **R1** for a sustained strike that paralyzes victims while maintaining contact. Although limited in range, there's no substitute when sidelining the enemy is the number one priority.

WEAPON STATS

Ammo Count	Ammo Upgrade Cost	Upgraded Ammo Count	Power Upgrade Cost
15	5000	30	10000

UNLOCKED AT:
Outside Receiving Station
ALDAROS PLAINS

Elite Upgrade Cost	Elite Ability
30000	—

UPGRADE

WARMONGER

WEAPON COST
06000

The Warmonger is a rocket launcher that lives up to its name. Each high-speed warhead is tipped with raritanium to guarantee utter annihilation. Its impressive blast radius turns massive mobs into mutilated mincemeat. The only limitation on this beastly bad boy is its low ammo capacity. Save it for large crowds and the toughest opponents.

WEAPON STATS

Ammo Count	Ammo Upgrade Cost	Upgraded Ammo Count	Power Upgrade Cost
6	10000	10	25000

UNLOCKED AT:
Orthani Gorge
THE DEADGROVE

Elite Upgrade Cost	Elite Ability
60000	Each rocket splits into multiple warheads

UPGRADE

BLITZER

WEAPON COST

06000

Good, old-fashioned fisticuffs get a raritanium-enhanced upgrade in the form of the Blitzer. Normal melee attacks get supercharged, propelling their owner into battle with pulverizing strikes. This close-range weapon tears up ground-based enemies but proves useless against aerial opponents.

WEAPON STATS

Ammo Count	Ammo Upgrade Cost	Upgraded Ammo Count	Power Upgrade Cost
18	10000	36	25000

UNLOCKED AT:
Mining Camp
THE DEADGROVE

Elite Upgrade Cost	Elite Ability
50000	—

UPGRADE !

MR. ZURKON

WEAPON COST

10000

Misery loves company and Mr. Zurkon loves misery. Bolster the team's numbers with this snarky synthenoid that doles out damage, destruction, and demeaning disses. Mr. Zurkon's highly advanced targeting systems are so accurate there's no need to keep an eye on him. While activated, cutting-edge renewable energy powers this robotic rapscallion to guarantee he never runs out of ammo during his uptime.

WEAPON STATS

Ammo Count	Ammo Upgrade Cost	Upgraded Ammo Count	Power Upgrade Cost
1	5000	2	10000

UNLOCKED AT:
Elerox Pass
N.E.S.T.

Elite Upgrade Cost	Elite Ability
30000	—

UPGRADE !

PYRO BLASTER

WEAPON COST
10000

Roast and toast enemies with the scorching heat of a thousand white-hot suns coming from the Pyro Blaster. Kerchu technology has allowed for the transport highly volatile, compressed gasses in a convenient, portable package that spews its superheated suffering with ease. Its range is limited but there's no better way to clear the immediate vicinity than to cover it in flames. It's always a good time for barbeque when packing the Pyro Blaster. BBQ sauce not included.

WEAPON STATS

Ammo Count	Ammo Upgrade Cost	Upgraded Ammo Count	Power Upgrade Cost
30	5000	60	10000

UNLOCKED AT:
Elerox Pass
N.E.S.T.

Elite Upgrade Cost	Elite Ability
30000	Flames travel farther

UPGRADE

CRITTER STRIKE

WEAPON COST
10000

Neuter the most ferocious foes through the amazing transmogrifying technology that powers the Critter Strike. Hold **R1** and watch a focused energy beam reconfigure the target's molecules, eventually transforming them into completely non-threatening critters. These newly neutered creatures merrily forget their animosity and actually make tempting targets for any aggressors still in the area. Thin the enemy's numbers and create distractions with ease thanks to the Critter Strike!

WEAPON STATS

Ammo Count	Ammo Upgrade Cost	Upgraded Ammo Count	Power Upgrade Cost
30	5000	60	10000

UNLOCKED AT:
Elerox Pass
N.E.S.T.

Elite Upgrade Cost	Elite Ability
30000	Creates tougher critters that attack enemies

UPGRADE

DARKSTAR FISSION TETHER

WEAPON COST
15000

The Terachnoids don't worry too much about their energy bills when it comes to weaponry and aiming isn't their strong suit. The result is the Darkstar Fission Tether, a defensive weapon repurposed on the battlefield by various alien species. It automatically locks onto nearby enemies to unleash arcs of energy. Using one near a teammate allows their arcs to link together and focus on a common target for even more devastating damage.

In contrast to the Arc Lasher's ability to electrically lock down opponents, the Fission Tether is a weapon of pure devastation. A constant stream of electrical energy automatically lances out toward the nearest target and continually applies damage until they are destroyed. Because electricity follows the path of least resistance, allies that are also using the Fission Tether add their electrical energy to the same stream, pooling the damage with explosive results and causing the energy to expand to other nearby targets.

WEAPON STATS

Ammo Count	Ammo Upgrade Cost	Upgraded Ammo Count	Power Upgrade Cost
30	10000	60	25000

UNLOCKED AT:
Rehabitation Center
N.E.S.T.

Elite Upgrade Cost	Elite Ability
60000	Increased attack range

UPGRADE

OMEGATECH FROST CANNON

WEAPON COST
25000

When the cold shoulder approach simply isn't enough, cool off pesky enemies with a sub-zero dose of mediation. Hold **R1**, and Frost Cannon, like other beam-type weapons, quickly acquires targets and begins delivering a constant stream of ice. When enough of a target's core temperature has been sapped, they become encased in a cocoon of ice and can be shattered with a simple melee strike. When partners join the deep freeze, the resulting Overdrive explosion sends out an area effect wave that can instantly freeze nearby enemies, leaving them just as vulnerable to shattering.

WEAPON STATS

Ammo Count	Ammo Upgrade Cost	Upgraded Ammo Count	Power Upgrade Cost
15	10000	30	25000

UNLOCKED AT:
Cove
OCTONOK CAY

Elite Upgrade Cost	Elite Ability
60000	Frozen targets eventually shatter and damage nearby enemies

UPGRADE

THUNDERSMACK

WEAPON COST

25000

A storm is coming, and your heroes are the ones who created it. The Thundersmack's purpose is simple: form a dark and stormy cloud, then zap nearby enemies with intermittent lightning strikes. Using multiple Thundersmacks causes the single storm cloud to grow into a whirling tornado with far more frequent lightning.

WEAPON STATS

Ammo Count	Ammo Upgrade Cost	Upgraded Ammo Count	Power Upgrade Cost
10	10000	20	25000

UNLOCKED AT:
Feeding Dock
OCTONOK CAY

Elite Upgrade Cost	Elite Ability
60000	Summons an additional, temporary cluster of low-flying storm clouds

UPGRADE

CHARACTER-SPECIFIC WEAPONS

Like any good team, each member of this foursome brings something unique to the table. In the course of their adventure, all four of them gain access to a fantastic gadget only they can use—provided they can afford it. These one-of-a-kind gadgets can dramatically alter strategies as the quartet cuts a swath of destruction through the evil forces assembled against them.

RATCHET

CLANK

QWARK

DR. NEFARIOUS

DOPPELBANGER

WEAPON COST
05000

UNIQUE TO:
RATCHET

There are plenty of times in the furious carnage of battle that a hero needs to take a breather. Unfortunately, most villains don't acknowledge the need to take bathroom breaks every once in a while. Buy some breathing room with the Doppelbanger in these situations. It a launches a convincing robotic decoy of everyone's favorite Lombax for the enemy to focus their energy on.

WEAPON STATS

Ammo Count	Ammo Upgrade Cost	Upgraded Ammo Count	Power Upgrade Cost
4	10000	8	10000

UNLOCKED AT:
Archipelago
ALDAROS PLAINS

Elite Upgrade Cost	Elite Ability	
30000	Doppelbanger gains Plasma Cannon Arms and will fire at enemies	**UPGRADE!**

ZONI BLASTER

WEAPON COST
05000

Run circles around the enemy with the Zoni Blaster. What it lacks in damage-dealing properties it more than makes up for with its one-of-a-kind temporal distortion properties. Zap the enemy with it and they're slowed down to a snail's pace. Wipe the floor with them as they futilely attempt to do combat in slow-motion.

UNIQUE TO:
CLANK

WEAPON STATS

Ammo Count	Ammo Upgrade Cost	Upgraded Ammo Count	Power Upgrade Cost
4	10000	8	10000

UNLOCKED AT:
Archipelago
ALDAROS PLAINS

Elite Upgrade Cost	Elite Ability
30000	Time dilation affects all enemies on screen

UPGRADE !

QUANTUM DEFLECTOR

WEAPON COST
05000

No one's ever satisfied with the President considering every bill, amendment, and policy are hotly debated and highly divisive. It can be dangerous being the figurehead of the entire government and it's always better to be safe than sorry. The Quantum Deflector lets heads of state breathe a sigh of relief in public, confident in its ability to provide top-notch protection that can withstand the most dangerous attacks. The Quantum Deflector grows to surround other characters when Captian Qwark stands still.

UNIQUE TO:
QWARK

WEAPON STATS

Ammo Count	Ammo Upgrade Cost	Upgraded Ammo Count	Power Upgrade Cost
4	10000	8	10000

UNLOCKED AT:
Archipelago
ALDAROS PLAINS

Elite Upgrade Cost	Elite Ability
30000	Quantum Deflector lasts twice as long

UPGRADE !

CLOAKER

WEAPON COST
05000

Being one of the galaxy's most wanted comes with certain liabilities. For one thing, it's hard to pick up magazines at the store without being spotted. For the many times when it's just more trouble than it's worth to appear in public, there's the Cloaker. This gizmo bends light rays to provide a perfect, albeit temporary, camouflage to allow for stealthy trips to the corner store or behind enemies' backs. While cloaked, Nefarious can execute a powerful ambush strike against his unsuspecting victims.

UNIQUE TO:
DR.
NEFARIOUS

WEAPON STATS

Ammo Count	Ammo Upgrade Cost	Upgraded Ammo Count	Power Upgrade Cost
4	10000	8	10000

UNLOCKED AT:
Archipelago
ALDAROS PLAINS

Elite Upgrade Cost	Elite Ability
30000	Cloaked melee attack gets supercharged

UPGRADE !

UTILITY **GADGETS**

Not every problem is solved with high-yield ordnance—just most of them. But for those times when a big boom won't get the team anywhere, there are handy utility gadgets. Each of these tools serves a valuable purpose in helping the team in their quest to stop Ephemeris.

GLOB LOBBER

The Glob Lobber was originally a tool for spacefaring traders that needed to anchor their starships in a wide variety of low-gravity environments. However, it surged in popularity among the spelunking and climbing crowds for its ability to manipulate natural terrain to create new routes. A patented biomass fuels the mechanism that replenishes itself so fast it's impossible to run out.

UNLOCKED AT:
Village Entrance
ALDAROS PLAINS

QUAKEHAMMER

Tharpod explorers trail blazed new frontiers throughout Planet Magnus in search of treasures and resources. Rather than give up when faced with the dense rock prevalent throughout the murky Deadgrove, they developed Quakehammer technology to break on through to the other side. Effective on their own at breaking up smaller rocks, using multiple Quakehammers increases their power output exponentially to cause Mega-Quakes that shatter the toughest surfaces. Warning: Shaky hands are common after operation, so avoid any delicate tasks like making model ships in a bottle or pouring a cup of tea.

UNLOCKED AT:
Orthani Gorge
THE DEADGROVE

REFLECTOR

Gifted with little in the way of fanfare, the Reflector is actually the most life-saving of the gadgets the foursome comes across. By deploying a single Reflector, energy beams are either negated or, as the name suggests, reflected back toward the source. Any allies standing behind a deployed Reflector are protected as well, and reflected beams can be re-angled to attack enemies and weak spots alike.

UNLOCKED AT:
Phonica Craters
PHONICA MOON

ENCYCLOPEDIA ATTACKTICA
THE BEASTIARY

The unlikely foursome may have run the gamut from enemies to allies in the past but, for now, there exists an uneasy alliance between them. This is a good thing, as all manner of enemies both docile and dangerous alike are all too happy to attack the quartet and bring an early end to their quest to discover who or what has left them in their current situation.

ORGANIC ENEMIES

LUMENOID

A source of light and power for the towering metropolis, Lumenoids are normally more helpful than harmful, but when the Z'Grute frees them from their normal city-powering operations, they become a bit more menacing. "Menacing" here means they'll slowly move toward your characters and attempt to zap them.

ATTACKS: ELECTRIC SHOCK

FIRST ENCOUNTERED
Rooftop Amphitheatre
LUMINOPOLIS

CAN'T TOUCH THIS

Lumenoids are indeed as innocuous as they seem. So long as they don't actually touch anyone, they can't offer much in the way of danger. Take them out from afar by using a thrown melee attack (**R2**+⬤). Don't bother wasting valuable ammunition on them; a thrown weapon is just as effective.

Z'GRUTE

Ordinarily held in stasis, the Z'Grute turns decidedly dangerous—and smash-happy—when Dr. Nefarious' faithful butler Lawrence re-animates the Critter, turning it loose on the city for a non-stop parade of destruction. Though it must ultimately be apprehended, the foursome must chase the Critter through the city, at times avoiding the chaos caused by the Z'Grute.

ATTACKS: ELECTRIC PROJECTILES, GROUND ELECTROCUTION

FIRST ENCOUNTERED
Rooftop Amphitheatre
LUMINOPOLIS

GRAVOID

These purple, bulbous Critters flying throughout Aldaros Plains are both ornery and destructive. But rather than attack head-on, they prefer to undermine their targets' footing. Gravoids tug and pull at the unstable rocks throughout Aldaros Plains, causing the ground under their victims' feet to collapse and send them tumbling to their doom. Blast them before they can rip up the rocky road.

ATTACKS: GROUND EXTRACTION

FREEZE, SUCKER!

To stop a Gravoid before it can pull the rug out from under Ratchet, turn to the Arc Lasher. Its high voltage freezes Gravoids in their tracks and leaves them completely vulnerable to teammates' attacks.

FIRST ENCOUNTERED
Archipelago
ALDAROS PLAINS

OCTOMOTH

One of the intimidating Critters collected by Ephemeris, the Octomoth is unceremoniously dropped by Commander Spog into the path of Ratchet and his teammates. This multi-limbed monster didn't take too kindly to being stranded and eagerly picks a fight with the gang. A passive predator, the Octomoth uses the spear-like tentacles to pierce the ground underfoot. Tearing away at its victims footing, it lets gravity do the rest. Its normally impervious shielded mouth is its only weak point. The tentacle-touting threat exposes it only in anger and pain after getting its tentacles violently beaten back.

ATTACKS: GROUND-PIERCING TENTACLES

FIRST ENCOUNTERED
Village Outskirts
ALDAROS PLAINS

GRAVOID BRUTE

These inventive Gravoids have managed to scavenge technology to build their own offensive weaponry. Instead of turning the environment into their weapon, they have armed themselves with rockets and armor plating. Avoid the red crosshairs on the ground indicating their rockets' destination and knock these goons out of the sky.

ATTACKS: **ROCKETS**

FIRST ENCOUNTERED
Archipelago
ALDAROS PLAINS

DREADGRUBS

These pests bug visitors to the Deadgrove's to death! They appear in groups, curling up into a balls and roll at potential victim with their spikey bodies. These creepy crawlies deal more damage they can take and are easily squashed before they can get close enough to do any harm.

ATTACKS: **ROLLING MELEE**

FIRST ENCOUNTERED
Orthani Gorge
THE DEADGROVE

GROVE BEETLE

Thick, chitinous armor protects the Grove Beetle from the many dangers found within the Deadgrove. As a result, it's one of the most resilient and fearless of the native denizens in the area. Its only weaknesses are its fleshy underbelly and an overzealous attitude. When the Grove Beetle's charging attack is stopped short by the terrain, it literally bowls itself over and winds up on it back to expose its weak point.

ATTACKS: **CHARGING STRIKE**

FIRST ENCOUNTERED
Orthani Gorge
THE DEADGROVE

RECON RETREAT

Have one teammate drop into the path of the Grove Beetle when possible to get its attention. Once it's riled up enough to attack, hookshot back to the safety of the main party and let the Grove Beetle knock itself out.

WIGWUMP

Little is known about the massive Critter that lurks in the deepest depths of the Deadgrove. Even Commander Spog steers clear of its stomping grounds, risking only a small number of his robotic minions to maintain a security presence. The uncontested top of the food chain, the Wigwump navigates a labyrinth of tunnels with ease to strike with little warning. It relies upon its superheated magma breath and powerful jaws to slay its targets.

ATTACKS: MAGMA BREATH, SNAPPING JAWS

FIRST ENCOUNTERED
Abyss
THE DEADGROVE

FLABBERFISH

Flappy-jawed though they may be, Flabberfish have the pesky habit of latching onto their unsuspecting prey's head. Otherwise, though, these amphibious Critters attempt to overwhelm targets through sheer numbers.

ATTACKS: BITING SNAP, CRANIAL ATTACHMENT

WEEVOID

Weevoids are dangerous predators on Magnus, producing a non-lethal toxin to paralyze its prey. They then attack their helpless victims with their sharp claws and tail. A formidable opponent, they tactically curl up inside their armored shells to withdraw from combat temporarily and are invulnerable during this time.

ATTACKS: TOXIN SPIT, CLAW AND TAIL MELEE

FIRST ENCOUNTERED
Cove
OCTONOK CAY

FIRST ENCOUNTERED
Elerox Pass
N.E.S.T.

HEAD START

Flabberfish, like many of the species on and around Magnus, are plentiful, but weak. Deal with them quickly using thrown melee strikes or, in a pinch, a weapon that has plenty of ammo like the Combuster. It'll only take one hit to take each of them down, but keep an eye out for any allies that have come into a new hat.

SLORG

Sometimes the best offense is a good defense. In the case of Slorgs, their electrified bodies make them impervious to damage. Instead, they simply react to impacts in the most Newtonian way possible: by producing an equal and opposite reaction—in this case sliding like a pat of butter on an exhaust port until they impact a wall, bouncing back toward their attackers.

ATTACKS: ELECTRIFIED BODY

FIRST ENCOUNTERED
Cove
OCTONOK CAY

ON STRIKE

The Critterstrike is the heroes' best friend when dealing with these docile denizens. Simply apply some of the rainbow-colored beam to get a Slorg moving, then let loose with a few more hits to re-adjust them should they start bouncing oddly. Toss all the Slorgs in Octonok Cay into the drink to earn a Trophy!

ARMORED SLORG

Effectively identical to their non-armored brethren, Armored Slorgs have an addition layer of metallic plating that much be destroyed first. Once their protection is gone, deal with them like any other Slorg.

ATTACKS: ELECTRIFIED BODY

FIRST ENCOUNTERED
Cove
OCTONOK CAY

SEPIAD

The Sepiad is often seen, but rarely encountered face-to-face, preferring to use their tentacles to drag food into the aquatic domain of the King Sepiad. Avoid any tentacle strikes while exploring the Cay, but get ready to take one on in a proper battle before making it onto the W.A.S.P.

ATTACKS: TENTACLE SLAM, TORSO SLAM

BIG, DUMB AND UGLY

When the Sepiad finally pulls its generous frame up onto the docks for a mini-boss fight, remember that this thing isn't especially bright. It tries to slap at your heroes, but after just a bit of damage it heads back into the water. Use this opportunity to ring the nearby sonic pylons to lower bait. Then take advantage of the poor, entranced Critter's distracted state by peppering it with short-range attacks. Just look out for when it's finished with the bait and slams its body back down onto the dock!

FIRST ENCOUNTERED
Cove
OCTONOK CAY

KING SEPIAD

So this was who the "smaller" Sepiads were handing over all their spoils to. No matter, despite the larger size, all it really adds in terms of attacks is a bit of aquatic danger (in the first wave) and more idle slapping when he hoists himself onto Octonok Lighthouse. Large though he may be, the massive critter seems overwhelmingly drawn to bright, shiny, electric things. Perhaps something to nibble on while it is trying to nibble on your heroes?

ATTACKS: VARIOUS TENTACLE STRIKES

FIRST ENCOUNTERED
Octonok Lighthouse
OCTONOK CAY

ANTHROPODS

The first encounter with Terawatt Forest's local fauna fits rather nicely with the firsts of the other parts of Magnus. These guys could be considered cute if not for the fact that they attack in groups and for their propensity to appear in the middle of encounters with much more dangerous locals. Use the same techniques as before: melee throws, ammo-rich weapons or employ some judicious Vac-U application.

ATTACKS: PINCER ATTACK

FIRST ENCOUNTERED
Kaleero Trail
TERRAWATT FOREST

SHARD BEAST

Shard Beasts have gained a nasty side-effect from munching on the local indigenous rock: they're electrically charged, giving them an impenetrable shield they can raise, powered by the spikes. What's worse, those spikes pose a shocking danger on their own. Talk about a bad combo!

ATTACKS: LIGHTNING BURST, INVINCIBLE BARRIER

ELECTRO-CLASH

Don't bother trying to attack the Shard Beast unless he's first appearing in the world. The shield he erects almost immediately nullifies any attacks. Instead, focus on the spikes that punch out of the ground (but don't get too close). Shatter them, and the shield goes down.

FIRST ENCOUNTERED
Kaleero Trail
TERRAWATT FOREST

RAZORMOTHS

Magnus' fliers are prone to swooping in at the most inopportune times—usually when your heroes are trying to do something important like stay alive. Though not terribly dangerous, they follow the common pattern of strength in numbers. They're weak, however, so just pepper them with beam weapons to render them a non-threat before they can even get in range to attack.

ATTACKS: SWOOPING ATTACK

FIRST ENCOUNTERED
Kaleero Trail
TERRAWATT FOREST

CRATERPEDE

This multi-segmented threat doesn't seem so dangerous at first. For one, it seems to move slowly, but that movement is aided by the ability to do a 180 with almost no effort. They constantly zero in on targets, rendering normal strafing movements ineffective. Worse, they must be taken down a segment at a time.

ATTACKS: SLOW MARCH SLAM

REAR WINDOW

Trying to take on a Craterpede from the front is a mistake plenty of would-be heroes have attempted in the past. They never lost the "would-be" status for a reason. You should avoid the weapon-deflecting carapaces and instead lock onto the rear segments. Keep chipping away at them to expose the head, but always remember that they move in a more or less straight line to attack their targets. Jumping here helps.

FIRST ENCOUNTERED
Phonica Craters
PHONICA MOON

LURKER

Oh great! An enemy that chills in a crater filled with acid. Worse, they seem to be able to move between craters, which means they can simply duck out of sight right as the foursome are trying to lay on the damage, only to pop out in another place and spit their seriously dangerous acid. The key is to look for the eyestalks peeking out of the acidic stew; they're a clear indication of intent to pop out and spit anew.

ATTACKS: ACIDIC SALIVA PROJECTILES

FIRST ENCOUNTERED
Phonica Craters
PHONICA MOON

GUNGROTH

The Gungroth is teased for the entire length of the trek through the Polar Sea. Imprisoned by Ephemeris' Collectors, yet never properly gathered, the beast escapes and actively tracks your heroes until a final showdown. Given their arctic-friendly fur and ability to clamber over even icy outcroppings, they should be regarded as a true threat.

ATTACKS: SWIPE, BELLY SLAM

FIRST ENCOUNTERED
Polar Ice Floes
POLAR SEA

SLAM DUNK

Gungroths are quick, powerful and seem to love going airborne. When they leap, watch the ground for their telltale shadow and move to the side of that direction. Flanking (or even moving to the rear) helps avoid the impact and the swipe attack that's soon to follow.

GRIVELNOX

One of the most fearsome beasts of Rykan V, the Grivelnox is an imposing sight. Gifted with multiple bony tendrils that are more than capable of taking out smaller prey, their real power lies in the ability to absorb particular traits of the things they ingest. Needless to say, eating some of the more terrifying things found in this galaxy is a bad, bad thing. Thankfully, the Grivelnox doesn't tend to stray far from its normal attacks even when bolstered by elemental effects.

ATTACKS: TENTACLE SWIPES, TENTACLE STABS, FIERY MINION SPAWNS, ELECTRICAL BLASTS

FIRST ENCOUNTERED
Ephemeris
UZO CITY

TORANAUX SPIRIT

The purest form of whatever was carried on the asteroid that slammed into Magnus millennia ago, these Critters exist as ephemeral forms that can only survive and truly interact with their realm by possessing and controlling a local Critter. Originally bound to the lovable, simple critters littering the Magnus landscape, Dr. Croid inadvertently awakened them, only to force Nevo to help them find a far more powerful body…

ATTACKS: NONE

FIRST ENCOUNTERED
Ephemeris
UZO CITY

177

ROBOTIC ENEMIES

CLEANER MINION

Creating more messes than they tidy, these maintenance robots have been overhauled for combat duty. They are equipped with laser beams that have a limited reach and generally appear in groups. Despite their poor attack range, they are sturdily built and aren't easily dismantled.

ATTACKS: SHORT-RANGE LASER

FIRST ENCOUNTERED
Skyway
LUMINOPOLIS

SCOUT MINION

A versatile attack unit, the Scout Minion is a lethal blending of toughness and power. Each one is equipped with twin cannons integrated into its arms that can fire off plasma pulses at a high rate of fire. They are protected by several layers of armor plating that have to be worn down before these enemies go down. Using long-range weapons to eliminate them and avoid being caught in a tight space with these resilient foes.

ATTACKS: PLASMA PULSE CANNONS

FIRST ENCOUNTERED
Skyway
LUMINOPOLIS

MORTAR MINION

The heavy-duty cousins of the Scout Minion, Mortar Minions are armed with high-yield explosives that they lob from a distance. Often attacking from behind cover, they can be frustrating to deal with at long range. Face them head on, using the time it takes for each of their shots to arc to dodge the bright bullseyes indicating their mortars' landing sites.

ATTACKS: MORTARS

FIRST ENCOUNTERED
Mining Camp
THE DEADGROVE

MORTAR TOSS

Mortar Tosses are more like tax men rather than foot soldiers: they exist to slow things down but don't do any real fighting. They are usually found restricting access to sensitive areas and doorways. Defeating them requires Ratchet to team up with an ally and perform a mortar slam. Pounding the robot operating the Mortar Toss on top of its head and into its place overrides the mechanism it's securing.

ATTACKS: NONE

FIRST ENCOUNTERED
Minion Training Center
ALDAROS PLAINS

RIFT-JUMPER MINION

Rift-Jumper Minions are low-level lackeys in the robotic hierarchy. They rely on large numbers and the element of surprise to defeat their targets. Equipped with short-range teleportation technology, they arrive on the scene suddenly and in force to swarm potential victims with melee strikes. The very definition of cannon fodder, they are easily destroyed by any counter-attack.

ATTACKS: MELEE STRIKE

FIRST ENCOUNTERED
Minion Training Center
ALDAROS PLAINS

ENEMIES AS AMMO

These lightweight robots are easier to clean up with the Vac-U than are dust bunnies. Even better, once one is firmly lodged in the Vac-U, it can be turned into a projectile and launched at its brethren. Use Rift-Jumper Minions to destroy their own kind and save on ammo.

BLADE MINION

These aptly named robots move around like giant, deadly spinning tops. Their rapid rotation keeps them balanced and mobile as well as driving the titular blades that serve as their offensive weaponry. Blade Minions beeline for their targets and try to shred them with ramming attacks. Slam attack their green tops to destroy them.

ATTACKS: SPINNING BLADES

2V2

It takes two slam attacks to take out a blade minion, but only one mortar slam. An agile single player or two players attacking in quick succession can perform the former. However, the latter requires two players to work together to take the threat out faster.

FIRST ENCOUNTERED
Minion Training Center
ALDAROS PLAINS

PYROMITE

Overwhelming force is the strategy employed by Pyromites. These flying explosive payloads lock onto their targets, close in, and then self-destruct. They are churned out at extremely high rates by manufacturing hubs that independently assemble and launch them in large numbers. Destroy the production hub to stymie the flow of flying enemies.

ATTACKS: SELF-DESTRUCT

A BOLT BUFFET

There is no limit to the Pyromite producer's output. To pick up extra bolts, ignore the source and let the hub provide wave after wave of bolt-awarding targets.

FIRST ENCOUNTERED
Outside Receiving Station
ALDAROS PLAINS

PROTON TURRET

The Proton Turret is a stationary enemy unit that sprays deadly plasmas pulses at an astounding rate. Fortunately, their operators control the turret from an open-air cockpit, leaving them vulnerable to attack. In addition, the turning speed of the turret is low enough that it's relatively easy to run circles around them.

ATTACKS: RAPID-FIRE PLASMA PULSES

FIRST ENCOUNTERED
Orthani Gorge
THE DEADGROVE

TURRET MINION

A much tougher cousin to the Proton Turret, the Turret Minion is surrounded on all sides by shield panels. These protect it from all manner of attacks. The only way to take down a Turret Minion is with three mortar slams to the green-topped robotic operator at its center. It only exposes itself to check its targets between waves of attacking with a 360-degreen, close range shower of plasma and a slower-firing plasma cannon.

ATTACKS: CLOSE-RANGE PLASMA SHOWER, PLASMA CANNON

FIRST ENCOUNTERED
Vertigus Cliffs
N.E.S.T.

PROTON EXCAVATOR

The old Tharpod mining equipment has been co-opted by the robotic minions as defensive emplacements. These stationary units are mounted along the access shaft leading deep within the Deadgrove and their mining lasers have been converted to offensive weaponry. Their lasers sweep within a limited arc

ATTACKS: CONTINUOUS LASER BEAM

DOUBLE TROUBLE

When dealing with two Proton Excavators facing each other, a wall slam can be overkill and leave Ratchet exposed to attack from one enemy while dealing with the other. Instead, use a mid-air melee attack by pressing ● while flying right next to the control pod.

FIRST ENCOUNTERED

Access Shaft
THE DEADGROVE

HUNTER MINION

Hunter Minions buzz about through the air in swarms looking for targets. Individually, their light-weight construction offers little resistance to concentrated weapons fire. However, they are a force to be reckoned with in groups when they focus their individual laser beams on a single target.

ATTACKS: FOCUSED LASER BEAMS

CLEANING AIR POLLUTION

Hunter Minions stay airborne through advanced plastics used in their construction. This makes them vulnerable to being sucked up by a Vac-U. The real challenge lies in jumping high enough to reach them with the Vac-U's suction.

FIRST ENCOUNTERED

Elerox Pass
N.E.S.T.

BOUNCER MINION

Close-range combatants, Bouncer Minions are the heaviest hitting melee units Spog has under his command. Built to withstand the grueling, intense combat conditions, they bounce back easily from most attacks. They use only melee attacks that require them to be close to their victims, so attack them from a distance outside their attack radius. It takes teamwork to take these bruisers down, so coordinate with teammates to focus fire on one at a time.

ATTACKS: PUNCHES, GROUND STRIKES

THE BIGGER THEY ARE

Despite their toughness, Bouncer Minions' high center of gravity and heavy weight make them easy to knock over. If your character is surrounded on all sides and feeling the pressure, perform a slam attack to force them back and temporarily stun them.

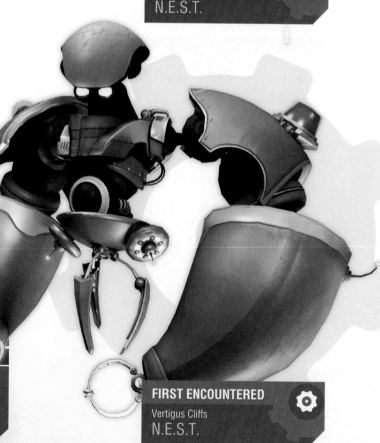

FIRST ENCOUNTERED

Vertigus Cliffs
N.E.S.T.

SENTRY MINION

An intimidating robot standing guard over the most crucial areas, the Sentry Minion packs a wallop. Sweeping its assigned area with a glaring spotlight, the Sentry Minion's death ray instantly drops any targets caught in the spotlight with a single shot. In addition, a front-facing energy shield protects it from incoming attacks.

ONE AND DONE

Despite their impressive attack power, Sentry Minions aren't built to last. A single plasmabomb easily arcs over its shields to destroy it in a single shot.

ATTACKS: **DEATH RAY**

FIRST ENCOUNTERED
N.E.S.T. Entrance
N.E.S.T.

TANK MINION

The Tank Minion is designed to soak up damage like a sponge while dealing out plenty of its own. Its massive robotic torso makes it easy to spot at a distance and conceals an unlimited supply of mortars it launches from long range. Equally deadly at a distance are the laser beams that emit from its arms that sweep across the battlefield.

ATTACKS: **SWEEPING LASER BEAMS, MORTARS**

FIRST ENCOUNTERED
N.E.S.T. Entrance
N.E.S.T.

MR. PERKINS

An advanced revision of the Tank Minion, an energy shield generated by two adjacent Mortar Tosses protects Mr. Perkins. An upgrade over the standard sweeping laser beams, Mr. Perkins has enough power to emit two at a time—one from each arm. He discourages close-range attacks by emitting an expanding electrical discharge along the ground in its immediate vicinity.

ATTACKS: **SWEEPING LASER BEAMS, MORTARS, ELECTRIC DISCHARGE**

FIRST ENCOUNTERED
N.E.S.T. Entrance
N.E.S.T.

COMMANDER SPOG

A fierce and experienced warbot, Commander Spog is the supreme commander of the robotic minions faced by Ratchet and his allies. Equipped with a deadly arsenal, this towering behemoth is a no-nonsense soldier at heart. Nothing gets his circuits fired up quite like intruders or a plan gone awry. Spog attends to his duties somewhat begrudgingly, following orders to the letter despite feeling underutilized by Ephemeris.

ATTACKS: SWEEPING LASER BEAMS, TIMED BOMBS, SAW BLADES, GROUND POUND

RETURN TO SENDER

Commander Spog's bombs are light enough to be sucked up with a Vac-U. Pick them up to create room to maneuver and launch them back at Spog when you're low on ammo.

FIRST ENCOUNTERED
Rehabitation Center
N.E.S.T.

BOMBER MINION

Contrary to their name, Bomber Minions are actually as adept at (and in fact employ) more missile-based attacks. They pepper your heroes with a stream of projectiles that are seriously aggressive—meaning just side-strafing won't work. Instead, they spit out their payload in a hero-seeking stream that necessitates waiting until the last moment for a double-jump to safety.

ATTACKS: CLUSTER MISSILE STRIKE

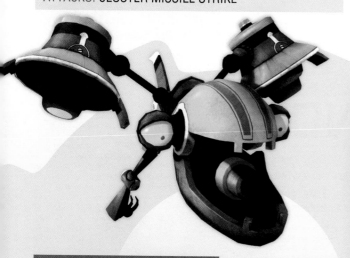

FIRST ENCOUNTERED
Cove
OCTONOK CAY

MISSILE MINION

So if Bomber Minions spit slow-seeking rockets, Missile Minions—that's right—spew earthbound projectiles. Thankfully, the targeting systems seem to paint a pretty clear (and weirdly compromising) bullseye on the ground. Move far enough away and, nope, no effect. Then again, they are minions instead of criminal masterminds…

ATTACKS: BOMB ATTACK

8 IS GREAT!

See something on the ground with a suspiciously target-like shape? Yeah, something bad and explosive projectile is headed there—often in a boss fight. The secret? Just skirt the battlefield with a figure eight. Contract the circles to avoid buddies if you must, but always, always keep on the move.

FIRST ENCOUNTERED
Feeding Dock
OCTONOK CAY

CROID BOT

Yes, this is happening: bots are indeed jumping into other bots to pilot them. Casting aside the observation of a hard hat for bots, instead consider the fact that Croid Bots are not to be messed with. They are capable of unleashing twin streams of energy, but are equally happy with just projecting single-fire masses that do plenty of damage.

ATTACKS: TWIN BEAM ATTACK, PLASMA FIRE, VAC-U CATCH AND RELEASE

TOO CLOSE FOR COMFORT

Croid Bots are fairly slow—so much that one might assume that a melee-range attack is prudent. It isn't. Oh how it isn't; these bots have a form of the same Vac-U your heroes employ and can suck up a friend, turning them into a projectile that damages not only them, but your hero if struck. Wait until the last second, then jump out of range of a buddy should they become inadvertent ammo.

FIRST ENCOUNTERED
Kaleero Trail
TERRAWATT FOREST

ION TURRET

It seems the hard hat-sporting bots of previous days have gotten a better job. In this case, they can spray an octet of laser beams with a simple press of a button. Employ the Reflector to render their attacks pointless, and then beat the bolts out of the machine they used to cause so much high-powered pain.

ATTACKS: EIGHT-WIDE BEAM ATTACK

FIRST ENCOUNTERED
Phonica Craters
PHONICA MOON

GROUNDPOUNDER

This machination was designed for a singular purpose and, hoo-boy, does it do it well. The Groundpounder shatters any sort of platform most travelers would traverse, but for the purposes of your heroes' encounter, it's actually pretty single-minded. Jump to a nearby iceberg and its attacks are nothing.

ATTACKS: ICEBERG DUNK

FIRST ENCOUNTERED
Middle of Nowhere
POLAR SEA

SCORCH MINION

Sporting twin spouts of impressive (and deadly) flame, the Scorch Minion seems all too ready to create a Lombax BBQ—with some sides of Qwark fritters on Clank and Nefarious skewers. The twin beams of heat have to be either jumped over or carefully ridden between. Either way, it's not easy.

ATTACKS: FIREBALL SHOT, TWIN FLAMES

FIRST ENCOUNTERED
Polar Ice Floes
POLAR SEA

SWARM BEACON

The Swarm Beacon is something of a jerk. The longer it stays around, the simpler (but not weaker) minions float in, heeding the call of the message the beacon sends out. The only real recourse is to slip in, avoid the friends it calls in, and Vac-U (with an ally, remember) to suck it into oblivion.

ATTACKS: MINION SUMMON

FIRST ENCOUNTERED
City Ruins
UZO CITY

THE POWER OF CRITTER COMPELS YOU!

The single most effective (and hilarious) method for dealing with the Scorch Minion is to simply apply overwhelming Critterstrike payload in the face of this pyro-machine. Turn it into something a little more friendly with easy application.

WHEN SAVING THE GALAXY ISN'T ENOUGH
SKILLPOINTS & TROPHIES

Sure, getting a ragtag foursome to work together long enough to escape the fate thrust on them is all well and good, but sometimes one needs a little more—in this case there's the added challenge and reward of Skill Points and Trophies. One offers immediate in-game rewards, while the other festoons a PSN profile with the spoils of their accomplishments.

SKILLPOINT LIST

Skill Points are classic *Ratchet & Clank*, offering bonus optional objectives on top of the main level goals or Trophies. Earning Skill Points isn't just about bragging rights; successfully pulling off these extra challenges can unlock.

SKILL POINTS LIST

NAME	DESCRIPTION	LOCATION
A Band of Weirdos	Get through Luminopolis without a single hero dying.	Luminopolis
Public Menace	Destroy all of the consumer bots.	Luminopolis
Better Luck Next Time	Defeat a Gravoid Brute without getting hit by a missile.	Global
Judgment Day	Throw Clank or Nefarious into the incinerator.	Minion Training Center—Aldaros Plains
Gold Stars for Everyone	Dispose of all the trash balls in the first incinerator in seven seconds.	Minion Training Center—Aldaros Plains
Hold Your Ground	Don't let the Gravoids take more than five pieces of ground.	Aldaros Plains
Deadlocked and Loaded	Defeat all of the arena enemies with your melee weapons.	Aldaros Plains
Have You Two Met?	Get one Proton Turret to kill another.	Orthani Gorge—The Deadgrove
Treasure Hunter	Quakehammer all of the ground.	The Deadgrove
Back to Work	Break the water cooler.	Orthani Gorge—The Deadgrove
Terminal Velocity	Don't use the jetpack for 30 seconds.	The Deadgrove
Crate Hater	Break all of the floating crates.	Access Shaft—The Deadgrove
Jetpack Master	Don't touch any of the hazards using the jetpack.	The Deadgrove
It Burns When I Touch It	Don't touch the lava floor.	Abyss—The Deadgrove
100% Pure Adrenaline	Make it up the wind tunnel in 20 seconds.	N.E.S.T. Entrance—N.E.S.T.
Master Infiltrator	Get through the sorting facility without being spotted by the Sentry Minions.	N.E.S.T. Entrance—N.E.S.T.
Paging Mr. Perkins	Don't get hit by Mr. Perkins.	N.E.S.T. Entrance—N.E.S.T.
Grind Rail Ace	Avoid all of the hazards on the final grind rail in N.E.S.T.	Rehabitation Center—N.E.S.T.
Gone Fishin'	Get all of the goody reels.	Octonok Cay
The Conductor	Avoid being damaged by the conductor panels.	Feeding Dock—Octonok Cay
Rusty Pete Would be Proud	Navigate the waters of Octonok without damaging any of the rafts.	W.A.S.P. Control Room—Octonok Cay
Team Spirit	Save a hero from the spotlight.	Kaleero Trail—Terrawatt Forest
On Planet Magnus, Vegetables Eat You	Don't get eaten by a Venixx.	Terrawatt Forest

NAME	DESCRIPTION	LOCATION
Ace Pilot	Reach Phonica Moon without taking damage.	Ornithopter Ascent—Phonica Moon
Keep it Green	Skip a fuel tank during the flight to Phonica Moon.	Ornithopter Ascent—Phonica Moon
Cold Hearted	Destroy all of the icicles.	Polar Sea
Demolition Expert	Destroy all of the Pyromite generators in Polar Sea.	Polar Sea
Pain Don't Hurt	Beat the Grungoth with only your melee weapons.	Polar Ice Floes—Polar Sea
The Pacifist	Get past the Sentry Minions without getting killed or killing them.	Uzo City
Combuster Apprentice	Kill 50 enemies with the Combuster.	Global
Combuster Master	Kill 100 enemies with the Combuster.	Global
Combuster Legend	Kill 200 enemies with the Combuster.	Global
Arc Lasher Apprentice	Stun five enemies with the Arc Lasher that another teammate kills.	Global
Arc Lasher Master	Stun ten enemies with the Arc Lasher that another teammate kills.	Global
Arc Lasher Legend	Stun 15 enemies with the Arc Lasher that another teammate kills.	Global
Thundersmack Apprentice	Kill 25 enemies with the Thundersmack.	Global
Thundersmack Master	Kill 75 enemies with the Thundersmack.	Global
Thundersmack Legend	Kill 150 enemies with the Thundersmack.	Global
Warmonger Apprentice	Kill five enemies with the Warmonger.	Global
Warmonger Master	Kill 15 enemies with the Warmonger.	Global
Warmonger Legend	Kill 30 enemies with the Warmonger.	Global
Plasmabomb Launcher Apprentice	Kill 20 enemies with the Plasmabomb Launcher.	Global
Plasmabomb Launcher Master	Kill 75 enemies with the Plasmabomb Launcher.	Global
Plasmabomb Launcher Legend	Kill 200 enemies with the Plasmabomb Launcher.	Global
Pyro Blaster Apprentice	Kill 30 enemies with the Pyro Blaster.	Global
Pyro Blaster Master	Kill 60 enemies with the Pyro Blaster.	Global
Pyro Blaster Legend	Kill 120 enemies with the Pyro Blaster.	Global
Blitzer Apprentice	Kill ten enemies with the Blitzer.	Global
Blitzer Master	Kill 20 enemies with the Blitzer.	Global
Blitzer Legend	Kill 30 enemies with the Blitzer.	Global
Frost Cannon Apprentice	Freeze 25 enemies and then destroy them.	Global
Frost Cannon Master	Freeze 50 enemies and then destroy them.	Global
Frost Cannon Legend	Freeze 75 enemies and then destroy them.	Global
Critter Strike Apprentice	Turn 25 enemies into critters with the Critter Strike.	Global
Critter Strike Master	Turn 50 enemies into critters with the Critter Strike.	Global
Critter Strike Legend	Turn 100 enemies into critters with the Critter Strike.	Global
Poor Mr. Perkins	Critter Strike Mr. Perkins.	N.E.S.T. Entrance—N.E.S.T.

NAME	DESCRIPTION	LOCATION
RYNO Apprentice	Kill 25 enemies with the RYNO.	Global
RYNO Master	Kill 50 enemies with the RYNO.	Global
RYNO Legend	Kill 100 enemies with the RYNO.	Global
Fission Tether Apprentice	Kill 30 enemies with the Fission Tether.	Global
Fission Tether Master	Kill 75 enemies with the Fission Tether.	Global
Fission Tether Legend	Kill 200 enemies with the Fission Tether.	Global
Zurkon the Apprentice	Kill 25 enemies with Mr. Zurkon out.	Global
Zurkon the Master	Kill 50 enemies with Mr. Zurkon out.	Global
Melee Apprentice	Kill 50 enemies with the melee.	Global
Melee Master	Kill 100 enemies with the melee.	Global
Q-Force Apprentice	Kill ten enemies in a row using melee without taking damage.	Global
Q-Force Master	Kill 25 enemies in a row using melee without taking damage.	Global
Doppelbanger Apprentice	Destroy ten enemies while they're distracted by the Doppelbanger.	Global
Doppelbanger Apprentice	Destroy 20 enemies while they're distracted by the Master.	Global
Quantum Deflector Apprentice	Absorb 75 shots with the Quantum Deflector.	Global
Quantum Deflector Master	Absorb 200 shots with the Quantum Deflector.	Global
Zoni Apprentice	Kill five enemies that have been slowed down by the Zoni Blaster.	Global
Zoni Master	Kill ten enemies that have been slowed down by the Zoni Blaster.	Global
Cloak & Dagger Apprentice	Kill five enemies while using the Cloaker.	Global
Cloak & Dagger Master	Kill ten enemies while using the Cloaker.	Global
Overload Apprentice	Use Co-op overload to kill 15 enemies.	Global
Overload Master	Use Co-op overload to kill 30 enemies.	Global
Medic	Revive other teammates five times.	Global
Nurse	Revive other teammates ten times.	Global
Doctor	Revive other teammates 15 times.	Global
Guardian Angel	Revive the same teammate twice in a row with at least two additional human players.	Global
Making the Grade	Buy your first upgrade.	Global
Galactic Scout	Kill 100 enemies.	Global
Galactic Adventurer	Kill 200 enemies.	Global
Vac-U Apprentice	Kill ten enemies with the Vac-U 4000.	Global
Vac-U Master	Kill 25 enemies with the Vac-U 4000.	Global
Mortar Slam Apprentice	Mortar Slam ten enemies.	Global
Mortar Slam Master	Mortar Slam 30 enemies.	Global
The Bolt Collector	Have 25,000 bolts banked.	Global
Dream Crusher	Double second place's bolt count.	Global
The Green-Eyed Monster	Get Bolt Master at four Most Wanted screens in a row.	Global
The Qwark Award for Excellence	Get the n00b award at four Most Wanted screens in a row.	Global
Forever Alone	Beat the game with the bot.	Global
Good Grief	Beat the game in Grief Mode.	Global
Son of Kaden	Complete Game with Ratchet.	Global
Son of Orvus	Complete Game with Clank.	Global
Master of Evil	Complete Game with Dr. Nefarious.	Global
Hail to the Chief	Complete Game with Qwark.	Global

TROPHIES

Trophies, while certainly similar to Skillpoints, have the added benefit of boosting a player's overall Trophy level on their PSN Trophy card. After all, what good are bragging rights if they can't be seen outside of a game?

RATCHET & CLANK: ALL 4 ONE TROPHIES

NAME		TYPE	DESCRIPTION
	Platinum Trophy	Platinum	Earn every other trophy
	Keep the Meter Running	Bronze	Don't let the Air Taxi take damage in Luminopolis.
	Intergalactic Tool of Justice	Bronze	Defeat the Z'Grute
	Bomb Disposal	Silver	Blow up 85% of the exploding crates in Aldaros Plains.
	El Matador	Bronze	No one gets hit by a Grove Beetle in the Deadgrove.
	Now We Need a Really Big Tissue	Bronze	Defeat the Wigwump.
	Spog 2.0	Bronze	Defeat Commander Spog.
	On Some Planets They're a Delicacy	Silver	Shoot all of the Slorgs back into the waters of Octonok Cay.
	Night Lights are for Wimps	Bronze	Get through Rossa Fields without using any of the energy repositories.
	It Was Like That When We Got Here	Bronze	Destroy all of the towers in Gorthon Crater.
	A Moment of Reflection	Bronze	Use only Reflectors to destroy the generators in Phonica Moon's security tunnels.
	Mission Improbable	Bronze	Get through the laser walls at the end of Uzo City in 45 seconds.

NAME		TYPE	DESCRIPTION
	The Mad Plasmabomber	Bronze	Kill eight enemies with one shot.
	Pyromancer	Bronze	Barbecue four enemies at the same time using the Pyro Blaster.
	Knockout Artist	Bronze	Kill three enemies with one attack using the Blitzer.
	Fine, But You're Cleaning Up After Them	Bronze	Get ten critters on screen at once.
	Eight Seconds	Bronze	Kill eight enemies in eight seconds using the Darkstar Fission Tether with two or more teammates.
	Zurkon the Legend	Bronze	Kill 100 enemies with Mr. Zurkon out.
	Melee Legend	Bronze	Kill 150 enemies with melee.
	Q-Force Legend	Bronze	Kill 50 enemies in a row using melee without taking damage.
	Doppelbanger Legend	Bronze	Destroy 30 enemies while they're distracted by the Doppelbanger.
	Quantum Deflector Legend	Bronze	Absorb 500 shots with the Quantum Deflector.
	Zoni Legend	Bronze	Kill 15 enemies that have been slowed down by the Zoni Blaster.
	Cloak & Dagger Legend	Bronze	Kill 15 enemies while using the Cloaker.
	Quick Killer	Bronze	Kill eight enemies in two seconds.
	Overload Legend	Bronze	Use Co-op overload to kill 60 enemies.

NAME		TYPE	DESCRIPTION
	Life Support	Bronze	Revive a teammate with one second left on their timer.
	Friendship through Firepower	Bronze	Buy your first weapon.
	Upping your Arsenal	Silver	Buy half of the weapons.
	For the Zombie Apocalypse	Gold	Buy all of the weapons.
	Tricked Out	Silver	Fully upgrade one weapon.
	Upgraded	Gold	Fully upgrade all weapons.
	Galactic Hero	Silver	Kill 500 enemies.
	Vac-U Legend	Bronze	Kill 50 enemies with the Vac-U 4000.
	The Bolt Banker	Silver	Have 100,000 bolts banked.
	The First Million is Always the Hardest	Gold	Have 1,000,000 bolts banked.
	Waiting Room	Bronze	Reach the lobby.
	Connected	Bronze	Play an online game.
	Old-School	Bronze	Play a single-player game.
	Couch Potato	Bronze	Play an offline-only game with 2 or more players.

INTERFACE CHARACTER PORTRAITS

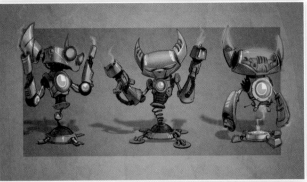

CONCEPT ART

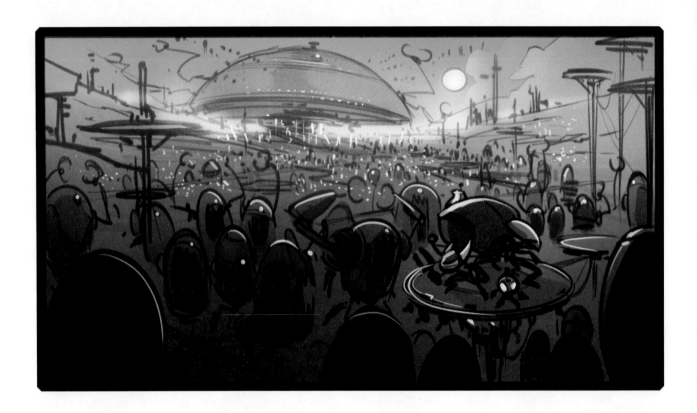

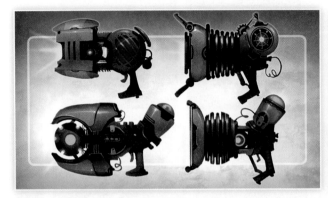

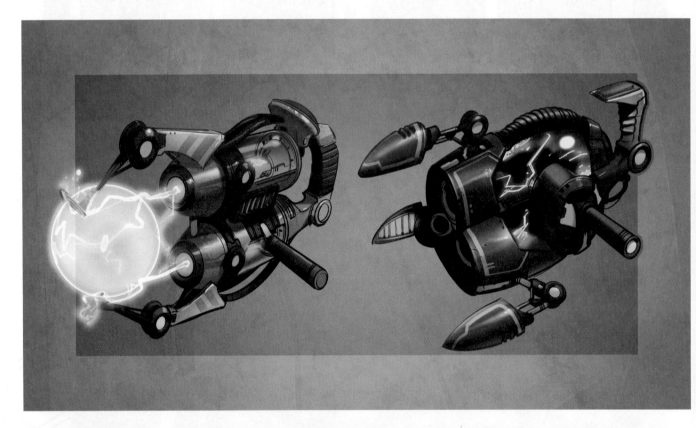

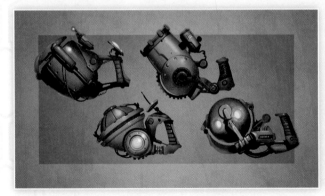

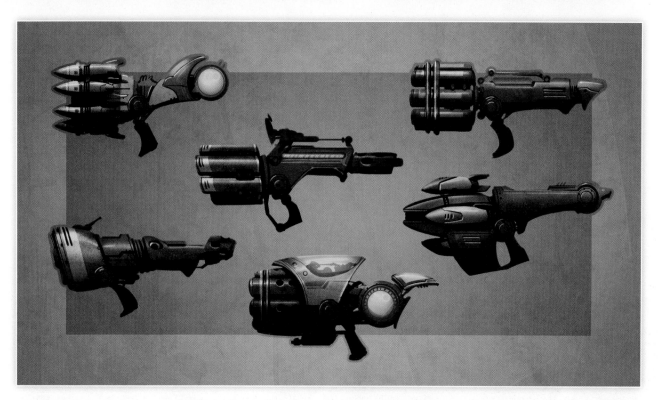

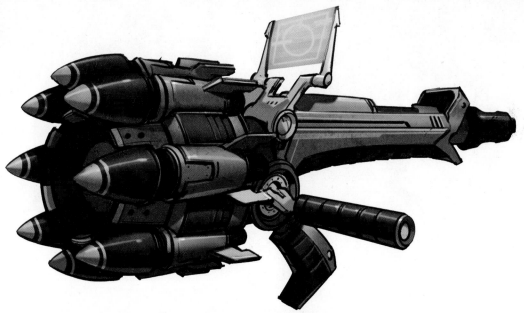

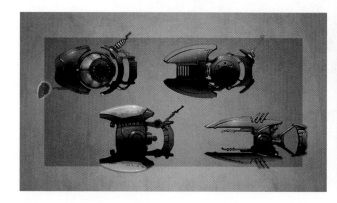

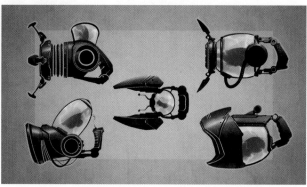

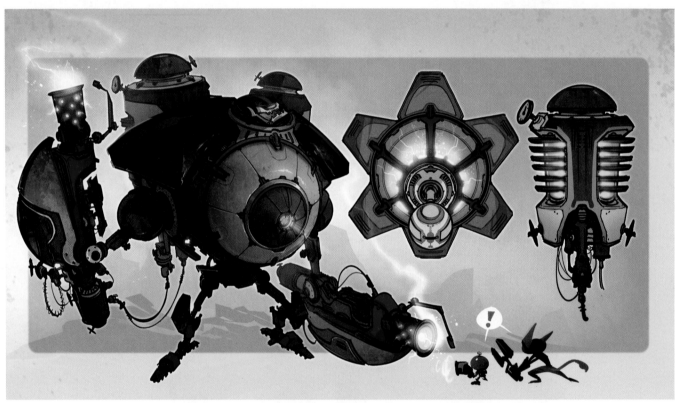

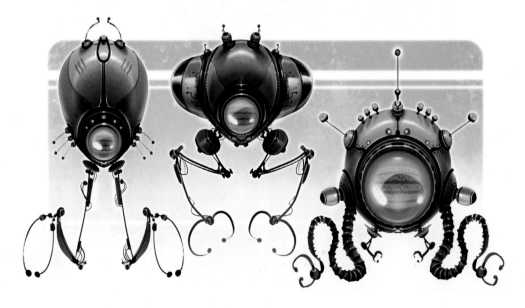

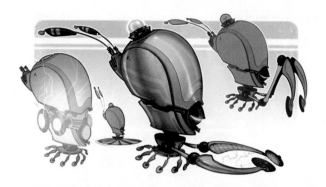
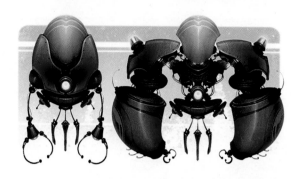
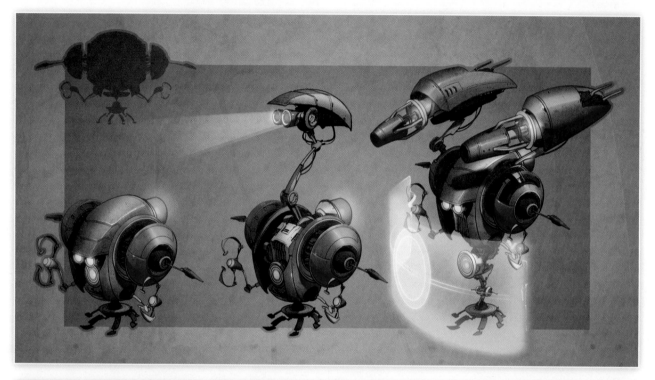
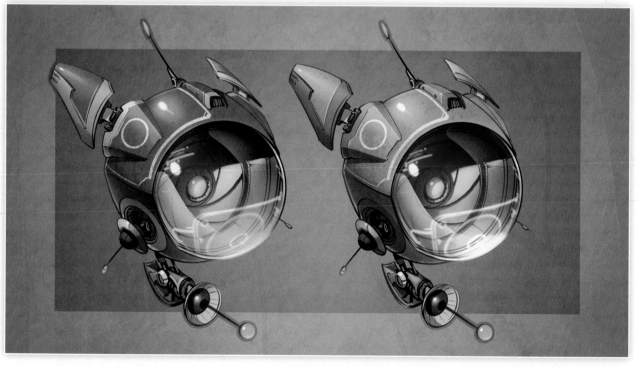

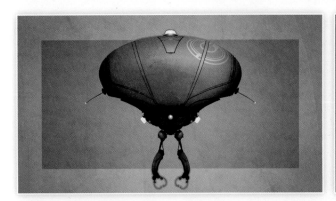
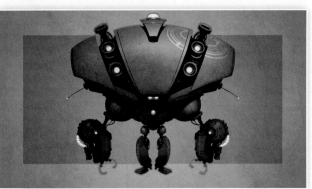
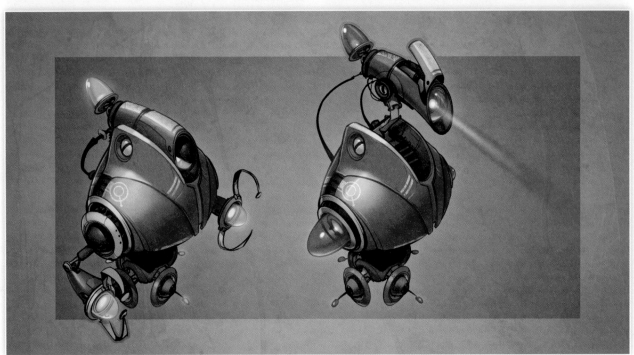
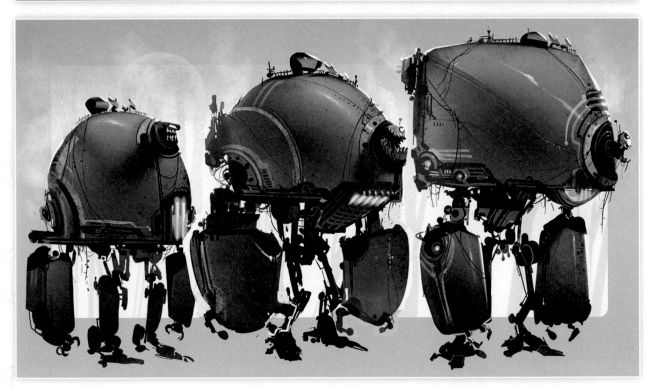

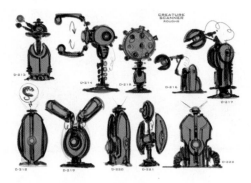

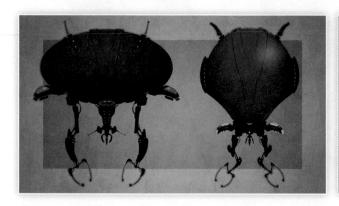

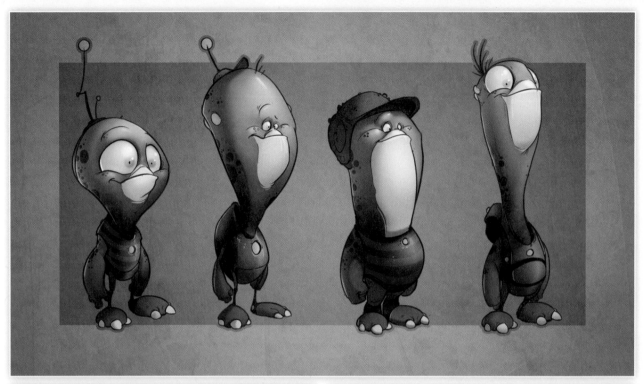

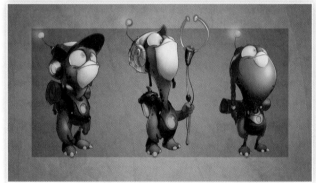

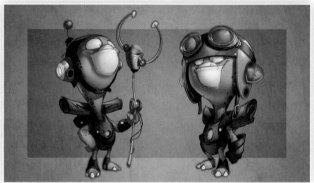

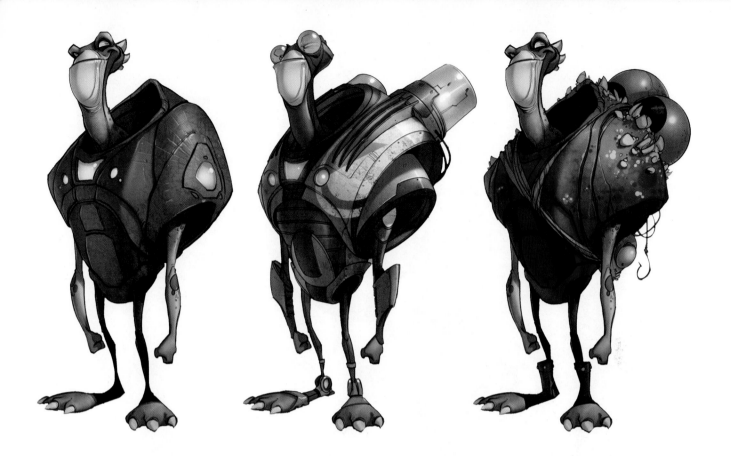

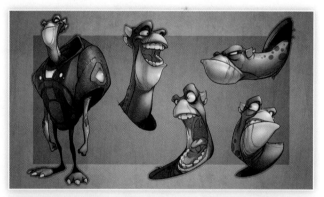

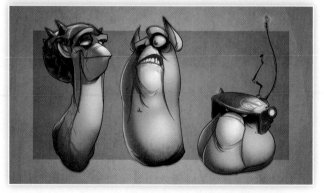

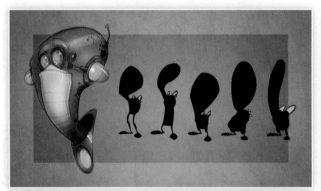

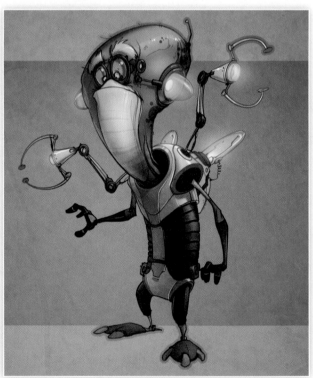

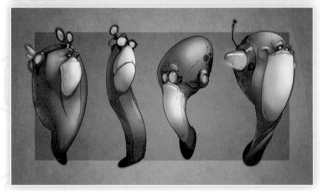

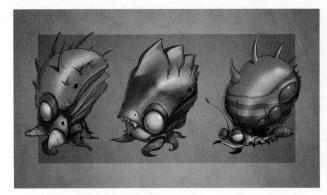

Mr. Dinkles
ACTION CHART

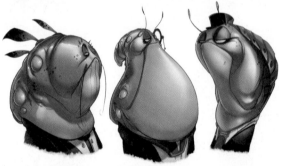

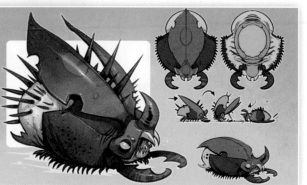

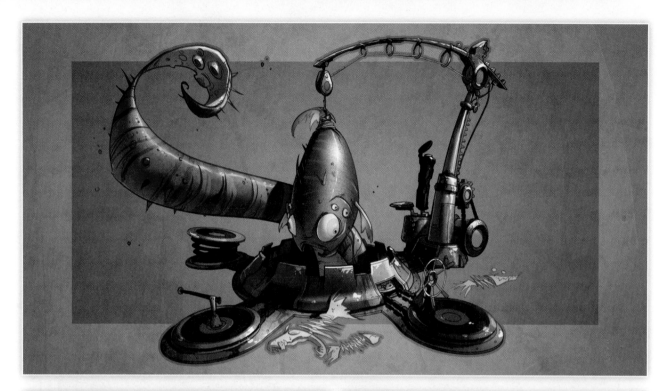

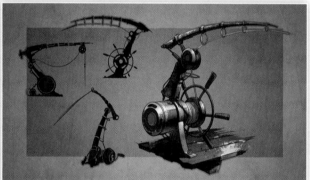

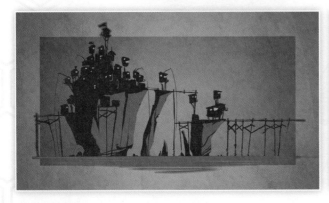

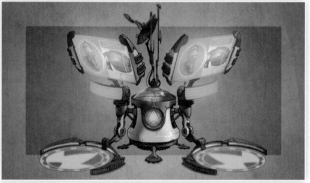

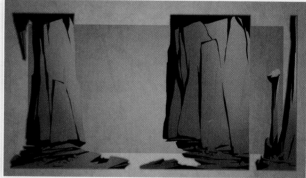

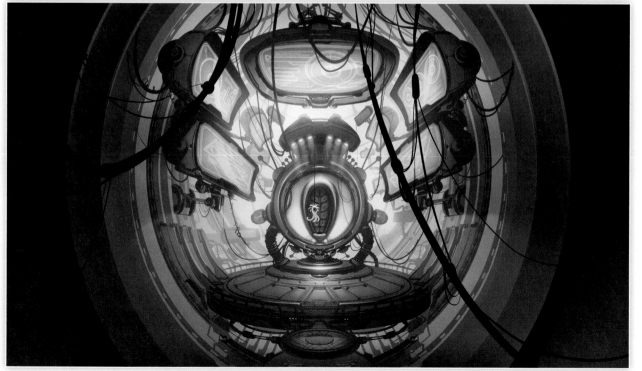

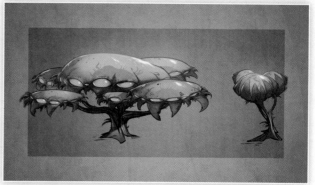

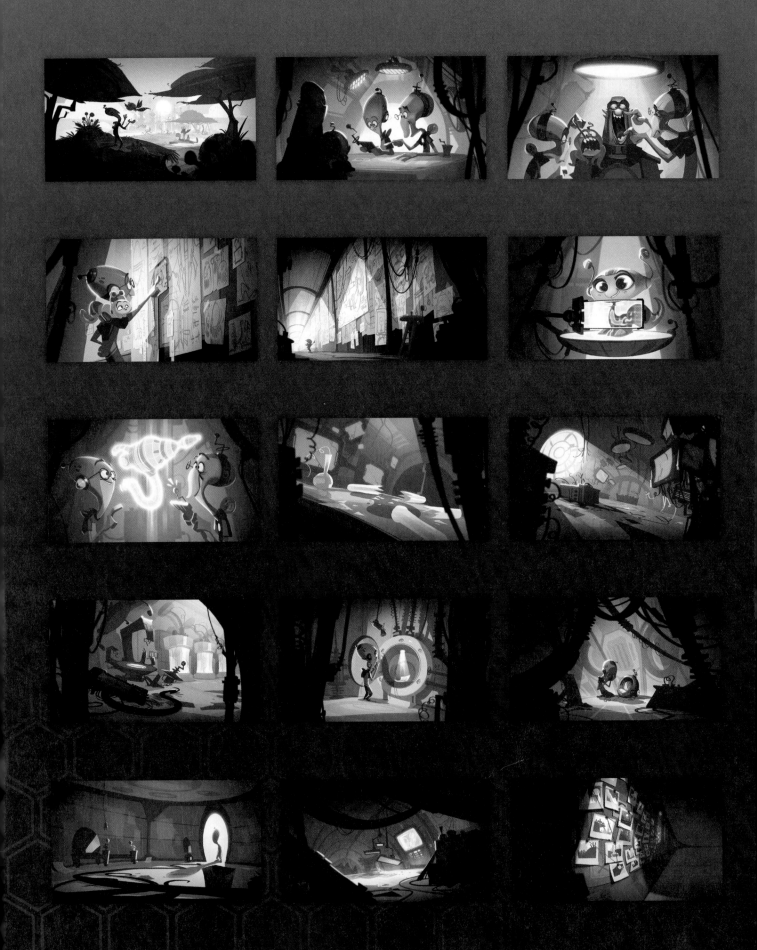

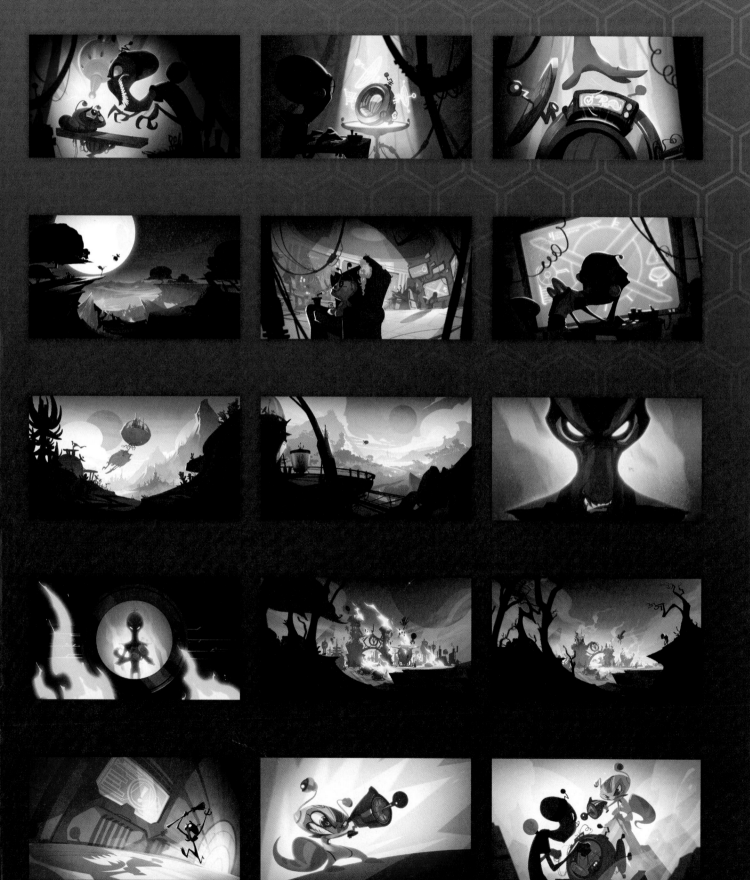

OFFICIAL STRATEGY GUIDE

BY OFF BASE PRODUCTIONS

© 2011 DK/BradyGAMES, a division of Penguin Group (USA) Inc. BradyGAMES® is a registered trademark of Penguin Group (USA) Inc. All rights reserved, including the right of reproduction in whole or in part in any form.

DK/BradyGames, a division of Penguin Group (USA) Inc.
800 East 96th Street, 3rd Floor
Indianapolis, IN 46240

Ratchet and Clank: All 4 One is a trademark of Sony Computer Entertainment America LLC. Developed by Insomniac Games. "PlayStation", and the "PS" Family logo are registered trademarks and PS3 is a trademark of Sony Computer Entertainment Inc. The Sony Computer Entertainment logo is a registered trademark of Sony Corporation.

The ratings icon is a registered trademark of the Entertainment Software Association. All other trademarks and trade names are properties of their respective owners.

Please be advised that the ESRB ratings icons, "EC", "E", "E10+", "T", "M", "AO", and "RP" are trademarks owned by the Entertainment Software Association, and may only be used with their permission and authority. For information regarding whether a product has been rated by the ESRB, please visit www.esrb.org. For permission to use the ratings icons, please contact the ESA at esrblicenseinfo@theesa.com.

ISBN 10: 0-7440-1343-7
ISBN 13 EAN: 978-0-7440-1343-6

Printing Code: The rightmost double-digit number is the year of the book's printing; the rightmost single-digit number is the number of the book's printing. For example, 11-1 shows that the first printing of the book occurred in 2011.

14 13 12 11   4 3 2 1

Printed in the USA.

CREDITS

Senior Development Editor
Ken Schmidt

Senior Book Designer
Keith Lowe

Production Designer
Areva

BRADYGAMES STAFF

Global Strategy Guide Publisher
Mike Degler

Digital Category Publisher
Brian Saliba

Editor-In-Chief
H. Leigh Davis

Licensing Director
Christian Sumner

Operations Manager
Stacey Beheler